TURN UP
the HEAT

TURN UP
the HEAT

A COUPLES GUIDE TO SEXUAL INTIMACY

DR. KEVIN LEMAN

Revell
a division of Baker Publishing Group
Grand Rapids, Michigan

© 2009 by Dr. Kevin Leman

Published by Revell
a division of Baker Publishing Group
P.O. Box 6287, Grand Rapids, MI 49516-6287
www.revellbooks.com

Printed in the United States of America

Library of Congress Cataloging-in-Publication Data
Leman, Kevin.
    Turn up the heat : a couples guide to sexual intimacy / Kevin Leman.
        p.   cm.
    Includes bibliographical references.
    ISBN 978-0-8007-1903-6 (cloth)
    1. Sex—Religious aspects—Christianity. I. Title.
BT708.L47 2009
    613.9′608655—dc22   2008044869

ISBN 978-0-8007-3402-2 (ITPE)

To protect the privacy of those who have shared their stories with the author, some details and names have been changed.

In keeping with biblical principles of creation stewardship, Baker Publishing Group advocates the responsible use of our natural resources. As a member of the Green Press Initiative, our company uses recycled paper when possible. The text paper of this book is comprised of 30% postconsumer waste.

green
press
INITIATIVE

To John Young and his lovely wife, Marlene.

Thank you for your friendship
and encouragement over the years.
You have only one assignment:
to take loving care of each other
for the rest of your lives.

Contents

Acknowledgments   10

Introduction   11
Have a great sex life—by Saturday night! (Or Thursday night, if you're really frisky.)

1 Shootin' for the 'Moon   15
Some honeymoon symphonies are like the Boston Philharmonic. Others are like "Twinkle, twinkle, little star, where the heck are ya?"

2 The Beginning of Happily Ever After?   30
You're back from your honeymoon. . . . Now what about the next 48 years?

3 Lights On or Lights Off?   43
What makes you a couple: vive la différence!

4 What's Your Mom Doing in Bed with Us?   54
Why more than two of you walked down that flower-strewn aisle to say, "I do."

5 You're Frisky Again? Didn't We Just Have Sex— in April?   62
How often should you do it—and do you have to do it?

Contents

6 Turn-Ons and Turn-Offs in the Bedroom   69
   What your spouse really cares about . . . and what you shouldn't.

7 Inquiring Minds Want to Know   79
   The truth about women and orgasms.

8 Men Don't Think Just about Sex   90
   They think about food and ESPN too.

9 Ahh, the Sheer Delight of a Quickie   101
   Sometimes it's just what you—or your spouse—needs.

10 What's on Your Menu?   108
   Scintillating appetizers and delicious desserts for your marital palate.

11 And Then We Had Children   118
   How to keep Mr. Happy happy, keep the ankle-biter battalion in check, and let Velcro Woman still get a good night's sleep.

12 Shh! It's a Secret!   131
   Why good communicators have a better sex life.

13 Not Now, Honey, We'll Wake the Children . . . (But We Don't Have Any Children Yet!)   150
   What those excuses really mean . . . and what to do about them.

14 Ms. Boring Meets Mr. Predictable in the Bedroom   159
   Breaking out of the predictability rut.

15 Love Handles Can Be Sexy!   169
   Why not cut yourself some slack?

16 Help! I Married Judge Judy   175
   Tackling the biggest sex killer—criticism.

17 Too Pooped to Whoop?   185
   What to do when your spouse is giving you that Bullwinkle the Moose look . . . and you're already in hyperdrive.

18 Romancing the Stone   195
   How to turn up the heat without getting burned.

19 Yesterday, When I Was Young . . .   210
   What happened to you in the past has everything to do with how much you enjoy sex.

Contents

20 Why Jack or Jill Is Still on Your Mind   221
You can't change your past relationships. But you can choose to move on.

21 Starving for Sex!   230
How to know if your spouse is a sex addict—or just has a high sex drive.

22 The Grass on the Other Side May Look Greener . . .
But You Still Have to Mow It   246
How to handle life when it isn't quite what you expected.

23 After an Affair   265
How to rebuild what's good after the carnage.

24 There's No Such Thing as Over the Hill . . . Unless You Act
Like It   277
How to combat the sexual effects of job loss, depression, and aging.

25 If Mick Jagger Can Still Sing, We Can Still Do
the You-Know-What   286
There's many a tune in an old viola, and it's some of the best music around.

Conclusion: Grow Old Along with Me   292
The best is yet to be. So go ahead—turn up the heat!

Notes   295

Suggested Resources for Couples   296

About Dr. Kevin Leman   297

Resources by Dr. Kevin Leman   299

Acknowledgments

To my Revell editor, Lonnie Hull DuPont: You are an amazing woman. Simply stated, your creative talents are greatly appreciated.

And to the other woman in my life (my other editor), Ramona Cramer Tucker, who understands my heart . . . and my humor—many thanks.

Introduction

Have a great sex life—by Saturday night! (Or Thursday night, if you're really frisky.)

When Adam saw Eve for the first time, what do you think he said? "Holy moley, will you look at that!"

To Adam, beautiful Eve was a wonder—the one creature in Eden perfectly suited to be his mate. What did Adam do next? What comes naturally to us men: He stared. He appreciated. Then he couldn't help but touch this gift from almighty God. And what happened next was very, very good.

Sex—God's awesome invention—got a great start in that beautiful Garden of Eden. But whatever happened to the garden where a man and a woman—true partners, together for a lifetime—were naked and not ashamed?

You know what happened. Just one little bite of the forbidden fruit, and all of a sudden what almighty God created got labeled "dirty." Adam and Eve quickly realized they were in the buff, so they slunk off into the bushes to hide themselves until they were clothed. Their perfect world of paradise was ruined. Their lov-

11

ing heart connection with almighty God was severed. And their innocent, peaceful relationship, as well as their sexually satisfying exploration of each other, was interrupted. All at once they *knew* their differences—and found them downright shameful and embarrassing.

But when it gets right down to brass tacks, what do we all dream of? Getting back to those days in the garden, where God's perfect invention of sex surrounded both the man and the woman in a mutually satisfying, forever relationship. What does every godly man want? A godly woman who loves sex. What does every godly woman want? A godly man who provides the intimacy that her soul longs for. You see, men need only a place, but women need a reason. As a husband and wife understand and learn to appreciate those crucial differences, they can turn up the heat in their relationship and have great sex—*all the time.*

Sex inside the bounds of holy matrimony was God's idea, but today folks are just a little afraid to ask questions about it, for fear of embarrassing themselves. (It's kind of like Adam and Eve hiding naked in the bushes.)

So I've made it easy for you.

Packed into this book are the hottest questions about sex and intimacy—questions I get asked every day as I travel, speak, and counsel married couples and soon-to-be-wed couples—and my straightforward answers. (To protect the privacy of those who have shared their stories with me, some details and names have been changed.)

Have you ever wondered how often you should do it—and if you *have* to do it? Why she likes the lights off, and you want them on? What to do when you're too pooped to whoop and he's giving you a look like Bullwinkle the Moose? If depression or aging can affect sex drive? If he's a sex addict? If you are, because you've just got to have it? What's okay—and what's not—in bed? If there's sex after children? How you compare to his exes? Why he's so boring in bed? If you'll still be able to . . . you know . . . when you're eligible for the seniors discount at McDonald's?

And that's just for starters.

If you want to have a great sex life by Saturday night, just read on. *Turn Up the Heat* will take you and your spouse to new, scintillating heights of mutually enjoyable satisfaction. I bet you'll even save money on your heating bills.

You can thank me later.

1

Shootin' for the 'Moon

Some honeymoon symphonies are like the Boston Philharmonic. Others are like "Twinkle, twinkle, little star, where the heck are ya?"

You might be about to embark on the long-awaited event of your honeymoon. Or maybe you have already taken the long walk down that flower-strewn aisle, are now nestled together in your romantic getaway, and have brought this book along to read together. Either way, good for you. If you're already thinking about what you can do to make your marriage the best it can be, you're starting your marriage out right!

Most people think, *Wow, the honeymoon. I can't wait!* After all, that's when the bells, whistles, and sirens all come together at the same time. And that mighty crescendo is the sign, of course, that you'll live happily ever after. All you need to do is save up to buy that little house with the white picket fence and your top-of-the-line Beemer, and eventually have a couple of those . . . what do you call 'em . . . children. Oh, of course. (On second thought, maybe a schnauzer would be cheaper.)

But does life always turn out as you expect? Has it so far? Just as life has its surprises, your honeymoon is likely to have its surprises as well. If you're like most couples I talk to, you're going to find that the honeymoon isn't quite what you thought it would be.

If you are sexually inexperienced (possibly 20 to 25 percent of the people reading this book are virgins), I can guarantee you that you're not going to create a symphony. You're going to have something a little more like "Twinkle, twinkle, little star, where the heck are ya?" But think about it. If there's a job that requires good ol' on-the-job training, and lots of it, what job would you rather have? What would be a more fun career than learning to master this one, I ask you?

Others of you have had sexual experiences previously with one or more partners. You might have been married before. You might have gone through the loss of your first spouse through divorce, death, or abandonment. You might have experienced things in your childhood you never should have experienced—abuse that was not your fault. Because the very nature of sexual experiences is so intimate, those memories will also be a part of your relationship with your spouse. (We'll talk more about all these issues in this book.)

Some of you are past that first honeymoon night already and have had a great experience. You're thinking, *That was incredible. I never thought sex would be so great!* And then there's the other 95 percent of you who are thinking (and a little embarrassed to admit it to your spouse), *So that was it? That was the best he had to offer?* Or, *You gotta be kidding me. Did she think that was going to turn me on?* And, *Oh my goodness, what have I gotten myself into! I have a lifetime of this?* Some of you, out of desperation, may have even picked up the phone to call Mom, Dad, or a friend for some quick advice. Or maybe you went to the local bookstore to find one of those how-to-do-it-right books, because deep down inside, you feel just a bit panicked.

If you're one of those who have pushed the panic button, rest assured that you're not alone. You'd think that sex would be one of the easiest acts to master in life—after all, get a male and a female, and the rest should be natural, right?—but, quite frankly, it takes some doing. You need the timing of a major league baseball player, the precision of the finest jeweler, and the capacity to be like Arthur Fiedler incarnate in the bedroom. And here's the kicker: even if you *could* be all those things rolled up into one, there's no guarantee that those bells, whistles, and sirens will be wailing away in your bedroom.

> *You need the timing of a major league baseball player, the precision of the finest jeweler, and the capacity to be like Arthur Fiedler incarnate in the bedroom.*

So how can you prepare yourself emotionally, physically, and mentally to become one on your honeymoon—and beyond?

I'm so glad you asked. Because your questions have everything to do with how sexually experienced or inexperienced you are prior to your honeymoon, you may want to skip to the section that best applies to you. (And it's okay if you want to peek at the other one too.)

A. You're virgins or very inexperienced sexually.
B. You're experienced sexually (you've had prior partners or been married before).

A. You're Virgins or Very Inexperienced Sexually

Q: My husband and I are both virgins. We started dating when we were in college and dated for three and a half years until we were both through college and grad school. Both sets of parents agreed to fully fund our educations if we agreed to wait to get married until we graduated. But sometimes I wonder if we waited too long. We couldn't do it for so long (there were some nights it was so, so, so hard to not get . . . uh, *close* . . . you know what I mean), and now that we're on our honeymoon, all of a sudden we can. I just can't seem to make the switch in my head. Neither one of us can relax. Help!

A: Kudos to you and your husband for waiting—and for asking for help in this area while you're still on your honeymoon! That says a lot about the type of people you are—and the married couple you will become. If you controlled your desires for that long and waited for sex, it's not likely either of you are going to be worried about your spouse finding sexual fulfillment somewhere other than in each other because you've built trust and a mutual respect. But I agree with you. My wife, Sande, and I were both virgins when we got married. It *is* hard to flip the switch, especially for a woman. Why is it harder for women than for men? Because for a man, Mr. Happy is ready to go at just about any time, any place. (So kudos to your guy for keeping himself purely for you—that says more than words ever could about his love and respect for you.) A woman? She needs the atmosphere, the environment, the cuddling, the words, the right timing. Everything has to be right for her to feel cherished and loved.

So here's my suggestion to both of you. So many people make their honeymoon a time when they have to go see places. "Oh, hey, let's go to Puerto Rico." "What about an Alaskan cruise? I've always wanted to go there." "Paris? After all, it's the city of love, and I've always wanted to see the Eiffel Tower." Sure, you might be in an exotic location (many folks are when they're on their honeymoon), but instead of focusing on the sites, why not instead make it a time to "see" each other in a beautiful and romantic spot?

Instead of rushing off to a local tourist attraction, a special dinner, or the beach, take things slow. Take your time. Wake up and cuddle. Spend a day completely, totally naked. Touch and revel in each other's bodies. Don't answer the phone. Order room service. Take time to explore and get to know each other's bodies for the fun of it. Don't make it your aim to always get the goal into the net. This isn't your time to have to figure out everything about sex and perfect the act. It's your time to laugh, stroke, have fun. It's your time to relax and just enjoy being together.

Q: I started taking birth control pills about three months before our honeymoon because we want to "plan" our family—not have it be a surprise. It has been really hard for me to wait for sex over all the years I've been single; sex has been constantly on my mind. But now that we're married, my sex drive seems way lower. In fact, it's hard to even get interested in sex. I hate seeing the hurt look on my husband's face. Is something wrong with me—or could it be that the birth control pills are making me less interested?

A: The first thing you need to do is explain to your husband what's happening in your mind and your body so that it becomes "our" problem—not "your" problem. Go together to the ob-gyn, explain the situation, and discuss other options. There are many formulations of birth control pills; you could easily try other

19

For Women Only

What *Not* to Expect from Your Lover

1. That he's George Clooney. Fred Flintstone might be closer. Most men are lousy lovers; they don't innately understand what turns a woman on.

2. That he's knowledgeable, just because he's a guy (and especially if he's had sex before). I've talked to a lot of men and asked them if they knew what a clitoris was, and they said, "A what?"

3. That he'll know the roadmap to please you. He'll have no clue what feels good to you unless you tell him . . . not only once . . . but time after time after time. "Oh, honey, I just *love* it when you do that!" And, "It felt good for you to start there yesterday, but today would you start . . . here?" And then just watch Lover-Boy enjoy pleasing you!

---

ones. And there are also other forms of birth control (including diaphragm, condom, IUD, and natural family planning). The most important thing is that the two of you are now a unit, and you have to work together toward the goal of a healthy, satisfied sex life. Magazines gossip about how taking birth control pills inhibits your sex drive. And there might be some truth to that for some women. But the real issue, to me, is what's happening in your mind and in your heart and how the two of you are working together, as a couple, to turn up the heat on your passion.

Q: The first time my wife and I had sex, I'd wanted it to be so beautiful, so perfect for her. I thought I was being really gentle, going really slow (we're both virgins) . . . then she started crying. So I stopped and ran a long, hot bath for her (she says that helps her relax) and even ran to the store to get some lavender, her favorite scent. She sat in the tub and cried some more. Then she called her mom and talked for two hours.

What am I doing wrong? I really love her, so how could I hurt her? Is my penis too big? Am I going about things wrong?

I don't ever want to see my bride cry—ever again—especially if I'm the cause of it.

A: Wow, a guy who actually asks for help, is thinking of his wife instead of himself, runs her a bath, and goes to the store to get her favorite scent? Hang in there, buddy. You're doing everything right! We could auction you off on eBay for big bucks.

The truth is, you're a male, and she's a female. And when you enter her, with Mr. Happy all puffed up and energetic, she *is* going to be sore. As a virgin, she hasn't had any visitors there before.

Did your bride go to her ob-gyn before your honeymoon? Some women get their hymens stretched; some have them broken for a more pleasurable experience. Others use two or three fingers to begin stretching the opening before their first experience with sex so the muscles are more flexible.

As her husband, you're now in a position to help her . . . gently. There's nothing you can do about the size of your penis, but you can use a lubricant for easier entry. Also, as your wife adjusts to sex, realize that there will be some times when you won't "go all the way." Keep the emphasis on your love and care for her and what feels good to her. Focus on long sessions of cuddling and closeness without sex when she's sore. Realize that for women, processing thoughts and feelings is extremely important. So don't feel bad if she calls Mama for some advice now and then. Mama herself was most likely in a similar position, say, 20 to 30 years ago, and I bet she remembers that time and can give some long-term perspective.

If I handed you a viola and said, "Play it," you'd probably look at me, surprised, and say, "I can't play the viola. I don't know the first thing about it."

So I'd encourage you further, "Come on, just try it. I want you to play it. Take the bow and play it."

So you do, and you make this rather awkward sound. I might look at you and say, "Good, that's good!" My guess is that you'd look back at me and say, "Good? That's terrible! I told you I can't play the viola."

"Yes," I'd say, "but you made noise, and that's the beginning." You too can make beautiful noise.

And one last thing: keep up the lavender baths. They're a great path to your wife's heart—and your growing love for a lifetime.

Q: I grew up in a really conservative, religious home. I was never told this in so many words, but the message came across loud and clear: *Sex is dirty. And you're dirty if you even think about it.* Sometimes I wonder how on earth I ever came to be, because I never saw my parents in anything less than their bathrobes. I still remember getting in trouble as a 7-year-old for running out of the bathroom in my underwear without a robe on. Bible verses about staying pure were held over my head during my teen years.

My fiancé (husband in three days) says he can't wait to see me nude. I know this sounds stupid, but that idea panics me. I really love him and trust him, but I've never revealed my body to anyone. The only sex education I've really had is from books—the ones I've purchased in the last year since Ryan and I got engaged. I really, really want to be married, but being naked just seems . . . *dirty*. Okay, so I said it. How can I get that out of my mind?

A: Thanks for your honesty. And you're right. The way you were reared has everything to do with how you view your body. It sounds like your home was extremely strict. For example, most 7-year-olds wouldn't think a thing about streaking completely naked from the bathroom and down the hall—and yelling happily as they go, "Hey, look at me!" You were wearing underwear and you still got in trouble. That hands-off approach has made you understandably skittish. It's time to adjust your thinking. You mentioned you're aware of Bible verses. But I'll bet anything that you weren't allowed the opportunity to read the Song of Solomon (also called the Song of Songs), unless you sneaked and did anyway. Here's just a little snippet:

> How beautiful you are and how pleasing,
> O love, with your delights!
> Your stature is like that of the palm,
> and your breasts like clusters of fruit.
> I said, "I will climb the palm tree;
> I will take hold of its fruit."
> May your breasts be like the clusters of the vine,
> the fragrance of your breath like apples,
> and your mouth like the best wine.

Song of Solomon 7:6–9

Whoa! That's in the Bible? you're saying. Yup, sure is. The whole book is a joyous celebration of married sex, showcasing all the delights that God has planned for one man and one woman in holy matrimony. May I make a suggestion? Take a Bible with you on your honeymoon and place a Post-it note on the Song of Solomon. On your honeymoon night, start reading slowly from the beginning of the book: "Let him kiss me with the kisses of his mouth" (Song of Sol. 1:2).

As you read together, caress each other gently and begin to undress slowly (in a low light, if that's what you're most comfortable with), and you'll begin to experience the delights of marital bliss with the one who loves you and has chosen you.

And, by the way, if you still need that bathrobe? (Old habits do die hard.) Ask your groom-to-be to handpick something out for you himself. I bet it'll look far different from the ratty pink one you've been wearing for years.

B. You're Experienced Sexually (You've Had Prior Partners or Been Married Before)

Q: I'm really embarrassed to write this letter, but here goes anyway. We just returned from what we thought would be the greatest time we'd ever have as a couple, in the exotic setting of the Bahamas. Sex was . . . a major disappointment. No, let me correct that. It majorly stunk. No fireworks. Nothing special. Just kinda . . . boring. We're both in our thirties and have had multiple partners before. I hate to even admit this, but all the

---

What to Expect on Your Honeymoon . . .

For virgins

1. A scared, apprehensive, nervous, somewhat fearful (see where I'm going here?) bride (who just might cry or call Mama)
2. A nervous groom (who may need a lot of cold showers)
3. A sore bride with a urinary/bladder infection and an unhappy (for awhile) Mr. Happy
4. Empty tubes of KY Jelly

For those who are remarrying or have had prior sexual experiences

1. A fresh new start, brimming with realistic or unrealistic expectations
2. A determination to make it work this time
3. A different partner than the one you had before (that may seem obvious, but think through that one . . .)
4. Old memories surfacing when you least expect—or want—them to

---

hot and heavy nights with my high school boyfriend in the backseat of my dad's car were much more sizzling.

After the first three nights, my new husband and I just found other things to do—like going to late-night luaus and lying on the beach to watch the stars. Surely there has to be more to this marital intimacy than what we've experienced.

A: No worries. Remember that your honeymoon was only the *beginning* movement of the symphony you're going to create together as a couple. If it was that boring and you're finding ways of filling time without having that closeness, I think there's something missing in your relationship. Are you really a couple who can share thoughts and feelings with each other? Do you have what I call the "intimate connection," where you could pick up a conversation two weeks later and not miss a beat? I think there's something wrong with your relationship, and coupled with that, you had some pretty high expectations of what your honeymoon would be like.

Think of men as violas for a moment. Violas can be made in the same factory and be built to the exact same specs, and they still have a different tone! What you're experiencing with your husband will be much different from what you experienced with your high school boyfriend. (And I would hope so! From what you've said, those nights were all about lust and certainly not about commitment, longevity, and communication.) Your husband is a different instrument than your old boyfriend. He'll play with a completely different tone—but it doesn't mean that he won't play with passion and excitement.

I have news for you. Great sex takes time to perfect, but what a fun ride it can be! So make time for sex in your marriage. If you both feel bored or feel like it's nothing special, talk about what would be exciting—and try it!

For Men Only
What Your Bride Needs Most from You

1. Don't think of sex as "the jackpot"—think of it as part of your relationship (albeit a very important part, says Mr. Happy quickly).
2. Think of your bride's needs *first,* before your own.
3. Realize she needs an environment of love, care, trust, and that she needs to feel safe, protected, and not rushed for her to have sex at the forefront of her mind.

Go beyond the standard missionary position and experiment with what feels good to each of you. Romance each other during the day. Go ahead and lay on the beach to watch the stars. But make a few adjustments. Lay a blanket over the two of you and let your fingers do the walking all over your spouse's body. Nibble on his ear. Get Mr. Happy's attention with a little rub. Whisper sweet somethings to her about how desirable she is and how she's the *only one* you desire.

Try some of these ideas for turning up the heat, and also invent your own. You might just find yourself walking a little more quickly back to your honeymoon suite. . . .

Q: Guess my dad said it best. "Paint or get off the ladder, son," he told me one day when I said I was debating whether to ask Cindy to marry me. He raised an eyebrow and added, "Well, you've been getting what you wanted—a little watoosie (my dad's word for *sex*)—for seven years. Don't you think it's about time to get a ring on her finger?" I couldn't argue with him; he was right. So we went ahead and did the whole wedding thing.

Now we're spending two weeks in our dream vacation spot: Hawaii (we've saved up for years to go at some point). Funny, though, I don't feel any different about her than I did before. Guess I was hoping we'd ramp up the sex now that we're married. But it just seems like the same old, same old. Am I just expecting too much?

A: The very tone of your letter shows that you're discouraged. Here are a few probable reasons:

1. You called your wedding (the event that should be the huge event in a couple's life—their joining) "the wedding thing."
2. You referred to your dream vacation spot instead of your honeymoon.
3. You mentioned that the sex was "the same old, same old."

Well, how different did you think sex in Hawaii would be from your home in Illinois? The two of you haven't changed, right? So sex in Hawaii is only going to be hotter and muggier!

The only thing that has changed is the piece of paper that declares you both have the same last name

Think of your honeymoon as a new chapter in your life and in your love story.

now. Let's face it: the surprise of sex and intimacy between the two of you has long been removed by your previous experiences. So if you're expecting a hot sexual interlude that's surprising and new on your honeymoon, you're a dog barking up the wrong tree.

Instead, think of your honeymoon as a new chapter in your life and in your love story. Because of your love for each other, you're taking your relationship to a deeper level. You're signing on the dotted line and pledging your troth to each other— whatever that is. I pledged mine years ago and still don't know what it is!

Your sex life doesn't have to be boring, though. Talk together about how to liven things up.

Q: I'm 40, and I just got married for the first time. All my friends say, "It's about time," and I guess it is. Brett's a great guy. We had been going together for four years (and yes, sex was a part of our relationship) and decided six months ago it was time to tie the knot. We'd both like to have kids someday, and I'm not getting any younger. And because I grew up with parents with two last names (my dad divorced my mom after he had an affair), I didn't want to do that to my own kids. So three weeks ago we got married and took a week off work for our honeymoon. I have to say, honeymoons are *nothing* like all the articles I've read. I just thought being married would be a little more exciting . . . *especially the sex part.*

A: Good for you for deciding to make the commitment to get married, especially with thinking about children on the horizon. You're right—it isn't fair to a child to be in a situation where there are no ties, where one of you can walk away scot-free at any time from the relationship. And that's what happens over and over every day in America (as you well know—you lived through it as a child).

In essence, you've had all the amenities of a marriage—without the commitment—over the past four years. By now you know each other quite well. You've been functioning as husband and wife without the paperwork, so you tell me what's going to be different on your honeymoon. You aren't working through the sex-for-the-first-time jitters or surprises such as, "I didn't know it would take you an hour to get ready to go to the pool!"

> *Developing your sex life in your marriage isn't something you simply win or lose. It's something you win for yourself and your mate.*

And you know what? You made a smart choice to get married. Research tells us that people who are married are happier, are healthier, and live longer than people who aren't. What a good step in the right direction! And down the road, your kids will thank you too.

Straight Talk

When you and your spouse leave on your honeymoon, it's so tempting for others to send you to the field of life with a pat on the back and the words, "Go win one for the Gipper." But the reality is, developing your sex life in your marriage isn't something you simply win or lose. It's something you win for yourself *and* your mate.

Your sex life has the potential to be one of the most, if not *the* most, satisfying and pleasurable parts of your marriage. Sex as the Creator intended it to be is a great gift that draws one man and one woman together for a lifetime.

The best things that honeymooners can do for themselves are read books about sex and communication, and talk about things before they get married, all through the honeymoon, and through the next 50 or more years of their life together.

So why not approach your honeymoon with the attitude of, "Hey, I'm not sure what we're getting ourselves into here, but I'm convinced it's going to be a great ride. So let's learn, laugh, and have fun doing it together!"

Now that's a honeymoon attitude for a lifetime.

2

The Beginning of
Happily Ever After?

You're back from your honeymoon. . . . Now what about the next 48 years?

You're in the midst of the first two euphoric years of your marriage (sans children messing with your sleep patterns, life, and general psyche—unless, of course, you're blending two families into one, then bless you). Enjoy those years! Your honeymoon might have been the best time of your life (or not—we've already looked at that in the last chapter).

After the honeymoon is the tremendously exciting time where you combine your individual lives into "couple life"—you move your possessions into the home you'll share; you combine finances, couches, cars, careers, and classes; and you juggle new activities on your Day-Timers.

You spend hours perusing stores or resale shops for just the right addition to your home decor. You have date nights, plan gourmet evening meals to celebrate, hold hands, and linger over dinner. You take moonlit walks with your brand-new schnauzer. You don't answer the phone after 8 p.m. (because you're snuggling).

You get to know each other's worlds and attend work picnics or gala events. You spend time doing things your spouse loves to do but you wouldn't normally be caught dead doing: like attending a Longaberger basket or craft show with your wife, or standing with your googly-eyed husband as he stares at a '67 Chevrolet 427 Corvette Stingray. (When you've been married a few years, you just might find yourself suggesting gently—or vociferously—to your spouse that he or she enjoy that activity with a friend.)

Life in general is adventuresome. You revel in your spouse and in being married—even if you're finding a few things you intensely dislike about him or her. Like the fact that he leaves the toilet seat up and you nearly fall into the bowl when you have to make a 2 a.m. potty run. Or like the fact that it looks like Mary Kay has visited the bathroom every time she gets ready for work in the morning. But even the dropped dirty socks by the bed are merely a brief annoyance before you shrug and drop them in the washer. Those are the little things, you figure. You have the man or woman you've dreamed of, so what's the big deal about picking up a sock? So what if your husband was late coming home for dinner the previous night? Or that your wife forgot to pick up Oreos for you at the store (though she *always* got them for you when you were dating)?

Then why do such little things bother you? Things like the bathroom looking like a water buffalo went on a stampede every time your wife washes her face, or the nail clippings your husband leaves on the carpet?

Ahh, could real life and your real spouse be intruding on your romance?

Q: When we got home from our honeymoon, I still had two days off, but Andy had to go back to work. I wanted to make things really special for him, so the first night I prepared a gourmet dinner. I'm talking Cornish hen, red potatoes, steamed broccoli, and a chocolate soufflé for dessert (and hey, normally I don't even cook). Andy was supposed to get home at 5:30, so I was all set up with candles and dressed in my slinkiest negligee . . . and he didn't come home until 8:00! By then I was a mess. Mascara was smeared down my face from crying, the Cornish hen looked like hen jerky, and the candles were stubs. When I asked him where he'd been, he told me sheepishly that he forgot he was married and that he'd gone home (to his parents' house) and was sitting around watching TV and joking with his dad. Finally his dad said to him, "Uh, aren't you supposed to go home for dinner?" That's when he realized he was at the wrong "home."

Ahh, could real life and your real spouse be intruding on your romance?

Okay, what gives? This new bride is really, really mad. How could he forget he was married? Does our marriage mean that little to him? Do *I* mean that little to him?

A: Whoa, Nellie. Who says that attention deficit disorder isn't present in adult males? I know you're mad now, but take the long view. Someday you'll have a hysterical story to tell your children. Bless his heart, your husband was simply doing what men do best: staying on one track. He probably had a long day at work and just did what came naturally—he returned to the cave from whence he'd come (translation: he returned to his parents' home, where he'd lived before you got married).

Put yourself in his shoes. Imagine how terrible *he* felt when he realized (1) what a dumb mistake he'd made; (2) how that would affect you, his bride; (3) how much worse he felt when he saw all the effort you'd gone to; and (4) how it tore his heart up to see your tears.

I can guarantee you something. That man of yours who probably looked like the saddest of all hound dogs when he returned home to you is going to be a faithful puppy dog from now on, returning home exactly on time for his bone. Why? Because he wants you, the woman he loves, to be happy above all things.

So cut the guy some slack. He wants to make up with you. He just pulled a dumb guy maneuver. Don't hold that Cornish jerky over his head for a lifetime. After all, he's put up with you when you were crabby during all those "special times" or when he was just taking up space on the wall while you talked with a girlfriend. Marriage is about loving . . . and forgiving. Making up can be awfully sweet too. Just give it a try. It's a lot more fun for both of you than being mad.

Q: Our sex life stinks. I can count on one hand the number of times we've had sex in the last six months. Is this our punishment or something for having sex before we got married?

A: When sex is forbidden, it can be awfully enticing. There's adventure, danger (in getting caught), and the thrill of the chase and the catch.

Then you get married, and things settle down. People tend to relax and let themselves go, quite frankly. Why do you think people gain weight after they get married? They're more sedentary. They watch more TV instead of meeting each other to go running or go to the health club. They don't always shower every day. They've "caught" their mate, so they don't have to be on display anymore.

Fast-forward a few years. When you have a 3-year-old son and a 4-year-old daughter in the next room, your thoughts won't be on getting it on. You'll be saying, "Can you roll over a little bit? I need to get some sleep."

Researchers say that honeymoon euphoria lasts about two years for most couples. That's why so many people write articles and books on how to keep the fire burning in a marriage relationship.

---

5 Great Tips to Dating Your Mate

1. Initiate it, plan it, and carry it out. It can still be spontaneous to your spouse, if he or she loves spontaneity, but *you* still need to plan it in your Day-Timer. Otherwise, with busy lives and cluttered schedules, it won't happen. Don't just pencil in the date; actually go to the work of planning it. Check your spouse's calendar, then make the reservation at the restaurant or hotel. By doing these details in advance, you're showing your spouse that you are thinking of him or her during the day, even when he or she is not around.

2. Accept your mate's attempts to do something unusual. (No one likes rejection. Reject your spouse and he or she may not try again.) I know one woman who took her outdoor-loving husband to an alligator-wrestling championship, and a husband who took his shoe-loving wife out on a surprise date to buy a new pair of shoes and a dress to go with them.

3. Be consistent. Set a regular date night. Just you two—no friends, no kids.

4. Splurge a little sometimes. Isn't your spouse worth something special?

5. Especially for guys: do *not* miss birthdays, anniversaries, Valentine's Day, or any holiday important to your wife. You may not care about Hallmark, but she does.

So what do you do for the next 48 years?

Sometimes you have to plan spontaneity, crazy as that sounds. You say that your sex life stinks. So I ask you: What are *you* doing about it? What have you done lately to make your sex life more exciting? When's the last time you kidnapped your spouse from work and took him to a hotel? When's the last time you sent the kids to Grandma's for the night, got her favorite dessert, and served it to her on your best china?

What you get out of marriage is what you put into it.

Q: Every time we have sex, it's really painful for me. Sometimes I bleed. I expected it to happen the first few times, because I was a virgin when we got married, but it's been over a year since our honeymoon. I'm always sore and stiff afterward (like I rode a horse for a long time). Will I just "get used to it," or is there something wrong with me?

A: I can't offer you medical advice because I'm not a medical doctor. But I have talked with enough couples to know that your situation of bleeding for over a year is unusual. It might be symptomatic of another issue, so I suggest you check with your ob-gyn right away. If your husband has a larger-than-average penis, that might account for the feeling of riding a horse, because every time you have sex, your muscles are stretched beyond what's comfortable for you. Some women aren't self-lubricating, so using a lubricant, such as K-Y Jelly, may help you to be more comfortable.

Also, I just have to ask: Is your husband aware that you are bleeding and so sore after sex? Is this something the two of you have discussed? If not, now's the time to talk about it. If he has a large penis or is thrusting powerfully into you, now's the time to talk together about how to vary your sexual position. Have you tried other positions that might be more conducive, such as you being on top, where the thrusting of his penis might be less forceful and more pleasurable to you?

A girlfriend once told me, "Keep dating them, honey, because once you marry them, it's not the same."

Sometimes pain associated with sex is also psychological because of a traumatic situation in your past, such as childhood abuse, a rape, or another previous sexual relationship. If any of these situations were realities in your life, talk to a counselor who can help you work through the issues, since they affect not only your sex life but the very way you see yourself in all aspects of your marital relationship.

So talk to your doctor, and talk to your husband. Those are your two best bets.

Q: A girlfriend once told me, "Keep dating them, honey, because once you marry them, it's not the same." Boy, was she right. When we were dating, Luke opened car doors for me, made phone calls to get my car repaired, took the day off to surprise me and paint the walls of my new condo, left a daisy on my car's windshield wiper—and many other thoughtful things. Then we got married, and Luke started working long hours. Somewhere along the way I seemed to have lost out in his priorities. I miss my boyfriend. I miss the romance. I miss feeling special. How can I tell him what I need without hurting his feelings? I know he's working really hard to provide for us.

A: Let me answer you with a story. It would be a great one to share with your husband too, to take the edge off what you want to tell him.

My wife loves nice restaurants. I'm talking five-fork kinds of places. Now, me? I like the one-fork variety. If it's plastic, so much the better. She loves the . . . what do you call it . . . the "presentation." She likes the nice evenings out with all those little forks. The same little forks that drive me up a wall as I wonder which one to use next. But Sande? She likes all that stuff. So, because I'm a good husband, I take her to nice restaurants.

One time, after a five-fork meal, I drove her to a resort hotel. She just looked at me. "Leemie, what are we doing here?"

"Honey, we're going to go into the hotel," I said calmly.

"I don't know what you have in mind, but I'm not getting out of the car," she said, arms crossed in that "No way, José" pose.

"Oh, c'mon," I said.

"We can't go out. I have no luggage. I'm NOT going in there."

I just smiled. I got out of the car, came around to open her door . . . and found out she'd locked it.

But I'm a smart guy. I had the key, so I used it to unlock the door. I literally lifted her up and said, "C'mon, dear, we're going in there."

"Okay," she said tensely, "I'll go, but you're not going to have any fun." So she wiggled down from my arms and started marching up to the main entrance like a soldier.

"No, not that way, this way," I said with another smile. I had the key for the room in my hand. After all, I had already been in the room that very afternoon.

When she walked in, she saw a king-size bed. She gave me the look. I could tell what she was thinking, and it wasn't nice. And it had everything to do with me and how exhausted I knew she was.

Then her expression changed. She noticed what was on the bed and moved toward it. I had purchased two books for her from Barnes & Noble—titles she'd mentioned she was dying to read sometime. I'd placed on the pillow three little sweetheart roses for the three children we had at the time.

That night, Mr. Happy went home sad.

And guess what else I did? I ordered room service for her: triple chocolate cake and a fresh pot of coffee. This was at 10:30 at night, mind you.

You're probably saying, "I hope it was decaf." Nope, it was regular. That's because I know my wife, and she's a raccoon—she's up half the night.

Then you know what I did? I told her, "Honey, you have a great time. I'll be back at 1:00 tomorrow to take you to breakfast."

She just turned and stared at me, surprise and tears brimming in her eyes.

And I went home and was Mr. Mom for the next 14 or so hours. (The truth? I don't carry out the role nearly as well as she does.)

Do you know how hard it was for me as a frisky husband to leave my wife alone in a hotel room with a king-size bed and the children elsewhere—my wife, who operates on the half-mile rule (we can't have sex if there's someone within half a mile of our home)? It was a golden opportunity for some happy times.

That night, Mr. Happy went home sad.

But guess what? Our marriage was the better for it, because my wife knew I cared about *her* as the cherished woman I love, not about what I could gain from her. I put her needs first, above my own. And the rewards of this kind of heart intimacy have been incredible in every area of our lives together, including our sexual relationship. (By the way, Sande had two more children after that—I got her pregnant when she was 42 and later when she was 47!)

So start the discussion by sharing this story with your husband. Then tell him gently, "Honey, I know you love me. I have no doubt about that. But sometimes I don't feel that I matter in your life anymore. I miss our times of closeness and the way we used to talk and laugh together. You made me feel so special, and I really miss that. I miss you. What can we do together to get that kind of passion back? Is there any way I can help you? Take some pressure off you? I know you've been so busy lately, providing for us."

For many busy husbands, just acknowledging that you long to matter in his life and that you miss the special way he made you feel will be enough to trigger his awareness that you need him. And that's one of the biggest needs of a man: to be needed.

---

10 Cheap and Memorable Dates

1. Visit the old train station in town.
2. Watch airplanes take off and land. Celebrate takeoffs with a gentle kiss.
3. Ride the city bus and check out the sights.
4. Take a walk by the river.
5. Take the afternoon off and have a rendezvous at home, then see a discount movie and have a picnic in the park.
6. Go to a library.
7. Watch a college athletic event (they're usually free and can be very entertaining).
8. Go out for coffee (it's cheap and can be nursed for a long, long time while you talk).
9. Get caught in the rain . . . and stay there.
10. Now figure out how to get those wet clothes off in a creative way. . . .

If you utter those precious words, "I love you. I respect you. I need you. I *want* you," your man will put you at the top of his priority list in a snap.

(Hint: For further insight into the way men think, read the next question and answer.)

Q: Sometimes I just don't understand women. I love my wife, but she complains I don't pay as much attention to her as I used to. But, you know, I spent a lot of time with her, getting to know her, when we were dating. Shouldn't she know by now that I love her, and that hasn't changed?

A: I agree with you. Sometimes I don't understand women either. And I love my wife too.

But there's something I've learned over forty-plus years of marriage. You're *never* done dating your wife.

"Whaddya mean, Doc? I told her I loved her once, when we got married. Isn't that enough?"

For you, evidently. For her, never.

Why the difference?

When you were dating your wife, you were doing what men do so well: moving in one-track, single-focus fashion toward winning your prize—your bride. You pulled out the stops. You tucked in your shirt, even bought a new shirt she said she liked. You combed your hair, brushed your teeth, even used breath mints before you kissed her. In short, you put on your very best appearance to win your bride. Then you walked down that aisle, and you smiled, thinking, *Hey, I got the marriage job done. Check one off my list.*

And what was she thinking? *We're going to have such a beautiful life together. We'll find a little house, have babies, be best friends forever. . . .*

The picture is different, isn't it?

So let me be blunt. If your wife has seen you at your very worst (in the buff) and still longs to connect with you and spend time together, as you did when you were dating, you'd be crazy not to go for it. For a woman, that longing to feel special is a longing to connect—with you. No one else will do—unless you step away from that role and decide not to fulfill it. (Then you leave her vulnerable to the attentions of other men.)

By longing to continue dating you, she's saying you are the greatest man in her life. You're her hero. The one she admires.

Now, come on. Isn't that worth far more than anything else you could be doing right now?

Straight Talk

Think of yourself as being in the 100-yard dash during these first two years. Virtually anyone can run the 100-yard dash—it's short, it's easy. It just takes a burst of speed, and dashing across that finish line is exhilarating.

But let me ask you: what are you going to do in the marathon, in the long haul of the next 48 years, when your relationship isn't as exciting or new anymore? These are the years in which your character and your spouse's character will come to the forefront. Just because you're married doesn't mean you should stop dating. These are the years where you focus on your marriage, building up your spouse, and working through any issues that may tend to rain on your marriage parade.

There will be times during those 48 years when you won't be sure you still love your spouse. But if you behave as if you do, your feelings will follow your actions. Love is not always a euphoric

41

feeling; it's a *decision*—a decision to remain committed to each other for a lifetime.

So what are you going to do for the next 48 years until you both (looking somewhat like raisins) get your picture in the local paper for your milestone fiftieth anniversary?

Following the advice in this book will ensure that you will mellow gracefully with age and that you'll have a great opportunity to enjoy each other throughout the years that God almighty gives you on this earth.

3

Lights On or Lights Off?

What makes you a couple: vive la différence!

Have you noticed that men and women are different?
"Duh, Dr. Leman," you're saying. "As if anyone wouldn't notice that."

I agree. It's easy to *see* the differences between men and women. But how much do you really know about just *how different* the opposite sex is in their approach to life, their thinking, the way they respond?

If you don't understand these differences—and learn to appreciate them—you'll spend way too much time banging your head against your spouse's, trying to figure out why he or she is not like you. Truth of the matter is, it's the *differences* between you that make you a couple. (I mean, really, would you want to be married to yourself? I shudder at the thought.)

Funny, isn't it, some of the differences between you? She likes to sleep late; you like to get up early. She likes movies that make her cry; you like testosterone ones. She likes her back scratched in

What do men need?
#1 need: to be fulfilled
#2 need: to be respected
#3 need: to be needed

an S-shape; you'd just take a massage anywhere. She needs the whole truth, the entire story, *and* the background; you'd rather have "just the facts, ma'am," or even a grunt in manspeak would suffice.

But these very differences are what give you a great shot at living a satisfying life together as a couple. What if you both liked to get up at 5 a.m. for coffee and reflection and wanted to be alone? I discovered it's not such a bad thing that my wife is a raccoon and is up half the night, and I'm an early bird.

Yet with all these differences, men and women were created sexually, in great detail, in such a way that they are a perfect fit for each other. So vive la différence!

Q: Maybe I'm just slow, but it's taken me two years of marriage to figure out just how different my wife and I are. Okay, I'll just come right out and admit it: sometimes we're *too* different. I have no clue where she's coming from. And that makes me more than a little nervous.

A: You're an honest guy, so I'll give it to you straight back.

You *are* slow, if you just noticed. Welcome to the reality of relationships! Men and women *are* different. They have very different needs.

What do men need?

#1 need: to be fulfilled (including sexual fulfillment)

#2 need: to be respected (your wife's respect is the highest priority)

#3 need: to be needed (what self-respecting guy wants to come home to a wife who is determined to do everything on her own and doesn't seem to need him?)

What do women need?

#1 need: affection (cuddling for the sake of closeness)
#2 need: communication (she needs words, sentences, and whole paragraphs when you get home from work—not grunts)
#3 need: commitment to family (she needs to know you'll be there at your son's soccer tournament and your daughter's ballet recital, and she won't have to wonder if you forgot)

See how different those needs are? Now why would the same Creator who put together the intricacies of the universe and the blood cells in our bodies not give men and women the same needs? Could it be that in the differences is some of the mystery, the attraction, that brought you together in the first place and now holds your marriage together? We are fearfully and wonderfully made. Truly, we are.

It is the differences that make you a couple. It's what attracted you to each other in the first place. After all, what fun would it be to be married to someone exactly like you? (I guarantee you wouldn't get along with two of yourself very long.)

What do women need?
#1 need: affection
#2 need: communication
#3 need:
commitment to family

Q: My wife and I have been married for five years. The first few years the sex was great. I know I'm doing it right—the same things I always do—but I don't get the same response I used to. Am I doing something wrong, or is my wife just not interested in me anymore?

A: Let's take a look at your letter for a minute. I couldn't help but notice all the times you used the word *I*. You didn't once refer to your wife's feelings or say that you'd talked to her about it. The focus seems to be all on yourself and your control of how your wife is responding to you. (Note that you didn't say, "My wife doesn't seem as excited about sex"; you said, "I don't get the same response I used to.") And you seem to be insecure about your role as lover. Is there a reason for that? If so, now's the time to talk to your wife about it. "Honey, I notice that you don't seem as excited about sex as you used to be. Is there anything I can do differently that you'd like?" You might be surprised at what you learn when you risk speaking those few words.

Also, you said, "I know I'm doing it right—the same things I always do." But do you really know you're "doing it right"? Or are you just guessing?

Years ago I worked with a guy named Jim, who told me one day, "I just don't get it, Doc. My wife likes this on Tuesday, but come Saturday, she says in a ticked-off voice, 'What are you doing?'"

If you're thinking of sex with your wife as a football play-book—you do this, then that—you're way off base. Sex with your wife isn't about the G-spot or the I-spot or the X-spot. It's about *relationship*. Think of it this way: sex is a gift from God, and it's something you have to perfect in accordance with whom? Your bride.

You need an adjustment on your perspective. Think of your wife as a Crock-Pot. She's going to warm slowly, so sex should happen ASAP—as slow as possible. Contrast that with yourself—you're ready to go instantly. One look at her, just one look, and Mr. Happy gets happy. You know what I'm saying?

Take the time to get to know your bride all over again. Ask her what she likes on Tuesday when you have sex, and then ask her again on Saturday when you have sex. I guarantee you that she'll want to be touched differently. So why not lead the way and start thinking, *What would my wife like?* rather than *I used to do this. . . .*

Marriage is all about giving yourself to the other person. When you got married, you agreed to become one, and that means giving up a lot of "I."

Q: I keep hearing all these things about a man's role and a woman's role. The man is supposed to be the take-charge person who handles the finances, brings home the bacon, likes to barbecue, and has sex on the brain. The woman is supposed to be the relational one who's good at remembering birthdays, taking care of the kids, and grocery shopping.

What Does a Woman Really Long For?

- Intimacy
- Security
- Being known and loved unconditionally
- Feeling like she can be whomever she wants to be
- Being freed from trying to please everyone

What Does a Man Really Long For?

- A 12-month football season
- A pocket satellite dish
- A wife who is assertive and aggressive in the bedroom
- A soul mate (someone who really understands how he feels when he dares to share his feelings)
- A wife who needs him (not others, just him)

In our marriage, our roles are nearly switched. I work full-time as an accountant downtown (so I have a lot of travel time), and my husband is a stay-at-home dad. He homeschools the kids, takes them on field trips, and even built a greenhouse in the backyard, but he couldn't identify a checkbook, much less write a check. He doesn't even know how to start a grill, but he can make an incredible tiramisu. And he's a great social networker, planning all the kids' birthday parties. In case you're wondering, he's not gay. He's as masculine as you get. (He even rides a Harley.) But in this relationship, we just seem to be the opposite of everyone else. In fact, *I'm* the one who pursues sex in our relationship. Otherwise I'm not sure he'd get around to it. (But he seems happy to oblige when I make the move.) I just have to ask: are we weird or something?

A: As I travel the country, I get asked that question a lot. A guy just walked up to me yesterday and said, "Uh, am I okay? I'm sorta the relational guy, and my wife keeps to herself. She's the one who tracks all our finances and investments. And"—here his voice got really quiet—"she's the one who's the most interested in sex."

You know what I say? "Okay? Sure you're okay! About 85 percent of marriages go with the norm. About 15 percent of us flow the other way. Is one right and one wrong? Nope. They're just different. So vive la différence!"

If your arrangement works well for you and your spouse, more power to you. That's wonderful. The problems in marriage come when one or both spouses are acting outside their comfort zones. For example, one guy I know just about took his family into financial ruin because he had grown up with the view that he, as the male, had to control the finances. When the electricity got shut off because he didn't pay the bill, he got the picture and handed off the bill paying to his very detailed wife.

So enjoy those differences! In fact, revel in them. Who says you can't pursue your husband sexually? From what you said, he sounds happy to oblige. He just may not think of it on his own. Don't feel like you have to explain yourself to anyone. It's you and your spouse who have to stand the test of time. The naysayers will come and go.

Q: I love my husband, but sometimes I get really frustrated with him. After sex, he rolls over and goes to sleep, like his job is done. But I feel empty. I wish he would just hold me and cuddle. To be honest, I could do without the sex and just keep the cuddling. Is that wrong?

A: Actually, you're very right. That's what the majority of women say. Men turn on instantly. Just the sight of their bride can get Mr. Happy flying ten stories high. But women aren't like that. They need to be held, cuddled, and talked to. In short, they need to feel cherished *before* there's any action in the bedroom—and they need to feel that way *afterward* too! After sex, your husband is satisfied, so he's ready for a good long sleep to recharge Mr. Happy for the next round. He may have no clue—unless you've told him—that his role isn't complete in the whole experience unless you can enjoy some cuddling afterward. Now's the time to have a little heart-to-heart with your husband. "Honey, I love having sex

> *After sex, your husband is satisfied, so he's ready for a good long sleep to recharge Mr. Happy for the next round. He may have no clue—unless you've told him—that his role isn't complete in the whole experience unless you can enjoy some cuddling afterward.*

49

with you, and I know it makes you happy. I really love it when we cuddle before sex. Do you think we could do that afterward too? That's really important to me."

Most red-blooded males would be thinking, *Hey, more time holding my wife's naked body? Oh boy, I'm there! Mmm, now why didn't I think of that?*

If he responds positively with just those words, you'll get all the cuddling you need. If he's a little more thickheaded, you might need another conversation that goes something like this: "Honey, I love having sex with you. You know I do. But cuddling afterward is so important to me. Otherwise, frankly, I feel a little empty and a little used. Like you got the sex job done, and now it's time for you to sleep. The sexual experience has been such a great thing to me that I need the cuddling to complete my satisfaction. Would you do that for me?"

If your husband doesn't respond to such a plea, you have other issues in your marriage that you need to deal with.

Q: We're trying to figure out the best time to have sex. My wife's a night owl, and I'm a morning guy. So neither of us is "in the mood" at the same time. It kinda puts a cramp on sex, if you know what I mean. Any suggestions?

A: When I talk about the differences between men and women, this question inevitably comes up. What do you think most men say when I ask, "When do you prefer to be intimate with your wife—in the morning or in the evening?"

Some will say morning; some will say evening. And some guys will laugh and say, "I'd take both!"

"Hey," I tell them, "not a fair answer. You have to pick one."

So the final answer? Most men say morning is the time they're most hot to trot.

When I ask women what the best time is for them to be intimate with their husband, what do they say?

"In June!"

That's correct. June.

No, seriously, it's the evening.

Isn't it interesting that almighty God, with all of his infinite wisdom, would do that: make men more interested in sex in the morning, and women in the evening?

Your mission, sir, is to figure out the time that works best for both of you. If your wife works outside the home, it's doubtful she's going to want a wild romp in the morning after she's taken a shower and is getting ready for work. So Mr. Happy may just have to adjust to evening (or another time of the day). And it may mean that you'll have to change some of your habits. Instead of putting up your feet after dinner in front of the TV, help your wife clean up the dinner dishes. Better yet, *you* make dinner *and* clean up the dishes. If you do, you'll have a grateful, happy wife who will be more than thrilled to inspire you in the bedroom because she has some energy left.

So figure it out—you'll be glad you did.

Q: Sometimes I'm really, really in the mood for sex. I mean, raring to go. Just one look at her, and I've already dropped my trousers. But Jen needs to talk—a lot—before I can even touch her. By then, I'm almost jittery with sexual energy. I feel like I'm going to explode.

A: Women and men both long for connections. For women, that connection is first of all emotional. She wants you to talk with her before she is ready for physical intimacy. For men, that connection is first of all physical and sexual. Oftentimes men have already used up their word count for the day, and they're basically done talking. They just want the action!

For your wife to feel prized and loved and to be a willing partner in bed for anything creative Mr. Happy may have in mind, she first needs to hear your words, your affirmation of her as a person, and your assurance that you love her and think of her during the day. She also needs to know that you consider her worthy of hearing about your day and that you trust her to risk sharing your thoughts and feelings with her.

> *Your mission for your entire marriage is to get behind your spouse's eyes and see how he or she looks at life.*

Think of Jen as a delicate plant that has to be cultivated, watered, and handled very carefully. Your wife is mysterious; she's not like you. Men are much more mechanical—they act on physical urges and do what comes naturally. They can tend to rush through the sexual experience to get to the climax. But if you do that with your wife, you'll turn her off. You'll make her feel used and abused. Your wife needs to hear your gentle words of love and appreciation; they're like water and light to a plant. If she does, she'll feel embraced by you, and she'll bloom. She'll come to that special place in your lovemaking where she'll say, "Don't stop. Right there. You've got it!" All of a sudden she's a cheerleader in the whole process. And guess what—that pleasure she's experiencing? It's all because of you!

Now isn't that worth waiting for?

Straight Talk

Men and women are different. To have great sex, men need a place; women need a reason.

It's interesting. We have a Creator who knew how to put the earth in outer space on exactly the right axis. One degree this way and we fry. One degree that way and we freeze. So don't you think he knew what he was doing when he made men and women? You should be on your knees thanking God that your spouse is different from you.

Your mission for your entire marriage—not just during dating or in those euphoric first couple years—is to get behind your spouse's eyes and see how he or she looks at life. It's not the lighting of the unity candle that magically makes you become one. Becoming one is a daily working out of your relationship. But turning up the heat is well worth it.

I can feel the temperature rising in your bedroom already.

4

What's Your Mom
Doing in Bed with Us?

Why more than two of you walked down that flower-strewn aisle to say, "I do."

What's the one thing you told yourself as a youngster growing up? "When I have kids, I'm never going to do to them what Mom (or Dad) did to me."

You can believe that with all your heart, mind, and soul. But if that day comes when you are blessed with children, my best guess is that you are going to say exactly those things to your children that your parents said to you. And you're going to use the same tone and inflection!

What am I getting at, and what does this have to do with sex and intimacy in your marriage? Fact is, the way you as a kid saw your parents treat each other has imprinted itself on your brain. Maybe you had an absentee father or mother. Whether you want to admit it or not, you have been positively and negatively imprinted by the behaviors of your parents.

So when you walk down that flower-strewn aisle to say, "I do," it's not just the two of you getting married. The pastor who turns to the congregation may say, "I introduce to you Mr. and Mrs. So-and-So." But the truth is, he didn't marry just two people. He married at least six people. If you both are products of blended families or are remarrying, the number goes up to at least ten.

"Now, Dr. Leman," you're saying, "you have a problem with math. Where are you getting all these people from? It's just me and my spouse."

No, it's you, your spouse, your mom and dad, and your spouse's mom and dad—at the very minimum. You marry your in-laws too. If you have any stepparents, they and their spouses are included too. If you're on your second marriage, then your previous spouse is included too. He or she affected you greatly.

Why do I include all these extra people in the marriage union? When you marry, you will reap the benefit or pay the price for what has happened to your spouse before you even met him or her. If your wife has a distant daddy, you'll pay for that. If she has a loving, warm relationship with her daddy, oh, the benefits for you and your entire family! If your husband has respect for his mother because he saw that from his father, you will be blessed with the same type of respect as a wife. If your husband saw his father walk all over his mother and chooses to do likewise, uh-oh. You will have to stand your ground firmly.

As a result of all his or her relationships in the past, your spouse comes to your marriage with a rule book. It's a private logic that informs everything you do. That rule book says, "This is the way things ought to be done, and the only way things ought to be done.

And if they're not done this way, I won't like it, and I'll make you pay for it."

Now, is this rule book posted in a public place—like on the refrigerator door or bedroom door? Nope. It's not posted anywhere. But that doesn't change the fact that we live by these internal rule books—they govern everything we say and do.

Here's an example of how internal rule books affect the dynamics of a relationship. Let's say carefree Louie and uptight Sarah marry. Join them in the bedroom and see what they're thinking (but not telling each other).

Carefree Louie: *Oh, wow, this is gonna be fun, fun, fun. I can't wait to experiment. And look at that new nightie I just bought her. I love it. It turns me on. We have all the time in the world.*

Uptight Sarah: *Okay, let's just get this over with. Same old, same old, except I have a new nightie on. My role is to just lie here, and your job is somehow to get me interested and then to pull my nightie down when you're through. Then can we please just go to sleep? I'm really tired. It's been a long day.*

See what I mean? That's a prescription for marital disaster. If he wants to explore your body from head to toe and discover everything about it, well, to you as a woman, that may be downright frightening. *Hey, I don't want him exploring anywhere!*

Some people are just more conservative. There's nothing wrong with them; they're just more traditional. Like my wife, Sande, who would shower with her bathrobe on if she could. Would I, the fun-loving guy that I am, love it if some night she came in swinging from the chandelier, buck naked? You bet I would. In fact, I'd have a repairman out the next day and reinforce that chandelier to make sure that the next time she did it, she wouldn't hurt herself.

But I'm a smart guy. I know, love, and respect my wife. We've been married for 41 years, and she's never swung from the chandelier. But there were many other times that she surprised the socks off me in different ways. She has gone out of her way to flex her rule book because she loves me. And, I tell you, that makes me really feel loved as a husband and the man she chose to spend the rest of her life with.

So what's in your rule book? What's in your spouse's rule book? Do you know?

One of the most important things to get straight in a marriage is to agree and act on these principles:

He is not your father. He is your husband.

She is not your mother. She is your wife.

If you don't agree on these principles, bitterness and resentment can begin to grow. Many of the hassles we experience in marriage are directly related to the kinds of things our parents have taught us (either overtly or subtly)—or the kinds of things they never bothered to teach us.

And many of them could be solved just by switching rule books with your spouse. Now there's some fine thinking. Wish I would have thought of it the day I got married.

This isn't rocket science. If it were, I couldn't explain it to you. Simply said, who do you want to please in your marriage? Your mama? Your papa? Or your spouse?

Whose Rule Book Are You Following?

If you're a woman, what 3 words best describe your relationship with your father?

If you're a man, what 3 words best describe your relationship with your mother?

Do any of those words describe the way you treat your spouse right now? Why do you think this is so? What's good about that treatment? What needs to change?

Q: My wife grew up in a very conservative home. We see the whole experience of sex completely differently. And when I say completely, I mean completely. Is there any middle ground? We're starting to disagree a lot—okay, so we fight. And it all has to do with our sex life. I want to talk about it, but she doesn't. She finds talking about sex really embarrassing. Now, me? I figure, *How can you do it and not be able to talk about it?* Or am I just stupid because I'm a guy?

A: Well, hello, Mr. Stupid Guy. You may not be as stupid as you think. You've already pegged the problem—that it has to do with your wife's inability and discomfort in talking about sex, due to her background. That's pretty good reasoning for a stupid guy, I'd say.

Let me add to your understanding of what's going on.

I had no idea that my wife had carried a tiny book—a rule book—down the aisle at our wedding. I had no idea she had such a thing tucked into her emotional purse. In fact, I didn't find out until our honeymoon, when she said to me, "What do you think you're doing?"

You see, I had violated a rule in her rule book—the unwritten book she'd brought with her into marriage, the book that contained her way of looking at life and her perception of what was sensual, sexual, right, and wrong. I had a rule book too, I found out. But our rule books were entirely different!

Where did our rule books come from? Good ol' Mom and Dad and the home we grew up in. Some of us were taught that sex is dirty. This sounds like the case with your wife, based on what you've told me. And that perception has colored not only her view of sex but the experience of sex in your marriage. No wonder, then, that she has a tough time talking about sex.

So when you try to talk to her about it, you're violating Rule #29 of her rule book (even if you didn't know she had one): *Thou shalt not talk about sex. Ever.* How does that translate to your wife? *He doesn't love me. He doesn't understand. He doesn't care what I think. I'm not important to him.*

And you, Mr. Stupid Guy, have no clue, right?

So let me ask you something: have you and your wife ever talked about those unwritten rules? I suggest it's time to get them out in the open. Air the laundry, so to speak, and you'll be far better off. Yes, your wife may be uncomfortable, so approach the subject as lovingly as possible: "Honey, I really love you. You are so treasured and important to me. I know you're really uncomfortable talking about sex, because that wasn't allowed in your home when you grew up, and I understand that. But I want to please you and give you joy. That's important to me as a husband. Would you honor me by talking about what would please you? What makes you comfortable? What makes you uncomfortable?" Your role is to listen and not to prod, then to gently share things that are important to you as well.

Why not simply exchange rule books? After all, isn't marriage about understanding each other and growing together? If you get both of your rule books out in the open, you can write a

---

What's in Your Rule Book?

1. What is a great evening to you?
2. How did your parents resolve conflict?
3. If you had an hour to do anything, what would you do?
4. Name 3 things married people should never do.
5. What would really disappoint you about someone you love?
6. Is honesty the best policy? Why or why not?

new rule book with the person you love. She'll never share her rule book with anyone she can't trust completely.

To have a healthy, lasting marriage, you have to be willing to grow and mature—together. You have to be willing in heart to see things differently and to change your behavior to benefit your spouse. Yes, it's work, but it'll be worth it—the first time you hear her say, "Oh, that's great. A little more there!"

Q: I always thought it was just one of those goofy things people say in magazines: "You always marry someone like your mom." But you know, now I'm thinking it might be true. I grew up in a home where my mom always took care of everything. Even though she worked full-time, she was always there to drop us kids off at school and to pick us up. She was at all of our soccer games and school concerts. Dad traveled a lot, so I guess she had to be independent.

My wife of seven years, Lisa, is a lot like my mom—really independent. It never bothered me until this year, though, when a friend joked, "Hey, do you ever get to see Lisa? Seems like she's always running somewhere. Do you guys ever have time for sex?" And then it hit me. For the first time ever, I realized how lonely I had felt as a kid, because I missed my dad being around. I spent time with my mom, but it was always because we were going somewhere, not just to be together. I want things to be different in my family when we have kids (something we're talking about), and I want sex to be part of our relationship. But where do I start?

A: You start right where you are. First, you figure out your rule book (in your home growing up, Dad was on the sidelines and Mom was chauffeur, but neither had emotional involvement) and how it has influenced your life. Then talk with Lisa and get her ideas about how to move toward the changes you long for in your life together.

But tread carefully. You love the wife you married, and nothing has changed about her. It's *you* who has changed (evidently you were okay with the status quo for seven years), so you can't expect her to immediately understand—or be on board with—that change in your perspective toward sex or anything else. Approach her gently, telling her how much you love her and that you'd love to do more things together. As you begin talking, share from your heart about how you felt growing up—very lonely. Assure her that she is the most important person in the world to you, there's no one you'd rather spend time with, and there's no one you'd rather have sex with—and that's important to you. Explain that when you have children, you want to be an active, in-the-game daddy, not a sidelined one.

Share your heart, in love, and you won't go wrong.

Straight Talk

If you view your spouse through the lens of your rule book—without letting your spouse in on why he or she is being judged that way—you're in for trouble. Why not make it easy on yourself? Simply exchange rule books. You'll be amazed at what you learn. Even a short rule book session at a Starbucks can bring a miraculous change in the way you relate to each other. So what are you waiting for?

If there's a battle going on in your marriage today, it would behoove you to take some time out to discuss your behaviors and expectations with your spouse.

5

You're Frisky Again? Didn't We Just Have Sex–in April?

How often should you do it—and do you have to do it?

My dear wife, Sande, is a low-energy person. In 40-plus years of marriage, we've taken approximately four walks—the longest of which was 400 yards. Recently she bought a bike. Actually, she asked for a bike for her birthday, and she got one. She rode it too. Once. Across the bridge to our property, which is a whopping 300 yards. That was a good start—for Sande. Come to think of it, it was several months ago that she took her grand first voyage. I should probably put some air in those tires before they go completely flat.

Contrast that with Carmen, a working-from-home mom who is the highest-energy person I know. What she accomplishes in a day is astounding. It makes me so tired just thinking about it that I have to sit down.

One of your kids is a fast eater; one is a slow eater. One needs a good ten hours of sleep; the other needs only five to eight hours.

My son-in-law, Dennis, can eat a large pizza by himself. Other folks I know can eat only one piece; it fills them up for the whole evening.

People are different. We all have different appetites. Some of us gag at the thought of a green bean in our mouths; others of us love those little suckers. (Even yellow beans, lima beans, any kind of beans—bring them on!) The reality is, we're all different, and that's a good thing.

We have no problem understanding different tastes in food and energy levels, so why do we have problems understanding different tastes in sex? Some people are low-activity people. They like to live life more gently, to take their time. Others are hyper, almost frenetic. And there are many of us in the middle.

Here's the funny part. Just like the four-foot-ten-inch bride finds a six-foot-three-inch guy to marry, many times in holy matrimony husband and wife are, by their very nature, very different. (Remember vive la différence?)

Of course, we assume that men are the ones with the most voracious appetite for sex. That simply isn't true. There are women who teach Sunday school who would swing into the bedroom on a chandelier if you'd let them. (My wife, as I said earlier, just doesn't happen to be one of them.)

Some people have sex 36 times a day . . . and then they die.

But many of you wonder, *How often should we do it? What's normal?*

Q: My husband and I are both in our late twenties, and we've been married five years. If it was my choice, I'd like sex once a day, but my husband is a twice-a-month (if that) kind of guy. When we have sex, it's really good. It's just that it doesn't happen enough to suit me. Could something be wrong with him that he doesn't seem to want it? What am I supposed to do if I'm in the mood and he's not? According to him, since he's the guy, he gets the say on when we have sex.

A: Though you'd prefer sex every day and your husband is a twice-a-month man, be careful that you don't start ripping on yourself or your husband. The truth? You have very different sexual appetites, and you'll need to work that out together.

Start by telling your husband that you would love to have sex more than once every two weeks. But you also hate to beg, "Please, honey, could we do it tonight?" That feels demeaning to you and takes the romanticism out of the experience. Getting it in a grudging way because you asked won't be psychologically fulfilling to you.

What a Woman Needs to Enjoy Sex

1. To feel loved, prized, and valued.
2. To be listened to and respected.
3. A romantic atmosphere. (It's why sex on the spot may work in the movies, but it's unrealistic in real life. A woman wants to feel clean—to pay attention to certain areas of her body before she wants to be touched. Hygiene is very important. All guys need is the sniff test.)
4. Privacy. (Absolutely not in her mother-in-law's house!)
5. To be understood and cuddled.

What a Man Needs to Enjoy Sex

1. To feel needed. (Being wanted by his woman is the emotional turn-on for a man.)
2. A place. (Anywhere will do.)
   It's a short list.

If your husband really loves you—he just doesn't have much umption in his gumption, as one old grandpa used to say— he will make an effort to please you more than he's naturally inclined to.

So tell him how you feel, then back off. Don't beat him up. And don't beat yourself up either. Women, especially because they deal much more strongly with body image, often begin to think, *There must be something wrong with me. I must not be attractive to him anymore. Maybe I should lose some weight or something.*

There's nothing wrong with you or your husband. You simply have different sex drives.

There's nothing wrong with you or your husband. You simply have different sex drives. And you know what? Be thankful for the times when you do have good sex! There are a lot of people who wish they had good sex once a month!

Also, do a bit of research on the idea that the man calls the shots. If you're married, it's not one person's right to make those calls. In 1 Corinthians 7:4, Paul says, "Your body belongs to your husband. And the good news is that your husband's body belongs to you!" (the Leman translation). If you take the "he has to be the aggressor" stance and put him in that box, and he doesn't become the aggressor, you'll find yourself criticizing him.

Instead, why not make this your challenge: you, wonderful lady, must create all sorts of fun ways to get your husband in the sack with you. He may be a low-sex-appetite person, but once you get his engines running, there shouldn't be a problem. Take things into your own hands . . . literally.

Q: I really, really want to know: how often should a married couple have sex? I've heard all sorts of answers, and some of them seem way out there. I'm honestly asking. Help! My husband has seemed a bit crabby lately, and I guess I'm just wondering if he's not getting enough action. Whoops. That was blunt.

A: I have to assume that you're asking because this has come up as a question in your marriage, so there's at least a minor skirmish over it. There are lots of "sources" for such a question—just check out *Redbook* and *Cosmo*. But are they right? And why is it so important to you to know?

Bottom line, what's normal is what you and your spouse are comfortable with and have agreed upon. There are many factors that go into how often a couple has sex: their health, their emotions, life changes, stress, depression, etc. Every person has a sexual rhythm. Your husband may be a 24-hour guy, a 48-hour guy, a 72-hour guy, or a once-a-week guy. And your job is to help him figure out what that rhythm is. If your husband is a little grouchy and irritable, it could be that he needs to release his testosterone. Maybe he's feeling overwhelmed or inept at work and needs some extra attention at home. If so, you're perfect for the job. So why not make yourself available? It's sure a lot more fun than doing laundry, I'll tell you.

That's what marriage is all about—working together to understand each other and turn up the heat to a vibrant, sexual relationship with your lifelong mate. And you are his perfect provision. Yes indeed, that's what marriage is all about—and the best years are ahead for every one of us.

So observe your guy carefully. Watch for signs that he needs some release, then surprise him with your attention. After a while, you'll have him all figured out. You see, men are easy. It's you women who baffle us men because you're so beautifully and masterfully complex. And we love you for it.

Q: I just can't help it. I see my wife in her underwear, and I'm ready to go. Sometimes I feel like I'm about ready to explode with sexual energy. Then my wife looks over at me and says, "Nuh-uh. You're not getting me in bed right now. No way. I have things to do." How can we come to some sort of agreement?

A: I know what you mean, brother. I feel the same way when I see my wife in her underwear, and I've been married 41 years! Traditionally men have been the aggressive ones in the sexual relationship because usually we do have sex on the mind—well, at least 33 times a day! So it's no surprise that you're jazzed and ready to go. However, if your wife feels that she *has* to be the recipient of your sexual advances at any time, I have news for you. She's going to feel disrespected and demeaned.

Sex is not something you use to take the edge off sexual tension. It's something to be enjoyed by both husband and wife. So I suggest you dial back your expectations a bit. Make love to your wife outside the bedroom. (I did a whole book on that subject, called *Sex Begins in the Kitchen*. You'd find it very helpful.) What does that mean?

Every morning of our married life—for 41 years—I've brought Sande a cup of coffee in bed. I've learned how to scratch her back exactly the way she likes it—on top of the nightie only, in an S-shape (Sande has lots of little rules). And you know why? Because I enjoy pleasing her, and I know how important those little things are to her.

Similarly, if you please your wife outside the bedroom and show her how much you care about her, she's going to be much more responsive to you, Don Juan.

Straight Talk

For many couples, twice a week is "normal." But do you really want to be *normal*? What's the fun or uniqueness in that? Why base your relationship on what everyone else is doing? Isn't this relationship based on you and your spouse?

Realize that Mr. Happy can get happy almost instantaneously. How long does it take a husband to get frisky? Probably not over two seconds. Women tend to take thirty minutes to get vaguely in the mood, and many, many pieces have to fall into place for her to be receptive to a sexual interlude. No wonder couples fight over the question of frequency.

Over a period of time, you and your spouse need to come to an agreement of what frequency is best for the two of you. It's the right—and the loving—thing to do.

6

Turn-Ons and Turn-Offs in the Bedroom

What your spouse really cares about . . . and what you shouldn't.

Let's be blunt. We guys can have a one-track mind. After all, when we get a signal from Mr. Happy that he's a ready teddy, that's all we care about. It doesn't matter if you haven't brushed your teeth. It doesn't matter whether you're just getting ready to get in the shower after working in the garden all day. You could be a sweaty mess. Mr. Happy doesn't mind.

But you do. You care. You can't think of sex without both of you brushing your teeth and having a clean surface to caress.

There are definite turn-ons and turn-offs in the bedroom, and every spouse is unique. Because both partners should be satisfied in marriage, this means it's time for negotiation.

Let's say your husband sees you in your bra and panties and wiggles his eyebrows. You know what that means. But you just got home from a long day at work, and you need to relax and eat dinner first. So what would you as a loving wife say?

"Honey, I love you, and I understand Mr. Happy is all ready to go. I'd be glad to oblige, but first I really want to take a shower and wash off my day. And I need to get something to eat since I had to skip lunch because of my meetings. If you could make some mac 'n' cheese while I'm in the shower, I'd appreciate it. Then we could eat right away, and soon we'll be in the fun zone. . . ." And you can wiggle your eyebrows right back at him.

Well, Mr. Happy might be momentarily disappointed, but I can guarantee you that husband of yours will zoom toward the kitchen and have that boxed mac 'n' cheese all ready and waiting for you on the table.

Is it a different kind of evening than you'd planned? Sure. You had thought something a little more gourmet might be nice. But mac 'n' cheese was the best solution, and you were smart enough to realize it. Good for you.

Or let's say you just went out to a movie with your guy friends, got filled with testosterone, and came home raring to go. Your wife is already in bed, reading a book. You take one look at her and you're ready to remove that nightie she has on. You married a wise woman, and she knows exactly what's going on. It's written all over her face. But you've also been married long enough to know that she's wrinkling her nose for a reason. That means her delicate sense of smell is a little overpowered by your male sweatiness. So she says, "Hey, go take a shower. I'll be waiting!" Want to bet you'll whip into that shower, get clean fast, and maybe throw on a bit of cologne in a sensitive spot for good measure?

Could you have responded differently in one of these situations? Of course! And if you were thinking only of yourself, your experience could have ended in a marital spat rather than an exciting sexual interlude.

Do you know what turns your spouse on? What turns your spouse off? You might be surprised. It may not be what you think at all.

Q: Ever since I was a kid, I've struggled with being overweight. My nickname was even "fat-face Cindy." I hated it. Even though I've worked hard to keep my weight down, there's no way I can compete with all the beautiful women in this world. Sometimes I look at myself in the mirror and think, *How could he love me? How could anyone love me?* It makes me not want to be naked . . . unless we have sex in the dark. Is there any help for me?

A: A lot of women needlessly beat themselves up about their weight. They read all the women's magazines, see the newest fashions on the young and slender models, and then look in the mirror and think, *Oh my!*

But think for a minute. Guess who chose you *just as you are*? Your husband! And if he truly loves you, he'll continue to love you just as you are.

But does that mean you should let yourself go? Overeat? Not take pride in how you look? Not shower? Not shave your legs? Not do those things your husband finds appealing (like wearing that hot-red number you have at the back of your wardrobe)? No, you do those things because you want to look your best for your husband.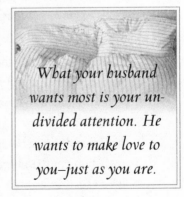

What your husband wants most is your undivided attention. He wants to make love to you—just as you are.

Does he expect you to be perfect? No. Does he expect a size 6? No. He knew you weren't perfect when he married you—and neither is he. And funny thing: he knew you weren't a size 6 when you got married. It didn't matter then.

What your husband wants most is your undivided attention. He wants to make love to you—just as you are. And he wants you to freely make love to him.

That's what turns him on.

Q: My husband is so dense sometimes. He comes home, drops his coat at the door, tracks his muddy shoes across the kitchen floor to where I'm making dinner, checks to see if our boys are in sight, then grabs my breast and pinches my bottom as if I'm going to drop right there on the kitchen floor—in the midst of steaming pasta and Ragú—and go at it with him. Can't he see that I'm in the middle of cooking dinner? I have two kids yelling, "Mom! When's dinner? We're STARVING!" And his muddy shoes just tracked mud across the floor that I spent the last hour cleaning! If he ever scrubbed the floor himself, made dinner, or did the dishes, he'd have a taste of how I feel. It's like I'm at his beck and call—a call girl—for whatever he wants.

But he never thinks about me or what my day is like. How can I get the message across, without banging him on the head with the pot of pasta?

A: Actually, I sort of like the idea of banging him on the head with the pot. But if that will get you three to six months in the local pokey, we ought to look at an alternative.

There's not a woman in the world who's ever told me behind the closed doors of my counseling office, "Dr. Leman, I just love it when my husband grabs my breast or my butt. It makes me feel so sexy, so wanted."

Women don't like to be grabbed. They like to be held, cuddled, and talked to. So you have every right to be offended. Here's something that might be worth a try (especially if your husband likes to be in control of the situation): When he starts his caveman move on you, just turn to him and say, "Oh, *honey*, when you grab my butt like that, it makes me want to take off my clothes and jump your bones right here on the kitchen floor, even if the kids are in the next room!" Then just sit back and wait for the dropped jaw and the shock. If he's the one who likes to be in control, that ought to put an end to his breast and butt grabbing, since you've taken him out of the driver's seat.

But it's also possible your husband is emotionally as dumb as a rock. Men can be like that sometimes. If that's the case, at some point you have to share with your husband how that makes you feel when he just grabs you—when there's no romance or cuddling, just grabbing.

Whenever I have a chance to talk to teenage boys about relationships with girls, I often talk about "Why It's Not Cool to Grab a Girl's Breast." And it's not cool. I've heard very few women in the course of my private practice admit that they liked their breasts touched in any way except for the most delicate, gentlest way possible. Some women said they liked the very top of their breast gently stroked—that could be pleasurable. But they did not appreciate a 20-, 30-, or 40-year-old male trying to act like he was an infant who needed her breast.

Men are not naturally good lovers, but they can be taught. It's just that you have to be a willing teacher (which means that you have to put up with a lot of antics along the way in the learning process).

You'd think that sex would be the most natural thing in the world, just as you'd assume that there would be nothing more natural than a baby at her mother's breast. But I'm here to tell you (after five children) that bringing a mother and baby together isn't always an easy thing. It's why hospitals today have lactation nurses to help moms and babies work together. It takes two to get into a rhythm. The same is true of your sex life.

It takes two, and it takes practice. It sounds like you're married to a bull-in-a-china-shop kind of guy. You're thinking (and seething), *What does he think I'm doing? Am I a lumberjack? One of his buddies he says "Good game" to and gives high fives to?*

You need to speak out. What have you got to lose other than a few less squeeze marks on your breasts and pinch marks on your butt?

I know what you're thinking: *Oh, great. I do everything around here. Now I have to teach him how to have sex too?*

Uh, yeah, you do. For better or for worse, remember? But it's worth the effort since men are highly trainable. Your husband has a willing spirit. He just may not know better. A little teaching can go a long way.

Hey, better check the pasta. It might be boiling over. . . .

---

10 Top Ways to Turn Off Your Wife

1. Wear the same boxer shorts for a week.
2. Belch.
3. Pass gas.
4. Be crude in any way.
5. Move too quickly.
6. Treat her like you own her.
7. Forget to brush your teeth.
8. Leave engine grease under your fingernails.
9. Notice your wife's new haircut . . . 10 days later.
10. Look at and comment about other women.

Q: I work out of the office three days a week and from home two days a week to avoid my long commute. But our house is just about to drive me crazy. It's so disorganized and such a mess that it's sometimes hard for me to work at home. When I say anything to my wife, she just gets mad. "Stop criticizing me," she says. "I'm doing my best." She works too, but only part-time, so she has more time than I do. She ought to do more of the picking up around here, don't you think? But every time I bring it up, she ices me, and I don't get any . . . you know.

A: Are you looking for advice, or are you looking for your behavior to be validated? Clearly you have an attitude. You come home to your little kingdom and expect it—*poof!*—to be in great shape. Let me ask you: what have you done to help it get that way?

Sure, you may work full-time and your wife may work part-time. But who does all the rest of the work around the house? Who does the laundry, cooks, cleans, grocery shops, mows the grass, takes out the garbage, and gets the oil changed in the car? From all the couples I've counseled, chances are pretty good that it's your wife who has all those jobs—and more. So that means she has one and a half jobs to your one.

Think about that for a moment. *Now* who should be taking more responsibility, do you think? If the mess bugs you, then *you* start organizing and picking things up (and without the attitude). There's nothing that will kill an intimate relationship faster than criticism. No one is going to want to do anything for you. Sounds like your wife is at that point, and I don't blame her. I sure wouldn't want to live with your constant whining.

And who knows? If you pick up the living room, organize the kitchen shelves, and clean the toilet, you might begin to understand what she does on a daily basis, and then you might get a little "you know."

Q: Okay, I'm new to this marriage thing. We just got home from our honeymoon a couple weeks ago. If you could give me advice on the most important asset a wife can focus on, what would that be, and why? This inquiring mind wants to know.

A: The most important asset would be a positive attitude about life. That helps in almost any situation, but particularly in marriage. And especially in your intimate life with your husband.

Here's what you have to understand about that man of yours: He wants to be your hero. He wants to please you. And if you give him just the tiniest bit of encouragement, he'll go to the ends of the earth for you.

But if you shoot him down, you might as well stick a dagger in his heart. He's going to slink away like a dog that's been beaten too many times and will just whimper by himself in his kennel. If you reluctantly accommodate his sexual needs, you will create a resentful husband who will seek pleasure, conversation, and intimacy elsewhere.

Now there's a scary thought. But it's also reality. And it happens every day in America to couples like you and your husband.

That's why a positive attitude is the most important asset. What does a positive attitude look like? It's opening your arms

---

5 Top Ways to Turn Off Your Husband

1. Talk nonstop without taking a breath.
2. Talk about him to your girlfriends.
3. Criticize him, especially in front of his buddies.
4. Let him find out important things thirdhand instead of from you.
5. Ask him, "Why?"

---

to your man and saying, "Honey, I'm so glad you're home. I'm so glad you're my man." It's saying in as many ways as you can think of, "I need you in my life. I want you in my life. You make all the difference in my life."

That kind of attitude will drive that man to a new desire. It'll turn up the heat on his wanting to please you in as many different ways as he can.

> *Women are picky—make that particular—about when, where, and how sex occurs. And your job as a husband is to figure all that out.*

And who wouldn't want that kind of man, right, ladies?

Q: My wife is so picky about sex. Where we do it. When we do it. What time we do it. There are so many stipulations that I get confused just trying to keep track of them. Then add to that her time of the month, and pretty soon a whole month has passed by. Somehow I thought sex would be easy after 11 years, but it just seems like it gets more complicated. Or is it just me?

A: You hit the nail on the head. Women are picky—make that *particular*—about when, where, and how sex occurs. And your job as a husband is to figure all that out. Think of it as a challenge to understand your wife, to unravel the mystery. But the mystery will never quite be solved, because for women, things change.

That woman of yours is a much more complex creature than you are. She might like one of your colognes on Friday and wrinkle her nose at it on Wednesday. Some days she might love a foot rub; other days it might annoy her. Your job is to watch for the signs and to ask for her guidance.

Don't fall into the trap of, "Well, that worked for the past 11 years, so it has to work now." Women are subject to many more hormones than us men, and that in itself is complex. Your job isn't to read my words and then do what I say. Your job is to read my words and then figure out what your wife likes. No one else can do it for you. She's your wife. Isn't it about time you really got to know her?

Straight Talk

Now's the time to talk with your spouse about what turns him or her on . . . and what turns him or her off. If it's hard for the two of you to talk about such intimate things, try making a list of "What I Love/What I Hate" first. Then grab a cup of coffee or tea and swap papers. You'll be amazed at what you learn. And you'll find that the starting point of a list will make things easier to discuss.

Part of learning to love your spouse is getting to know your spouse. It's delving deeper. When you got married, you chose to love your spouse. That means you chose to put him or her first in your thoughts and actions. It means you chose to respect his or her thoughts and feelings and that you promised to work together toward a mutually agreeable solution whenever any problems came up. You didn't see those things in the fine print of your marriage vows, but they're all there if you look.

If you want to turn up the heat on your sex life, you'll find out those turn-on/turn-off triggers.

How to Kill the Mood of a Sexual Interlude

1. Criticize each other.
2. Fight just before you make love.
3. Have unsettled issues between you.
4. Let your mother spend the night.

7

Inquiring Minds Want to Know

The truth about women and orgasms.

If you've ever waited at the grocery checkout (as I have many a time), and you've read just the titles on some of those magazines, by the time you pay for your bananas and skim milk, you'll have learned that it's possible for men and women to have not only three orgasms, but five, seven, and even nine orgasms—all in one lovemaking session.

Based on my experience as a psychologist who's helped thousands of couples with the intimacies of life, I've found that the multiorgasmic male or female is one rare bird. Yes, multiple orgasms can occur, but again, they are few and far between. The typical married couple is most likely to have a different kind of experience: a male who experiences one orgasm, and a female who, on a good day, experiences one orgasm.

Why do I say that about women? Because there's a lot of documentation in books on the difference between an orgasm for a woman versus an orgasm for a man. For men, an orgasm is more of a regular no-brainer. Mr. Happy just naturally and easily does his job in providing that experience. But for some (and most) women, it takes a lot of effort and practice to climax. So don't fall for what the magazines say. If you do, as a woman you'll spend your sexual life thinking, *Is this all there is for me? How come I can't do that?* And as a man you'll spend your sexual life thinking, *What's wrong with my wife that she can't have multiple orgasms? Or is it me? Am I not doing it right?*

Magazines set up dramatic statements that are overblown, yet how easily they can infiltrate your thoughts and hamper your *real* (non-airbrushed) sex life with the man you love. But take note of something. If you read most of the articles, you'll see that they say such things as, "Take charge of *your* orgasm . . . *your* love life." It's all about *you*, and I don't see much emphasis on *we*, the couple. Uh, doesn't the guy you're in love with have something to do with it?

No wonder so many marriages fail early—because we believe all those false, Hollywood expectations about what marriage is going to do for us. For example: *This woman I'm marrying is going to meet my every sexual and intimate need. We're going to have wild sex every night.* Or, *He's going to be just as romantic every day as the day he asked me to marry him. Talk about happily ever after. . . .*

I have news for you. Ain't gonna happen. A more realistic approach would be to agree together: "Some days will be better than others in our marriage. We won't always hit a home run. But we're going to stick with it, stay together, and bring each other pleasure."

Now that's the ticket.

Q: My husband's one of those guys that considers sex really important. Sometimes I'm so exhausted after the ordeal that I feel like I've had an aerobic workout. When I do get an orgasm, it's like he's hit the jackpot. But sometimes I just don't feel like going for it. Am I just a wimp, or is something else going on here? Frankly, I'd rather just cuddle. That means a lot more to me.

A: I think *all* guys see sex as really important, so your husband is a healthy member of the male species. But I'm concerned for you, since you're seeing this aspect of your relationship with your mate as an "ordeal." That means you're walking away exhausted and not feeling loved and satisfied. It sounds like having sex with your husband is something you're enduring because your husband wants it. And that's no good for you or for your long-term marital relationship.

Let me make a few educated guesses. You're probably a lower-energy person than your husband. You'd probably be happier with just cuddling and no penetration. You value closeness with your husband the most. And when you do hit that orgasm, you're done. Any further touching is almost painful.

Well, join the club. Ninety-five percent of women find more fulfillment in the closeness, touching, holding, and affection in lovemaking. They prefer the closeness rather than the sex itself. Those who have orgasms want them. Some say, "When he gets an orgasm, I want one too. It's only fair, right?" But most women would rather give up their orgasms than the feeling of closeness. One woman admitted to me, "I'm so glad my husband is impotent now, because I get the attention I need!" Has that ever crossed your mind?

You're very normal. You're not a wimp, and there's nothing wrong with you. Your husband just needs to understand that sometimes you'll want to go for that orgasm, and sometimes you won't. Either way, it's okay.

Q: I read somewhere that the best sexual experience is when both of you climax at the same time. Is that true? If so, we certainly haven't been able to do that.

A: Climaxing at the same time would be a great thing, but realistically, it doesn't happen that often. So why seek after what rarely happens? Why not enjoy the satisfaction of bringing each other to orgasm?

It's tremendously exciting and fulfilling emotionally for a man to work at pleasing his wife before himself. Quite frankly, if you're like me, you'll get more jollies out of watching your wife fully experience the pleasure you're giving her than from that pipsqueak little orgasm you experience.

So focus on being a good lover. Be a good friend. After all, she's your bride—the most special person in your life.

If you just happen to climax at the same time, all the more fun for you!

Q: My husband read an article about multiple orgasms, and he's been determined ever since to bring me to that point in our lovemaking sessions. All it does is make me tense, because the experience is too intense and I don't like it. But it's become his mission as a man to get me to orgasm more than once during sex. Help! I need a vacation.

A: You poor girl. You need a vacation in Tahiti by yourself. Your man indeed sounds like he's on a mission—and it's not working for either of you. It's making you exhausted, and he's probably critical of you and frustrated because you're not "performing" like he thinks you should. As if his bringing you to an orgasm more than once during sex is part of his trial of manhood or something. That's crazy, and your lover boy needs a wake-up call.

Just so we're clear on definitions here, "multiple orgasm" means having more than one orgasm in any lovemaking session. Your husband "getting" you to orgasm multiple times doesn't mean that he wins the Macho Man of the Year award. Some women may be able—and want—to have multiple orgasms. If so, they should go for it! But the truth of the matter is that most women can't have multiple orgasms. Some, like you, don't want them because of the intensity of the experience.

Most women struggle to have even one orgasm. So you have every right to be tense when you're forced not only to have one but to have more than one. Most women, after they have that one precious orgasm, just want to rest and bask in the afterglow. They want to relax and enjoy being close to their husband.

All women desire a heart connection and emotional intimacy. They want to know they are loved and cherished in a way that doesn't have to lead to a baby. They want to be recognized for the hard work they do, with no fear of becoming a notch in some guy's—even their husband's—belt.

> *The truth of the matter is that most women can't have multiple orgasms. Some don't want them because of the intensity of the experience.*

Your husband is dead wrong in pressuring you to do something you don't want to do and be something you don't want to be. Now is the time for him to show you love and consideration . . . and to transfer his drive to succeed and be at the top to another aspect of his life—the workplace.

Q: Is it normal for women to need manual stimulation of their clitoris in order to reach orgasm? My wife seems to be able to reach it only if I stimulate her clitoris with my fingers or mouth—not the natural way.

A: By "the natural way," do you mean your penis entering her and doing the Mr. Happy dance inside? A lot of men and women are confused about this one. They think all women should be able to reach orgasm by intercourse alone. But two out of three women need direct stimulation of the clitoris in order to reach orgasm. So if your wife is in that category, she's in the majority! And *how* you touch that delicate little instrument of your wife's will make all the difference in the world.

Many women like indirect stimulation followed by very direct stimulation. Some women enjoy being teased with just a very slight touch of this delicate area, combined with words and caresses that intimately share how much you love her. The clitoris is designed to be a very sensitive instrument—small but mighty. If you go right to the clitoris and put pressure on it, your wife isn't going to enjoy that. She needs you to work up to that point by delicately touching the surrounding areas of that wonderful little appendage. You can gently massage the hood over the clitoris. It's easy to tell when the clitoris is responding—it stiffens, becomes erect.

You can also massage the clitoris with your tongue. The nice thing about the tongue is that it has access to saliva, which is a good lubricant. Again, it's the gentle licking and sucking and touching that makes everything else fall into line. Some women prefer to have that kind of stimulation before intercourse; it's like the prelude to a masterful orchestra piece.

Will you "get it right" the first time? Well, it's like playing the viola. You don't end up in first chair the first time you pick up the instrument. It takes practice. And you train each other. Great sex means that a couple has had great training. So ask your wife what feels good to her and what doesn't—and realize that what feels good will change for a woman from day to day as her cycle and hormone levels change.

To put it frankly, your index finger is much more capable of bringing her to an exhilarating orgasm than is your little guy, Mr. Happy, on his best day. No offense to Mr. Happy.

Q: How do I know if he's early or I'm late? Sometimes he ejaculates before I'm ready for him. Any way to solve this problem?

A: Since it takes a woman longer to get frisky, to use my terminology, you might hit two or three pleasurable plateaus before you come to a full orgasm. That's especially true if you're new at the sexual experience, because a woman's pubococcygeus muscles—the PC muscles—aren't used to all the squeezing activity. That's why it may help for you to do Kegel exercises—squeezing and releasing of the PC muscles—which will assist you in reaching orgasm faster. It's the same muscles you would contract if you were trying to stop yourself from urinating.

---

4 Ways to Kill an Orgasm

1. Make sure your goal is to have an orgasm, not to make love to your mate. After all, the act is what's important, right? . . . Or could it be your spouse?

2. When you don't succeed, give up. Have the attitude of, *Well, we'll give this a try, but I know it won't work.*

3. Criticize your lover's efforts out loud. Or think things such as, *You gotta be kidding. This guy is so stupid.* Or, *I had no idea I married an ice cube. The North Pole's got nothin' on her.*

4. Put yourself down. *You're such a lug. You never do anything right.* Or, *I just don't deserve him.*

But such muscles take time to build, so what do you do in the meantime with your husband, who's hot to trot?

Over a period of time, you can help your guy learn to ejaculate at just the right time. It's called the squeeze technique, and you work together on it. When he feels like he's going to ejaculate, he withdraws from you, and you squeeze the underside of his penis. This stops the ejaculation from happening and gives him a chance to wind down, then go back into you again.

Your husband's orgasm is a piece of cake. Yours is the one that takes all the work.

The most important thing is communication—that you talk together and let each other know what's happening. So many couples don't communicate during sex, and that's too bad.

But now let me address the fallacy of "he's early; I'm late." Most couples do not have simultaneous orgasms. What happens most of the time is that a man tries to please his wife by bringing her to climax, and as she's beginning to enjoy that moment, sometimes his just having entered her at that point will increase the intensity of the climax for her. So she experiences her orgasm, and then he experiences his.

Your husband's orgasm is a piece of cake. Yours is the one that takes all the work.

Bottom line? People put all sorts of unreasonable expectations on their sex lives. It takes sophistication and work to bring a woman to full pleasure, but there are many levels of pleasure. Women don't have to have orgasms every time; couples don't need simultaneous orgasms to be sexually fulfilled.

So throw the expectations out the window, and just have fun.

Q: I've been married for two years to a really wonderful man, but he's starting to get on my nerves. It takes a long, long time for me to get interested in sex, and by then Mark is sexually frustrated. It's not like I'm withholding interest; it just takes me a long time to ramp up or something. What's wrong with me?

A: Nothing's wrong with you. You're absolutely, positively a normal woman. Yes, your husband may be hot to trot. Just hearing the shower run makes Mr. Happy get happy. But let me ask you something: What kind of lover is your husband *outside* the bedroom? How does he treat you? Could his lack of attention, his criticism, or his lack of helpfulness have anything to do with how long it takes you to get in the mood?

Bet it does. The truth of the matter is that your readiness for sex and your sexual satisfaction is as much about your relationship outside the bedroom as it is about what happens inside the bedroom.

So how's your lover doing outside the bedroom? Is there anything you need to tell him (nicely, of course) that would be helpful to you? And how about yourself? Are there ways in which you could show your guy how much you love him by saving time and energy for him and getting creative with how you please him?

Q: Sometimes my husband is a little rough during sex. Frankly, even though we're married, I feel a little abused. It makes me want to avoid sex any chance I get. And I admit—I've even faked an orgasm once or twice, just so I could go to bed. I hate to think that life is going to be like this for the next 20 years. Do I just have to put up with it?

A: Absolutely not. There is no excuse for a man *ever* treating his woman roughly. That special magic spot on a woman? It has to be touched ever so softly. And sometimes it doesn't want to be touched at all. Sometimes you just want to be left alone, and your husband—if he truly has your best interests in mind and not just himself—needs to understand that.

Having to fake an orgasm might work in the movies—remember when actress Meg Ryan faked an orgasm in *When Harry Met Sally*, and everyone in the restaurant wanted one of those? It sounded good, but it was fake. In the long run, neither of you will win with that approach.

You need and deserve gentleness—a gentle touch, gentle words. In order for you to experience a real orgasm—one that is a delight to you (if you're even interested)—you need a gentle leader who can bring you to that point of sexual exhilaration. A man you can trust.

Right now your husband's roughness is breaking down the trust in your relationship. That has to stop. If you talk to him about it and he doesn't understand why it hurts you, the two of you need to get some additional help from a qualified counselor. No woman needs to put up with roughness.

For women to be able to enjoy sex and to come to a powerful orgasm that engulfs them, they need a man with a slow hand, a gentle touch, and a kind, loving, loyal heart. A man who knows his bride so well that he senses when it's time for a little bit more pressure, a little bit more firmness—but never roughness. You are the one who needs to lead such a man into tuning the delicate little instrument he holds in his hand.

That's the kind of man you need to train your husband to be. If he can't be that kind of man, he needs help.

Straight Talk

If bringing your wife to orgasm is pleasurable for her, then go for it! And as you enjoy watching her, you can think, *I'm doing that to her. Yeah, me!* Yet keep in mind that on one day she may be willing to work for it, to go for it, but on another day she won't be interested. And that's okay too. You're not going for the gold every night; you're being sensitive to your wife's needs. So you can't think of her orgasms as another notch (or lack thereof) on your belt of male testosterone. If you do, your wife will start feeling the pressure, if she isn't already. On those nights when she isn't in the mood, she's happier just giving some pleasure to you, cuddling, and falling asleep. It's all about understanding her needs *at the moment.* With women, it's an ever-changing universe.

If you're a woman, what you're comfortable with will most likely change from day to day. You may want that rush of pleasure that an orgasm brings. Maybe you're one of those rare women who can—and want—to have more than one. If so, go for it! Have fun along the way. But there will also be times when you're too tired to go through all that work, and you won't want to be pushed.

The most important thing is that you both communicate during your lovemaking so you both walk away sexually satisfied on some level.

Orgasm—or not.

8

Men Don't Think
Just about Sex

They think about food and ESPN too.

We men are a lot more broadminded than you women give us credit for. We don't always think about sex. We think about sex, food, *and* ESPN.

Men, on the average, have 33 sexual thoughts a day. When I told my wife that, she said, "That's sick."

But think about it for a moment. Do you know how many breasts, thighs, and buttocks your husband has looked at today? Every day on his way to work he's bombarded with billboards and magazine ads selling everything from dog food to oil filters to cars. But they all share something in common—a smiling, sexy, partially clothed woman. Your husband can't even get his hair cut without being inundated by alluring women on the latest hairstyles magazines. No doubt about it: flesh sells. Madison Avenue knows that well.

And because men are designed by the Almighty to be visually stimulated by the female body, they look.

The wife who thinks, *Oh, how could you look at another woman?* is missing the point.

The woman who says to herself, *So you notice women who wear silk, huh? Mmm, let's see what I have!*—ah, now that wife understands her man.

And yes, she looks at cute guys with just the right amount of stubble on their faces.

Sex is energizing for a man. It builds his confidence and boosts his overall sense of well-being. If he's in an unfulfilling job, he gets the strength to keep on doing what he's doing because he knows that there is a purpose for his work . . . and a willing wife waiting as a reward at the end of his long day.

Sex is the great equalizer in a man's life. It's amazing the things great sex can cure for men—everything from viruses, bacterial infections, impetigo, chicken pox, and the flu, to a bad job review, being short on funds for income tax, and, most importantly, any problem in marriage.

If you are the one that man has chosen and he can't get enough of sex with you, you're one lucky woman. Even if he does sometimes act like a four-year-old who shaves.

Q: I'm happily married. I love my husband very much. But he drives me crazy when he looks at other women as they walk by on the street or in a restaurant. Shouldn't he look just at me? What's wrong with him?

A: What's wrong with your husband is that he was born a man. Men are very attracted to the physical. They're turned on by sight. When a young woman who is well put together walks by a man in a restaurant, he's not thinking, *I wonder if she likes Russian literature*; he's just drawn to her physical nature.

If your father, your pastor, and the person of the male species you most admired were all standing on a street corner, and a nicely built 29-year-old woman walked by, I can guarantee you something: all three of these pillars of male society would follow that young woman with their eyes as she walked by. Let's call a spade a spade. Men notice things like that. But just because he notices other women doesn't mean he doesn't love you.

Let me be quick to say, though, that there's a difference between simply looking at someone of the opposite sex and gawking at her with lustful intentions. All of us—male and female—look at people of the opposite sex every day. If you're in the business world, you're inundated with them.

It's important that your husband knows how you feel. Since evidently this is a sensitive area for you, he needs to be respectful of that and restrain himself as much as possible from looking at others of the opposite sex.

Here's an example. Carla is extremely sensitive to this issue since her first husband was a womanizer. So she told Paul, her second husband, "Honey, I know I'm a little loony about this, but you know that Mike cheated on me. He was a real womanizer. Because of that, I get really bothered when I see you watching other women when we eat dinner in restaurants. Can we figure out a solution together?" So she and Paul made an agreement. Now when they go to a restaurant, she sits in the booth next to the wall, and he sits facing her. That way during dinner, he is looking at her and not at the constant parade of people coming in and out of the restaurant. He does that because he loves Carla and understands the fears she carries from her first marriage. There's an added bonus too: they say their communication has improved because they're now focusing directly on each other during their dinners out. Now that's problem solving as a team!

In marriage, it's never "his problem" or "her problem." It's not 90/10. It's "our problem." If you both work on it together, you'll get it solved.

Q: I know sex is important in marriage, but I have to admit it's just not that important to me as a woman (well, other than getting my daughter out of it). I think it's a lot more important to my husband. I enjoy jogging and working out at the health club (it helps minimize the stress in everything I have to juggle in my life), but there isn't much point to having sex, unless we want another kid. It's just one more thing to have to find time for in the schedule.

A: I understand where you're coming from. Women have enough life stress to sink an elephant. You're juggling the ankle-biter battalion, the crabby hormone group, a career, and often a demanding husband. You're busy—no one can argue with that. And yes, you deserve and *need* some free time to do the things you love, like jogging and working out.

But there are more benefits to sex than you might think. Did you know that the perks of a healthy sex life equate to what you would get with consistently running 26 miles? Really, it's true. As I've counseled couples over the years, I've discovered something amazing: a woman who has a good sex life experiences less stress in her life. Why?

Ever heard of the slogan, "You're in good hands with Allstate"?

In marriage, it's never "his problem" or "her problem." It's not 90/10. It's "our problem."

---

5 Things a Man Can Do for His Woman

1. Use words, sentences, and complete thoughts, and share your feelings.
2. Draw bathwater for her, read to her, make her tea.
3. Write a poem and slip it in her car. Write a message of love to her on the mirror (then *you* clean the mirror yourself later).
4. Light scented candles in your bedroom.
5. Tell her how great she looks when she gets out of the shower (since nearly every woman I know struggles with body image of some kind).

Whoever invented that was a genius. It works the same way in marriage. If you sexually fulfill your husband, you'll be in good hands. You'll have a happy, satisfied husband who's willing to rearrange his schedule so you can have time to get to the health club. Who knows? He may even start jogging with you.

And if you are sexually fulfilled, you're going to be more appreciative of whom? Your husband. You're also going to appreciate life more, smile more, be a better mom, even be a better jogger.

Q: We've been trying for three years to conceive a baby, and I'm about ready to give up. To my wife, sex has become all about "getting the baby." There's no pleasure in it anymore. I can't stand to hear for another three years about body temperature and positioning—or especially to share her grief when she finds out she's *not pregnant again*. I really love my wife, but sometimes there's only so much a guy can take. I want to be more to her than her sperm donor.

A: Been there, done that. We waited five years before we really tried to have a baby, then Sande miscarried. After that point, my dear wife was taking her temperature every day. We'd go to

---

5 Things a Woman Can Do for Her Man

1. Tell him, "I love it when you're inside me. It feels so good."
2. Groan, pant, and breathe deeply during lovemaking—it's sweet music to his ears.
3. Say things such as, "Oh, go deeper, harder . . . you got it right there" to help satisfy your husband and wear him out. He'll never enjoy any workout more, though.
4. Take his hand, head, or mouth, and put it where you'd like it to be.
5. Explore his body . . . and find out what turns him on.

---

the grocery store, see a young mom with a baby, and my wife would tear up (she was nowhere near the onions, by the way).

This is an extremely emotional time for your wife. You have to understand that she wants to have a baby and be a mommy so much, and that's why she's doing what she's doing. I can assure you she doesn't see you as just a sperm donor. She just really wants that baby.

This is a time where you need to be her helpmate and not be critical of her. Be helpful, loving, and supportive. Ask, "What can I do to help?" I can think of all kinds of things you can do to help. So put on a happy face and don't be a four-year-old when your wife needs a man. Don't whine just because she's taking her temperature. Trust me, your wife has read every piece of literature on the planet about getting pregnant. I've been there and done that too.

For the record, after that miscarriage, Sande and I had our daughter Holly. In fact, we "stopped" having kids three times. We now have five.

Q: My wife treats sex like a carrot I can have when I'm a good boy, and one that gets yanked away when she's mad at me. How can I tell her that this really, really hurts me?

A: Sex is too special of a gift to be held out like a carrot or a reward for good behavior and withdrawn as punishment for bad behavior.

Your wife's behavior isn't showing you respect. It's a put-down, and that's why it hurts so much. It all goes back to a democratic society.

Here's how it works in marriage: "If you have a right to put me down, then I have a right to put you down." Soon a vicious cycle will have you at each other's throats (if you aren't already). Such behavior can't be tolerated in a marriage.

You need to talk with your wife immediately. Tell her how much it hurts you for her to withhold sex—how it makes you feel like a little kid asking for a treat and being unsure if you're going to get slapped for asking. Tell her bluntly that it makes you feel devalued and rejected as a man, and because of that you don't want to please her in other areas of your marriage. Tell her that you're more than willing to help out with things around the house, but her withholding sex isn't going to make you want to do anything.

Talk with her about the things that would make you feel loved and be willing to do anything to please her—like getting an email from her that says, "I can't wait for you to come home. I bought a brand new pair of sexy underwear that I want to model for you tonight." Or like overhearing her tell someone that you're the best husband in the world. Now those things would get your attention, right?

The idea of "Well, if you're a good boy and clean the garage and cut the grass, I'll have a treat for you" rarely works with children

---

Want Great Sex?

Here's a hint: As my lifetime buddy Moonhead says, "Hey, Leman, put a few hundred-dollar bills on her pillow for shopping. That'll help."

and never works with husbands. For the sake of your marriage, you need to risk your wife's anger and be blunt. Couples who operate on the "If you have a right to put me down, then I have a right to put you down" principle end up in divorce court seven years after they walk down the aisle. The health and longevity of your marriage is at stake. Don't let this one go.

Q: My husband wants me to initiate sex more often. I want to but get embarrassed. Any advice for me?

A: I'm impressed. You said "more often." That means you already are initiating sex sometimes. Good for you! So many women have grown up with the "guys chase after girls and not the other way around" scenario that they're extremely uncomfortable with initiating sex even within marriage. So you're not alone.

Think of it this way. Anything you do for the first few times will feel awkward. You aren't skilled at it yet. You're not quite sure what to do or how it will be received.

Here's the important thing to remember: the man you love just told you something he'd really love you to do for him. That man desires you, and all he's saying is that he wants to be wanted. How lovely and affirming for you! Of anyone in the world he could have chosen, he chose *you*.

So why not discuss what he means by initiation? Oftentimes a man will have fantasies that some naked woman will grab him by the tie, rip off his clothes, and make love on the hardwood floor. Some women in movies may do that, but are you comfortable with it? You don't have to have hot feelings to initiate sex or have wild sex in an uncomfortable spot. Find ways that work for both of you.

The important thing is that he desires *you*. So be creative. Risk a little. Do it for the man you love.

Q: We've been married for three years, and I'm worried. My husband must be oversexed, because he constantly has "doing it" on his brain. I thought he had high standards—that he was a moral kind of guy. He grew up in the church, and we attend church. But now I'm not so sure. Could something be wrong with him?

A: Lady, your husband is a poster boy for the male species.

How many more times does a man think about sex than a woman?

a. Twice as much

b. Five times as much

c. Ten times as much

d. Thirty-three times as much

And the answer is? Thirty-three times as much!

Here's what I mean. If I were to ask you who thinks more about sex in marriage—a man or a woman—what would you say?

If you said, "A man," you're right. Now here's the second part of the question (it's multiple choice): How many more times does a man think about sex than a woman?

a. Twice as much

b. Five times as much

c. Ten times as much

d. Thirty-three times as much

And the answer is? Thirty-three times as much! Men think about sex all day long.

So the question is not *if* he will think about sex, but *what* he is thinking about sex. Can he have pure thoughts about sex? You bet—if he's thinking about you, his wife. If he's thinking about getting in the sack with you as well as some creative ways to make it more fun, that is pure, holy, and good! You're his wife—your body belongs to him, and his belongs to you.

So why not live it up? Why not deal with your husband's sexual energy in a fun way? Get that guy home from work with a cryptic, sexy message. Surprise him. Send the kids to the neighbors for an hour. Kidnap him during your lunch hour. Did you know that one small touch in an elevator on the way to a restaurant can send the message, *I want you. Come home fast*?

Yes, sex is on your husband's brain. So why not give him *you* to think about? Now there's a smart wife.

Straight Talk

If you're a man, what's more fun to think about than sex with the one you've chosen for a lifetime? If you're a woman and your husband can't get enough of you, you're one lucky lady! Do you know how many women would love to be in your shoes? (A lot of women reading this book are saying, "You got that right!")

Ladies, remember the old Captain and Tennille song that says, "Do that to me one more time. Once is never enough with a man like you"? That's what your husband longs to hear you say. It's the language of his dreams, because it puts his needs first.

And did you know that anticipation is as good as or better than participation? It's the smart woman who includes a note with her husband's lunch or emails him a quick note that says, "I have an idea. You get home as fast as you can tonight and lock the doors, and I'll show you a new outfit I got." Think that man of yours will be late for the unveiling? I doubt it! What are you really saying by your actions? "Honey, I love you so much. It's been a long week, and I know just what you need."

Now, if I were going to give grades in marriage, I'd give you an A+. And your man would do anything to please you, because he's the hero in your life.

A man who is treated in such a way will knock down a wall for you. He'll go to Walgreens and get tampons for you during your "special time." He'll pace the floor with the baby at 2 a.m. so you can sleep.

Now isn't that worth a little of your time, humor, and creativity?

9

Ahh, the Sheer Delight of a Quickie

> Sometimes it's just what you—or your spouse—needs.

You can read all the books you want to prepare you for marriage and having a healthy sex life. But what happens when it's real life? What about when you as a husband are ready for a sexual interlude—but your wife's getting dressed for work and she wouldn't dream of getting messy? Or what about when you as a wife want to please your husband, but you're having extremely heavy periods that are lasting nine days each month, and he's looking at you with those "I can't stand it" eyes? Or what about when you have toddlers running all over the place and a baby (or teenagers) keeping you up at night, and you're both too tired for the full sexual experience?

That's when I suggest you get creative. Sometimes a quickie is just what you or your spouse needs. Are marriages always 100/100

101

in satisfaction for both parties? No. I have news for you. When your husband or wife is down with the flu, it's not 100/100. There are times in marriage where one of you gets satisfied physically and the other gets satisfied emotionally by making your mate feel good.

Frankly, quickies can help a marriage go around happily even in times of stress. They can be a relief for some wives, especially young mothers, who are completely exhausted and don't have the energy for a full sexual encounter. Quickies can make the best of situations when you're at your relatives' home and the two of you have to sleep on the couch in the living room for a week. No privacy there. Now, would you want to be rocking and rolling with your mother-in-law and father-in-law just a few inches of plasterboard from your bed of love? Probably not. That might be the perfect time for sex of another variety.

Q: Call me dumb (I'm new at this sex thing), but what's a quickie anyway?

A: Good question. A quickie is a fast and satisfying sample of sex. It's for when you can't have the whole enchilada for a number of reasons (time, exhaustion, etc.). Let's talk turkey here about what a quickie is. It can be a handjob (the common term used for rubbing your husband's penis and scrotal area to bring him to ejaculation, or stroking your wife's clitoris to bring her to orgasm), masturbation (your spouse can help you with that, and it's permissible if you're mutually agreed), or a quick sexual intercourse complete with a lubricated condom (available at finer drugstores near you) to take away the mess. See the difference? There's penetration on only one of those quickies.

Because of the way men and women are designed physiologically, it's more common for wives to give their husbands quickies. Since women often need at least 30 minutes to be in the mood, I don't often hear of women who want three-minute quickies. But husbands? Now that's a different matter.

Q: Dr. Leman, I'm really freaked out. Yesterday I walked into the bathroom and found my husband masturbating in the shower. What do I do? My husband is a sexual pervert!

A: What do you do? The next time you see him masturbating in the shower (or anywhere), throw off your clothes and say, "Honey, can I be of service to you?"

Masturbating is not the end of the world. You're not going to grow hair between your fingers. You're not going to go senile. All those things are flat-out lies.

About 94 percent of men admit they masturbate. The other 6 percent are downright lying. Lots of women masturbate. There's nothing wrong with masturbation as a physical act. It's a release for sexual tension.

But because the imagination is connected with masturbation, it can become a major problem. Look at it from this perspective. Let's say your husband is hot to trot, but he can tell you're not. So he gives himself a handjob in the shower. If he's thinking about you and what he'd like to do with you at your next sexual interlude, there's nothing wrong with his thoughts. But if, instead of thinking about you, he's thinking about the newest little item who just started working at his office, that's a problem. Also, if your husband is using the sexual release of masturbation to soothe his sexual needs, and then he's too pooped to whoop with you, that's a problem.

> *The next time you see him masturbating in the shower (or anywhere), throw off your clothes and say, "Honey, can I be of service to you?"*

Keep Your Man Happy . . . in 5 Minutes or Less

1. Give him a well-timed handjob.
2. Tell him what a great husband or dad he is.
3. Brag about him in front of others.
4. Tell him you need him home ASAP tonight, because you have something new to show him.

You are not simply a sexual organ. You are an individual who can relate, who has a heart, emotions, and an imagination. Typically you will find that when those aspects of your relationship with your spouse are managed well, the drive for masturbation will drift away. If masturbation becomes a replacement for your husband's relationship with you, it can be dangerous to your marriage.

So the question really is, who and what is your husband thinking about when he's masturbating? Is it you and what he'd like to do with you? Or is it someone else—a fantasy and desire that won't and shouldn't be fulfilled? Does his masturbation up the ante on wanting more sex with you—or take away his sexual drive for time with you? How is his masturbating affecting your relationship? These are the key questions you need to address as a couple.

Q: Is it wrong for us to have sex while my wife is having her period? Is there a medical reason not to? Or am I just an overzealous, overly sexed husband who can't stand waiting?

A: Every couple is different, and yes, I know of couples who have had sex during the wife's period. But is that something you *really* need or want to do? I'd challenge you and your wife to think of other ways to enjoy the intimacies of married life during those times. Quite frankly, some of them are more pleasurable

---

5 Quickies a Man Can Do for a Woman

1. Clean both toilets and pick up the living room—without being asked.
2. Give her a foot rub with her favorite scented lotion.
3. Get your toddler dressed for preschool.
4. Call her to ask if there's anything she needs from the grocery store.
5. Leave her a note in the morning to say how much you love and appreciate her.

---

for a man than sexual intercourse. If you're one of those men who feels that the only sex you can have is in the missionary position, then you need to do some further reading to widen your expressions of love in marriage.

Have you talked with your wife about this? Most women aren't comfortable having sex while they're bleeding. It's that "Snuggle with me, bring me chocolate, but don't touch me sexually" time in a woman's life.

Most women I know have periods that last five days. Some have periods that last nine to ten days.

Yes, you as a man will still get frisky. I understand that. But instead of climbing the walls and forcing your wife to engage in something she's not comfortable with, you need to love and respect her enough to come up with new ways of making love. I won't prescribe them.

Q: It never fails. My husband always wakes up "in the mood" in the morning, when I'm getting ready for work. But if I let him have his way, I'd be late for work several times a week! Any suggestions?

A: Count yourself fortunate that you have a husband who desires you in such a way and can't get enough of you! Encourage him

105

to be a lover with finger and tongue. That way you don't get messy and need another shower, and you can get a quickie that will satisfy both of you for now, make you think of each other during the day, and anticipate an even longer lovemaking session some evening.

Quickies are designed especially to satisfy a husband who is as frisky as a male blue jay in spring, with little effort on your part—the no-muss, no-fuss, commonsense approach to loving your husband and meeting his needs. Let's say that you walk naked out of the shower toward your closet. All of a sudden you're very aware that Mr. Happy is standing straight up and singin' like a blue jay on a fir tree. But you have to get ready for work, get the kids up, and get them out the door to school. So what do you do with that eager husband of yours? You give him a quickie. What does that quickie say? "Honey, I understand your needs. We can't do the full thing right now, but I want to give you a little something special to hold you over."

By doing that, you've just landed that man solidly in your court. He'll be your hero, your protector, your helpmate. Isn't that worth a little effort on your part?

Q: I just gave birth a couple weeks ago and had a C-section. I'm still too sore to have sex, but my husband is *dying* for some action. I had a difficult pregnancy, so we couldn't have sex the last month of my pregnancy either. Any ideas for making the guy I love happy since he's been so patient in waiting?

A: In times like these, you just have to get a little creative. The two of you were smart to put that little unborn child's safety first. And kudos to your husband for being such a patient guy. Pregnancy, childbirth, and your period are times when you need a little creativity to keep Mr. Happy happy and fulfill yourself too.

These are the times when you need to get good at giving your husband loving expressions manually. Learn to give him a handjob—it's very permissible in marriage—for when he needs a quickie to release sexual tension. Just a little something to keep your guy happy and satisfied in the little nest that the two of you have built together. It's for those times when you're too pooped to whoop or you're too sore (like now).

Marriage is all about knowing what your loved one needs and meeting that need in a creative, loving way. You know that already, so you're off to a great start.

Straight Talk

Let's face it. There are times in a marriage when one partner will need more sexual satisfaction than the other one. When one partner will be exhausted or physically or emotionally unable to have a full sexual interlude. A husband and wife who are tuned in to each other will read those signs and turn up the heat in creative ways. Don't be afraid to risk trying new things, all for the sake of the person you love.

The name of the game for quickies? Use your creativity. If you as a woman are a nonmessy person and need to get out the door to work, why not use a condom in conjunction with a handjob to make your guy happy? He'll be eternally grateful . . . and I bet he might even cook dinner for you that night.

If you as a man know that your wife has a higher sexual interest than you do, save some energy for a sexual interlude. Pleasure her and bring her to orgasm (if that's what she wants) with your fingers of love. Stand next to her, over her—use your imagination. If it's mutually agreeable, go for it.

10

What's on Your Menu?

Scintillating appetizers and delicious desserts for your marital palate.

We all have to agree that there are different strokes for different folks. As a psychologist who has tracked a lot of sex lives over the past 40 years, I've seen the sexual appetites of many couples change over their years of marriage. Many couples who thought they'd never engage in oral sex have come to the point in their comfort with each other where oral sex is a satisfying part of their relationship. No pun intended, but I think it's an acquired taste.

Then there's right and wrong.

Because I get asked about oral sex and anal sex a lot, many times by the same people, I'm discussing them in the same chapter. But they are nowhere near each other . . . so to speak. For some of you, even the thought of oral sex and anal sex is repugnant to you. If this is the case for you, my suggestion would be to pass "Go" and skip right to the next chapter. However, if you're like most people and have some voyeuristic tendencies, read on.

Society today says anything goes, but anything doesn't go. There's a point at which I draw a line in the sand and say certain things are not right. Anal sex is that point. It's not natural and it's not healthy. It doesn't belong in the treasured relationship between a husband and a wife.

I've been blasted several times for taking this stance, but I hold the line. Usually it's the husband who makes the request, and the wife is literally berated and then acquiesces as a way of calming the storm. But she doesn't like it.

I would suggest to any woman that she also draw the line and stand her ground. Especially since she's the one who has the most to lose. Why is that? First of all, a penis is designed to enter a vagina, not a rectum. There is a high probability of physical damage to a woman's rectum because of the sensitive tissue there, and there's also a possibility of bacterial infections.

And most of all, there is the respect issue. If this is something you're not comfortable with, why is your husband, who is supposed to love you and be looking out for your best interests, forcing you to submit to this expression of sex?

It all goes back to this: love does not demand its own way—or it's not love.

Q: I'm a 51-year-old Sunday school teacher who's been faithfully married for 27 years. Our sex life has been hit and miss at best, but I read your wonderful book *Sheet Music* with my husband, Harvey, and he finally gets it. He found my "spot" after several years of hunting, so I owe you a big thank-you. I'm embarrassed to write this, but now I can't *wait* for the next time we have sex. And I'm going to be a grandmother this spring.

Here's my question. I would love to perform oral sex on my husband, but I don't have a clue as to the right way to do this. Again, I can't believe I'm asking this question, but I trust your judgment. You've really helped our marriage and our sex life so greatly up to this point. You're the only one I could think of to pose such a delicate question to. If there's any way you could respond to me, I'd greatly appreciate it.

A: First of all, there's no right way to engage in lovemaking with your husband as long as nothing is forced. I would suggest you start with just words of endearment and kissing and hugging, face-to-face, in any position that you and your husband feel is comfortable. Then, as you feel motivated, move down to kiss his neck or his chest, scratch his arms and his back, and caress his face. Move down to his genital area as slowly as you possibly can. Take the time to make little pit stops as you venture southward. Explore his portly body. (We're probably not talking Brad Pitt here, but who cares? He's all yours!)

Keep in mind: this is only one way to do it. There are all sorts of varieties in this sexual recipe—for men and for women. You can approach him from his feet or from his head. You can approach him from in front, from behind, or from the side.

When the time is right, gently caress Mr. Happy, making sure that you are the one making the movements at this point. This is not the time for your husband to be thrusting, or he could knock out a bicuspid or your partial. This is the time for you to use your delicate fingers and your lips and your tongue, not your teeth.

When you want to bring that man to climax, all you need to do is caress his scrotum area in one hand while holding his penis in your other hand and moving up and down gently along the penis shaft. My guess is that it won't be long before he'll be smiling like the alley cat that just ate the canary.

Of course, this is just one idea to get you started. After all, this is your husband, the man God has given you as your life-long mate. You've reared children together; you're even going to be grandparents soon. You know this man. So make love to him the way you want to make love to him. If he doesn't like it, he'll tell you. My guess? You won't hear a peep out of him other than some delighted moans and groans.

Bon appétit!

Q: My wife and I just celebrated our thirtieth anniversary this year. O.S. has never really been a part of our relationship, but I'd really like her to try it with me. When I suggested it, she just looked shocked and told me that wasn't natural, and that we should just do it the way we've always done it. Did I ask for something wrong? Is O.S. okay, or not? And if it is, how can I get my wife to try it?

A: I noticed you called oral sex "O.S." so you didn't have to spell it out, so that gives me a hint that you come from a more con-servative background.

Is oral sex okay?

Okay? Are you kidding me? It's *great*! It can be one of the coolest things in a marriage.

Now the bad news. It's not great if your spouse doesn't agree. You see, oral sex is an acquired taste, and some people just aren't comfortable with it (maybe not now, maybe not ever).

But I've also worked with thousands of couples over the years who would never have imagined, on their wedding day, that 10 or 20 or 30 years later they'd be engaging in oral sex.

Good for you for thinking of keeping the love between you and your wife fresh. But if your wife isn't comfortable with oral sex, you have to respect her position. Love doesn't demand its own

111

way. Acting like a four-year-old and having a temper tantrum (which I doubt you'd do since you seem like a gentle kind of guy) won't get you anywhere. But I suggest you do this. Take your bride by the hand and say, "Honey, I love you so much. I can't believe we've celebrated 30 years together. I want our love to always stay fresh and new. Would you be willing to experiment with me and try something new? Would you consider it out of your love for me? If you're uncomfortable at any time, we can stop."

Someone wise once said, "Cleanliness is next to godliness," and it's a consideration in oral sex. Many women (and men) will be happy to experiment with something new if they know that they're both clean—the soap-and-water kind of clean. Your bride may, in fact, be thinking, *Uh, don't we tinkle from there?* So why not remove that obstacle in your experimentation?

Love doesn't demand its own way.

Getting ready for sex—the anticipation, the process, setting the environment—is extremely important for a woman. So why not shower together? That might make oral sex more palatable for both of you . . . and lead to some interesting foreplay to get both your engines revving. That way she can be assured that Mr. Happy and Little Miss Delightful are as clean as she wants them to be.

Who knows? Your bride of 30 years might get the surprise of her life, and she might actually love it. And you might get the surprise of your life when someday she initiates it herself!

Q: We've been married for 20 years, and my husband wants me to engage in anal sex with him. He's never mentioned it before, but now he bugs me relentlessly about it. I'm really, *really* un-

---

Is Oral Sex for You?

Take this True or False quiz to find out.

__ 1. I'm eager to try it out.

__ 2. My spouse is eager to try it out.

__ 3. I'm willing to consider it.

__ 4. My spouse is willing to consider it.

__ 5. I don't want to sign on the dotted line to engage in oral sex forever, but sure, I'll give it a shot.

__ 6. My spouse doesn't want to sign on the dotted line to engage in oral sex forever, but sure, he or she will give it a shot.

__ 7. There is no way, José, I'm trying oral sex.

__ 8. There is no way, José, my spouse is trying oral sex.

So, is oral sex for you? Unless one of you wrote "T" for true for number 7 or 8, it sounds like you could give it a shot. Remember: the important thing is that both of you agree on what goes on in the bedroom.

---

comfortable with the idea. It just seems a little . . . well, weird, and even perverted. But what do I do? He's my husband. Don't I have to please him?

A: For your husband to bring this up as a big desire on his part after all these years of marriage is suspicious to me. Has he been viewing pornography? Where did he get the idea for anal sex all of a sudden?

I'm one who firmly believes there's a time to draw the line between good, healthy sex and kinky sex, and anal sex falls in the area of kinky sex—along with whips, black leather, chains, ropes, and other deviant types of sexual behavior.

Not only is anal sex unnatural, it can be very damaging physically to the woman. Here's a short course in physiology. Why do you think the clitoris is located in the vaginal area and not the rectum? The rectum was not designed to be the receiver of the penis. The rectum and the penis together score a sour note in anyone's orchestra. But the little area just north of the rectum was magnificently designed in such a way so that when the penis and the vagina come together, they can make beautiful music.

So to say it bluntly, anal sex is not only wrong, it's not good for you—physically or emotionally. If your husband asks you again about engaging in anal sex, tell him flat out and simply, "No, I will not engage in anal sex with you." Since he seems to be pursuing the idea, he's probably not going to be happy or satisfied with that answer. So explain why.

Anal sex is not only wrong, it's not good for you–physically or emotionally.

If he still doesn't get it, ask him what he thinks sex is. If you discover he has all kinds of perverted ideas about sex, chances are very high that he is viewing pornography, has viewed it in the past, or came from a home where he was exposed to pornography, kinky sex, or perverted attitudes. Interestingly, a lot of men who demand anal sex from their wives learned early in life that sex was a nasty, dirty thing. So sneaking out to look at a pornographic magazine with a buddy brought great delight.

Perhaps your husband feels pleasure only in situations where sex has a dirty, nasty feel to it. Isn't that a shame? If this is the case, your husband needs more help than you can give him.

You must say no—for your sake and for your husband's sake. Don't ever back down on this one.

Q: My husband wants me to swallow after oral sex. The very idea of swallowing all that ejaculate just makes me want to vomit. But he says I have to, if I love him . . . even if it makes me uncomfortable. But what about how I feel?

A: Whoa, hold it right there. Your husband needs a course in Love 101. Real love does not demand its own way. It thinks about the other person *first*, and it puts the other person's needs *first*. Every woman is different. Some women absolutely love oral sex. Some women hate it. Which are you? Are you only participating in oral sex because he's forcing you to? Or do you really like it?

And even if you do like participating in oral sex, no woman likes being forced to do anything. Frankly, that's abuse, and it has to stop. The idea that your husband would so demean you by pressuring to swallow his ejaculate is completely out of bounds with what love is all about. You need to hold your ground firmly here and say no. Explain exactly how it makes you feel. Explain that if that's the end result, you don't even feel like having sexual interludes with him anymore.

Your guy needs to be called up short. He does not own you as a love slave to do his bidding. You are his wife, and decisions about what you will do and not do in your sexual relationship have to be agreed upon by both of you.

Q: I discovered recently that my wife really loves oral sex . . . and I love giving it to her. The problem is, when I ask for it, she's too busy or not in the mood. If I give it to her, shouldn't she have to give it to me? What's the deal?

A: Simply said, your wife is being selfish. And so are you. Marriage isn't a "Listen, I'm doing this for you, so you need to do it for me" thing. That's competition, tit for tat. That's marital baseball, where the two of you play and keep score of all the runs in the seven-day ball game you call life. If that's what you think marriage is, good luck. You'll end up losing.

Although it's easier for a woman to accept oral sex than it is to give it, she can learn how to give it to you too. The two of you need to grow up and learn to work out your competitive edges in areas of life other than your sexual relationship. You need to find ways to love each other so you both feel sexually fulfilled. Does that mean you'll both get oral sex on the same day? Maybe, maybe not. But you have to end the competition. Right now. Marriage is not a competitive sport.

Q: My husband and I have been married for nine years and recently decided we wanted to experiment a bit more. We'd like to try oral sex. How do we start, and what do we do?

A: Do you remember when you didn't like green beans, and your mother said, "Listen, just try one"? That's good advice in this area of life too. Rarely have I talked with a couple who said, "You know, the first time we had oral sex, we absolutely loved it." But why not try something new and see?

You can begin by caressing or kissing the general areas that are special to each of you. For many couples, especially women who are more body conscious, this takes some getting used to. A man can stroke the belly and the thighs and up toward the clitoris to begin to bring a woman pleasure. A slow and gentle touching, rubbing, licking, or sucking of the clitoris can bring a woman to new ecstasies of sexual pleasure. (Note the key word: *gentle*.) A woman can encompass the man's penis in her mouth, blow on it, lubricate it with her hands, or put a condom on it. These are just some ideas for starters. I know you can get creative.

The important thing is to take your time. Don't hurry. To be a great lover takes practice, a great deal of trust, and some ingenuity. And just think—you have the rest of your married lives to experiment. That's some kind of fun!

Straight Talk

I want to borrow from good old St. Paul here, because he said it best:

> Love is patient, love is kind. It does not envy, it does not boast, it is not proud. It is not rude, it is not self-seeking, it is not easily angered, it keeps no record of wrongs. Love does not delight in evil but rejoices with the truth. It always protects, always trusts, always hopes, always perseveres. Love never fails.
>
> 1 Corinthians 13:4–8

What do those ages-old words mean? Words that have stood the test of time for generations upon generations of married couples?

Love does not demand its own way. Are you demanding yours?

11

And Then We Had Children

How to keep Mr. Happy happy, keep the ankle-biter battalion in check, and let Velcro Woman still get a good night's sleep.

No doubt about it. Children change the dynamics of a family. That's why I always tell couples that if one of you isn't ready yet to have children, don't have them. You both need to be agreed and unified to hold strong as parents.

When children enter the picture, there is less couple time, less sleep, more activity, more stress. There are physical changes in a woman due to pregnancy, breastfeeding, and exhaustion. (Do you know how much exhaustion counts against a young mom's interest in sex?) That's why a young father needs to be aware of the toll that all this chaos and exhaustion take on his wife and be additionally helpful. A young mom, for her part, needs to reserve some of her energy for her husband. Both of you need to be creative in finding time for each other and keeping your relationship a top priority—even with all your ankle biters' needs.

After all, when your parenting days are all over and the kids are out the door, who's left? The two of you, looking at each other.

Q: My husband and I aren't agreed on having kids. He's ready and says he wants to have four (he grew up in a home of five kids; he says that's too much, but one less would be good). I would rather wait a few years and have two kids (I grew up as an only child and always wanted a sibling). How can we come to an agreement?

A: This is a huge issue that bears having a lot of discussions before either of you act on it. There are some big discrepancies between your thinking, as you know. Parenting is such a big move that you both have to be agreed before you set out in that direction. You as the mom will be much more integrally involved than your husband will when the children are very young. He doesn't have breasts, so he can't help in the breast-feeding department. You're going to be the one on duty for long hours of the day or night just because you have the equipment. But that doesn't mean he shouldn't help with everything he can.

Was your husband's father helpful at home? Or did his mother do most of the work around the house? This will tell you a lot about what you're in for when you have children. Old habits (especially those lived out in a childhood home) die hard.

Let me be blunt. Children—the ankle-biter battalion in particular—will completely deplete the energy of the strongest woman of all time. When you have children, your greatest enemy to a sex life with your husband is going to be exhaustion. Does your husband realize that sometimes you're going to be simply too tired for *any* sexual interlude?

For a young mom, days and nights meld together. They don't end . . . for years. Children have no social awareness. They don't care about you—only themselves. They come out of the womb hedonistic. They want to be fed, to be held, and to have their diaper changed—now. Add to the mix a colicky baby, and that can put you over the edge.

Children—the ankle-biter battalion in particular—will completely deplete the energy of the strongest woman of all time.

Don't get me wrong. Children are wonderful. I have five of them and have lived to tell about it. I wouldn't trade a single one of them. But they are also a lot of work.

Both you and your husband need to be ready to take on that type of commitment.

Q: My wife gave birth a month ago, and she isn't interested in sex at all. Is this normal? Should I be worried?

A: Let me shoot it to you straight. For many reasons, medical doctors advise that you wait at least six to eight weeks to have sex. Your wife has just gone through an incredible event—one of the most traumatic and joyful experiences of her life. After being exhausted (and most likely morning sick) for the past nine months, she experienced giving birth, and that little 19½-incher who has been kicking around in her belly was laid across her breast.

Welcome to the world of motherhood! Going full-term with a baby and pushing for all those hours is absolutely exhausting. (I've heard it equated to running a marathon 24 hours a day for 9 months, and every woman I know agrees with that.) But guess what? The next 18 years are going to be grueling. Kids are hedonistic little suckers, and they'll drain your bride dry of time and energy. That's just the way kids are.

My guess is that if you're patient for another month or so (it takes women at least six to eight weeks to heal from natural childbirth; with C-sections, the healing can take longer), you might see some action. But there's a wide range of time between couples after they have a child. Some couples are back on track within seven weeks; some don't have sex for seven months after the birth of their baby. The important thing is that the two of you negotiate this together, because there are a lot of variables: the type of experience your wife had with birth, the baby's health, how the baby is nursing, how left out you are feeling, etc.

But let me give you a tip as a husband. This is a key time in your marriage. If your wife suffers from postpartum depression (as many women do after the incredible crash of hormones), this can tax your relationship. Pregnancy has been a time for you two to grow closer; now your wife is completely overwhelmed. She may have had an episiotomy; she may have had a C-section. In either case, she's recovering from surgery, and you're thinking about sex? Do you see what I mean here?

You need to understand that with this change in your family, your wife is going to be plagued with exhaustion—not just once in a while but most of the time. As that little 19½-incher grows to toddlerhood, he or she will demand a lot of attention and will drain the energy that your wife used to reserve just for you.

Now is your chance, more than ever, to be her knight in shining armor. Make sure your wife gets plenty of rest. Say, "Honey, I'll take the baby. Why don't you curl up and take a nap?" Give her time to shower in peace without worrying that one of the kids will fall down the stairs. Make an appointment for her to get her hair cut and her nails done, and you stay home with the kids.

There's a benefit for Mr. Happy too. He'll be happier if you're kind and compassionate toward your bride. So instead of pestering your wife about having sex, do things for her. Let her rest, give her time for herself. Things won't be the same from this day forward. They'll be different. There are more members in your family.

Your goal is to make your woman think every day, *Wow. I'm so glad I married that man. What a great guy.*

Q: I'm not quite sure what to do. I'm exhausted after being up with our colicky daughter nearly every night since she was born five months ago. The only thing on my mind is sleep—in the few minutes I can get it. My husband is getting cranky and whiny. He says he never gets any (he means sex) and he gets no attention either. But can't he see how exhausted I am? Do I always have to be the one who gives everything in this relationship?

A: Let me start with a story. Picture a salmon lying on her side upstream, gasping for her last breath. Six strangers huddle around the exhausted salmon and say, "Just one more push, honey. You're almost there!" Five months ago, you closely resembled that salmon as you birthed that precious little bundle who now demands so much of your time.

Frankly, you don't need a second child (your husband). He needs to step up to the plate and be a man, not a baby. That means he needs to be a helpmate to you—help with the baby, do housework, fix meals, be attentive to your needs, and be aware of your exhaustion level.

But you're not off the hook either. You need to be a smart cookie and realize that your husband needs and craves your attention. He can't be put off forever.

In order to have any energy for him and to show him that he's important in your world, find a support person. Grandma's great, if she lives nearby; good friends and trusted babysitters can also help. When your baby naps, *you* take a nap. Trust me, the housework and the dishes and the phone calls will always be there. Your relationship with your husband needs to come first.

Q: I know that sex is important, but there's always so much life stuff we have to get done. By the time it's done, though, I'm so tired that all I want to do is sleep. And I'm not the only one. My husband admits he feels the same way. His job is really taxing right now. So is it okay to just put the sex part on hold for a while? At least until the kids are grown up?

A: I admit there are nights in the Leman marriage where my head hits the pillow and I say, "Sex." And my wife's head hits her pillow and she says, "Sex." And then, since we've "had sex," we go to sleep.

Let's face it. Life is too busy. With his schedule, her schedule, and the kids' multiple-event schedules, couples don't make time for each other the way they should.

But if you care about your marriage (and you do, or you wouldn't be reading this), you have to fight

> *There are nights in the Leman marriage where my head hits the pillow and I say, "Sex." And my wife's head hits her pillow and she says, "Sex." And then, since we've "had sex," we go to sleep.*

for it. That means you make time, you take time. You get a babysitter and go on a date once a week. You even spend a few bucks on a hotel sometimes.

"Oh my goodness, Dr. Leman, what an outlandish recommendation that is," some might say. You know what I say? "Hey, you're the one who has a plasma TV set. You spend money for everything under the sun. Why don't you invest in your relationship with your husband or your wife?"

And by the way, many of you as parents seem to be driven to make sure your children feel they are the center of the universe. That's why you stack them high with activities that keep you running so they can "succeed." Let me ask you the question: if your kids are the center of the universe, where is there room for almighty God? And where is there room for a healthy sex life for you as a couple? Those kids are going to leave your little nest someday. But before that they can tear you apart.

Years ago I coined the expression, "We have seen the enemy, and they are small." Kids can consume every bit of energy that comes from your body. Make time, take time, for your "coupledom"—make it a priority. That's what will last for a lifetime.

Q: I'm a stay-at-home mom. I do all the stuff that keeps a house running . . . things that evidently are invisible to my husband. When he gets home from work, he expects me to drop to my knees in god worship (okay, so I'm dramatizing here, but sometimes it does feel like that), be in goddess dress (after the day I've had folding laundry and cleaning toilets and vomit), and be a ready teddy. How can I get across to him that I'm a worthy individual and that I have a REAL job—a 24-hour-a-day job? And that sometimes, like him, I'm too tired to be frisky?

A: Let's be blunt. One of the toughest jobs for women, who are so relationally oriented and see the whole picture, is to prioritize. There are some things that need to get done, and others that don't (or don't have to as much as you're doing them). So what if dust bunnies collect a bit in the corners of your house, or you have Hamburger Helper with pickles for dinner instead of the homemade soup you had planned? Will that kill anyone? (Well, maybe the sodium and MSG will if you have it all the time!) You have to stop feeling guilty about what you can't get done and just focus on what you can.

Now let me talk to that husband of yours, man to man. If your wife is unhappy, sir, it's your fault. You need to stand up to the plate and be a real man. A leader. Get behind your wife's eyes to see how she looks at life and what she does on a daily basis. Stay home from work for a day and take care of the home, the kids, the phone, the grocery shopping, and anything else on her to-do list for the day—while she's MIA at the spa and not within cell phone range. I bet that by about 11:00 that night, when she at last walks in the door looking radiant, you will be sprawled in your La-Z-Boy and flat-out exhausted, the living room will be a mess, and dishes will be scattered everywhere in the kitchen.

What kind of help does your wife need? What can you do that you're not doing? Do you need to hire a babysitter once a week? A house cleaner? I know what you're thinking. After all, I'm an economical kind of guy myself: "But, Dr. Leman, that'll cost money." Well, so do your La-Z-Boy and TV. And how much do those two things help your marriage? If your wife wants to talk to you, she has to hide the remote!

If you help her prioritize, take care of some things around the house that you wouldn't normally do, and make her feel special with some extra loving care, then watch out. She might be pulling your pants down any second.

Q: Before I became a mom, every other mom told me (laughing) that it was a 24-7, on-duty job with no end in sight. I didn't really believe them. Now I'm five years into parenthood with children who are 3 and 4. I even work part-time during the hours they're in preschool. By the time I get home at night, make dinner, and get it on the table, I'm sitting in a stupor and can't even eat. Then my husband walks in the door and gives me that "come hither" look. Is it selfish to just wish for time for *me*? Like a hot bath . . . by myself?

A: Wow, you have a lot on your plate. Young children and working part-time too. No wonder you're tired. Any way you can give up your job to have some time for just you when your kids are at preschool?

I want to say this very clearly: every woman needs time for herself. I call a woman like you "Velcro Woman," because everything sticks to you and everyone wants a piece of you. No wonder you feel frazzled sometimes. No person can be on duty day in, day out, 24 hours a day, without going just a slight bit cuckoo. After all, your husband puts in eight- to ten-hour days at his job, and then what? He comes home! You deserve a break too.

The catch is that you will have to take charge of that responsibility because no one else will. It's too easy for you to just take over. So make a plan. Ask a few trusted friends or neighbors if they want to have a babysitting co-op: "Hey, I'll watch your kids on Tuesdays if you'll watch mine on Thursdays." Start handing out lists of doable items to your family members. Even young children can be responsible for a few things.

For Husbands with Stay-at-Home Wives

You know it's been a bad day when . . .

- the kids have Mom locked in the basement when you come home.
- you can't smell dinner in the air.
- your wife is still in her jammies at 5:30 p.m.
- you don't recognize the family room.
- you notice the dog has gone potty on the carpet and no one has bothered to clean it up.
- the kids yell, "Dad's home!" and Mom yells, "Thank you, Jesus!" from the kitchen.
- you notice your 7 iron has peanut butter on it, and your putter is missing.
- you find a partially written note to you that begins, "I just couldn't take it anymore. . . ."
- you ask your wife, "Honey, what's for dinner?" and she says, "Check between the cushions on the sofa."

Make time in your schedule for something you do *by yourself*—whether it's jogging around your neighborhood, painting an antique desk, or bird watching. Everyone in the family will reap the benefits through a difference in your attitude . . . and that includes your husband, who'll be thrilled with the new see-through nightie you recently purchased just for him.

Q: I'm going to be really honest here. I hope I'm not getting myself in trouble (so I'm going to mail this before my wife sees it). Ever since my wife and I adopted our baby, she's had no time at all for me. It's always baby, baby, baby. It's like this little being has entered our lives and taken over. There's no sex, no anything. Am I crazy? This is my baby too, but I admit I'm a little jealous.

A: As a guy, I can understand what you're saying. Up to now you've been in the front seat—the driver's seat—of your relationship. All of a sudden you're sitting in the backseat, all by yourself, and your baby is in the front seat, snuggling with your wife.

You're honest. You can't be shot for that. You're saying you need some attention. And you know what? That's an okay thing to admit. Have you told your wife how you feel and that you miss her? "Honey, I'm so glad that we have Nadia in our lives now. We've waited so long, and she is really, really special. I love her so much, and I know you love her too. But I have to say that I miss you. I miss time with you. Sometimes I feel lonely and, as weird as it may sound, a little jealous of all the time she gets to spend with you. Can we figure out a way to carve out time for us? How can I help you make that happen? What can I do to make your work easier?"

When a woman is exhausted with the care of an infant (or any child, for that matter), the last thing she wants at night is that little touch on her foot signifying that Mr. Happy is now in the upright position and ready for blastoff. The only thing that woman wants to hear in the middle of the night is, "Honey, I'll get up and take care of the baby."

> *The smart husband knows that the number one enemy to his and his wife's sex life is her exhaustion.*

Are you willing to do that? If you want your bride as fresh as she can possibly be and willing to hop in the sack with you, you will be. Also, take note: Is there a time of day your wife seems more interested in sex? One day of the week more than another? Could you have a lunch romp? An afternoon romp? Could you cruise home for an hour during the baby's nap?

The smart husband knows that the number one enemy to his and his wife's sex life is her exhaustion. It's the smart husband who checks with his boss and then tells his wife, "I'm going to take off Friday so you can go shopping and go out to lunch with your sister. It's already set up. You deserve a break from the baby, and I can't wait to spend time with her."

When you do that, what are you saying? "Honey, I love you so much, I'd be willing to do anything for you."

You see, every day your wife is asking you, "Do you really love me? Do you really care?" And how do you think she knows whether you do or not? It's by your actions. They speak louder than words.

> *Marriage is a two-way street. You can't drive down the street and point out a problem without being part of the solution.*

Little things mean a lot. Women need and deserve time out. Just as men do.

Marriage is a two-way street. You can't drive down the street and point out a problem without being part of the solution. Working together and carving out time for the two of you will build intimacy and oneness in the marriage relationship. You can get your vibrant sexual relationship back. After all, it wasn't really missing. It was just on vacation for a while.

Straight Talk

There will be times when you are drop-dead exhausted as a parent. But you can't lose time with each other. Sure, that time (and the quantity of it) may look different than it did before, when it was just the two of you holding hands over a romantic dinner. Now you may have more quickies, take some one-night hotel getaways (so there's no little fist pounding on the door, asking for water), and dream of the days when you could have slow, leisurely sex. Keeping your sexual relationship strong is worth it—for you *and* for your kids.

Did you know how much your sex life affects your children? You can fool adults, but you can't fool kids. They have a built-in radar. They know when things are not well between Mommy and Daddy—they sense that disconnect. They see the anger on Mom's face when Dad comes up from behind to give her a hug and she snarls, "Not now. I'm busy!" They will sense Dad's coldness toward Mom. They will notice all those little things and take them to heart. Children then begin to feel insecure, uneasy. They will wonder, even if they can't voice the question, *How stable is our family? Will Mommy always be here for me? Will Daddy?*

The best thing you can do for your kids—to provide a loving, stable home environment—is to have a healthy sex life with your spouse. It's good for everyone in the family.

12

Shh! It's a Secret!

Why good communicators have a better sex life.

Did you know that on average, women use three and a half times as many words as men? So guess what that means? When we husbands are at the end of our workday, we've already used up our word count . . . and having a relationship with the remote control sounds awfully good. It doesn't ask us questions or get mad at us if we don't have a task done or don't answer a question a certain way.

That's why, when you wives talk to us about anything, it's not that we don't hear you or that we don't want to hear you. It's often that we're not equipped to *answer* you at that very moment. It may just take us a while to process. And you're so verbal that you're already three paragraphs down the track before we engage.

So it's no wonder that what we hear midprocess is a big, irritated sigh, and then, "Are you listening to me?" Yes, sure we were . . . kind of . . . but we're also unwinding from work.

Interestingly, scientific studies prove that a woman tends to be more relational and better at communication than her male counterpart. She actually has more connecting fibers than a man does between the verbal side and the emotional side of her brain. That means a woman's feelings and thoughts zip along quickly, as if they're on an expressway, but a man's tend to poke along slowly, as if he's dragging his feet on a dirt road. Eventually his thoughts will catch up with the woman's, but it may be miles down the road.

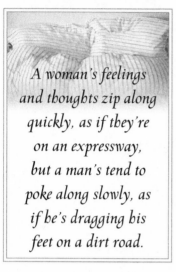

A woman's feelings and thoughts zip along quickly, as if they're on an expressway, but a man's tend to poke along slowly, as if he's dragging his feet on a dirt road.

The miles in between are where you women tend to get exasperated. After all, you're so good at expressing your feelings and jumping from topic to topic, who can blame you for rolling your eyes when all you get out of your guy is "the grunt"?

Because a woman's flow of words is so much more than a man's, we also (to be frank) sometimes tune you out when we get overwhelmed. We guys want the facts, not every blow by blow (unless, of course, it's about how to put the latest car engine together or problem solving on how to load Battlefield 2142).

Men and women, as I've said, are different. Perhaps it will help to know that a woman's top needs are:

1. Affection (translation: hugs, kisses, hand-holding, back rub—not sex)
2. Honest, open communication
3. Commitment to family

Ah, no wonder wives get so annoyed when we husbands can't follow the verbal train down the track. It's hard for us guys to talk—we're not used to it. When one of us exchanges a grunt with another man, we've had a whole conversation. But does that mean we can't do it? No, we just need a good teacher. And you women are the best at what you do.

But did you know that most couples spend 1 percent of their sexual relationship talking about it and 99 percent making love? They're missing out! I believe the ideal split should be 90 percent talking about sex and 10 percent engaging in a sensual, intimate activity. For why, read on.

Q: My wife hasn't been in the mood for sex a lot lately, and I can't figure out what's going on. I feel really rejected. But I'm too embarrassed to ask her straight out what's going on.

A: Although couples do it, many seem to have a hard time talking about it. As crazy as that sounds when you put those words down in black and white, you know what I mean, because you're living it. But you and your wife need to talk about it.

For starters, say to your wife, "Honey, I've noticed that you don't seem to be in the mood for sex lately. Now, I could be wrong, but I've just sensed that you're not as interested as you used to be. Is there anything you want to talk about?" Such an approach diffuses accusation and anger.

Most couples spend 1 percent of their sexual relationship talking about it and 99 percent making love.

You can't assume immediately that the problem is you. Your wife could be stressed, be overwhelmed at work or with your children and their activities, be going through a depression, or have changing hormones. There's also the possibility she's upset with you and feels like she can't say anything. Whatever the reason, isn't now the time to find out so you can address the situation before it grows into a bigger one?

Now's the time to be the husband your wife needs you to be and step out of your own embarrassment in order to talk to your bride.

Q: We used to talk all the time. We used to have sex several times a week. Now we have three kids—9, 12, and 14. We never talk— at least just the two of us—and sex is certainly not happening either. I really miss both. Any ideas about how to get them back?

A: If you miss talking and sex, go after them! Better yet, combine them. Having time for you as a couple is far more important than running your kids to multiple activities. You can improve your sex life if you start by improving your communication.

Make sitting down and talking together for a few minutes— just the two of you—your priority every night. And by that, I don't mean talking *at* each other. I mean talking *to* each other. You both must agree that while one of you is talking, the other one won't interrupt. For example, you talk, and your husband gives you his full attention (as he would if he were trying to woo you during the dating process). Then, after you've stopped talking, he says what he heard you say.

He may be right. He may be wrong. If he didn't get it right, then you clarify when he's done talking: "That's not exactly what I meant. What I meant was . . ."

The key is one person talking at a time while the other is fully engaged, listening.

By the way, one of the best places to talk is in the bathtub, with no barriers between the two of you. Now, if you're built like me—like a bullfrog on the side of a pond—or maybe you have a few bucks in your pocket, and you can have a Jacuzzi, all the better. You can relax in comfort while you talk. There's something about warm bathwater that just takes the edge off a discussion. And it can lead to other things too. . . .

There's no reason why you two can't take some time away by yourself, especially when your children are old enough to help themselves to the refrigerator. Your best bet is to get a lock installed on your bedroom and bathroom doors. Neither of you is going to be in the mood for sex if you're afraid your adolescent or teenager will walk in on you in your full glory at any time.

The point is to find a place where you can talk eyeball to eyeball, without interference and in a respectful way. If you do that, you might learn what many couples never learn—to communicate respectfully and lovingly.

Good communication is one of the keys to paving the road to good sex in marriage. You can't really have one—for long, at least—without the other. But combine them, and you two will find yourselves behind that newly installed lock on your bedroom door more often than you'd ever dreamed.

Q: We are a career-oriented couple, and we've always been happy with our lives that way. But lately, I've been feeling empty. I miss my wife, and I miss the playfulness of our sex life since her promotion has sent her jetting around the country. I respect her and don't want to hold her back from her accomplishments, but I'm lonely. How can I tell her that without giving her a guilt trip (which she doesn't deserve)?

A: Think of your working-outside-the-home and traveling wife as analogous to a stay-at-home mom with three little ones. But instead, the people your wife deals with are VPs, office managers, and other salespeople at the firms she works with. Just as those little ankle biters can strip the energy from a stay-at-home mom, the incredible pressure of a high-paced career (for both men and women) can have that same effect on energy, libido, and general demeanor.

So why not have some planned spontaneity during the times your wife is home? Take her to dinner and then to a resort or a nice hotel for the night (pack her a bag so she doesn't have to; she does enough of that already). Or, since she's gone so much, set up her own spa at home. Candles, bath oils, fresh towels warm from the dryer—all are wonderful mood setters that make a woman say, *He really loves me.*

Since you have enough time to be lonely, you have enough time to plan some things. Schedule a massage for her that takes some stress from her busy life. Then pay for the massage in advance so she can just relax.

Today's world is busy, and many couples are in dual-track careers. Leslie and Brian, one couple I know, both travel. She's in Hong Kong two weeks each month; he's in London one week each month. But they finagled their schedules so that he's gone one of the same weeks she is. During their two weeks together, they major on couple time and do fun things together four nights a week, just by themselves. The other nights are social times when they see friends.

Let me assure you that your wife already has guilt by the boatload for what she can't get done. She doesn't need an extra dose from you. So how you approach her will make all the difference in the world.

Maybe start with something like this: "Wonderful lady, I love you with all my heart, and there's something I want to tell you. I'm not telling you this to make you feel guilty, so if any guilt wells up, let's get rid of it. But sometimes I feel like a lost little boy. With me rushing one direction, you rushing another, and both of our challenging jobs, I miss the times we sit together and talk and make love. Those times seem to be less and less frequent, and I don't like that. I want to see it change. How do you feel about it?"

By using such words, you're zeroing in on the situation, assuring her of your love for her, and suggesting that the two of you work toward some kind of compromise that's doable for both of you.

There are many options. If she has a great job and loves it, and your job isn't so great or you don't feel as passionate about it, perhaps *you* could consider changing jobs or staying home. There are lots of stay-at-home hubbies and dads these days.

In the long run, what's more important? Things or people? Career or marriage?

Sad to say, I can answer that question for most of America: career is #1. And look at the divorce rate.

If you want to stay married and be happy in that marriage, you'll do everything you can to work on communicating your heart to your spouse and sharing your lives.

Q: My husband is a workaholic. His driven nature has taken the spark out of our relationship and has made our house a tense place to be (if he doesn't make a deadline, the whole family gets the brunt of his frustration). When he does take the time for sex, it seems like that's driven too . . . and lacks the warmth, spontaneity, and love that we used to have. How can I tell my husband, without offending him, that I want the man I fell in love with back?

A: Because a man is so driven to succeed by today's culture, and that's also the way God almighty made him (to provide for his family), it's easy for him to fall into workaholism. But workaholism can destroy the very foundation of the marriage you are working to build together. Sometimes husbands overwork because they fear being out of work (and so want a cushion) or because they need the encouragement that a bonus or a slap on the back for a job well done brings. Sometimes husbands overwork because they feel they aren't needed—and sometimes aren't wanted—at home. So why bother to be there? Why not bury yourself in a career where you get visible rewards?

First you need to figure out why your husband is overworking. Oftentimes men have no idea how their workaholism is impacting their marriage and family. If you are a woman of faith, pray that God will change your husband's heart. The hard thing is that at this point there is little you can say that won't sound confrontational.

What you *can* communicate, however, is how much he is needed and wanted at home. You can create an atmosphere of welcome, warmth, gentleness, and tenderness. You can ask questions that help you understand his world. As much as you might want to give him a lecture, don't. You're his wife, not his mama. Those are two completely different roles.

Instead, be his lover. Make your home the place where he longs to be and where he's most comfortable. Let your love and gentle words of welcome draw his heart toward home.

Q: I work ten-hour days on construction sites and have a hard time switching tracks to home. My wife complains that I'm MIA

Attention Getter

If you want to get a man's attention, touch him.
If you want to get a woman's attention, whisper.

---

from our family when I get home—that my brain is somewhere back at the job site, and it doesn't kick in until I start thinking with "my other brain" when I want to get her in bed with me. I can't argue with her. She's right. I know I'm a one-track kind of guy, but how can I make the switch? She gets ticked, and this really affects our sex life.

A: Wow. Sounds like you have some pretty intense, long days. You must be physically and mentally tired by the time you get home. No wonder you're MIA sometimes. But here's what's really going on. Your wife, sensitive soul that she is, is picking up on the fact that you're headed somewhere else in your mind and that you aren't tuned in to her or her needs. She's like every other woman in the world—she wants to be number one in her man's life. That's why the fact that you don't engage in life at home really bothers her. And because you aren't engaged in her life, she probably figures, *Why should I bother pleasing him?*

Sex is not just an act; it's a relationship. The way you interact with your wife—your loving touches and nurturing words—will set her up emotionally to not only enjoy but also pursue sex with you.

So let me ask you: how long is your drive home? When you leave the job site, you need to emotionally and mentally leave it. How about putting on some calming music or stopping at a local park and just sitting on a bench for a few minutes to reorient your thinking?

There are lots of ways to unwind from the workplace and turn your thoughts toward home. One female lawyer I know doesn't accept any clients past 4 p.m. She uses the 4 to 5 p.m. time to clear her head on the way home. Another couple agreed that the husband needed 20 minutes at a local coffee shop as downtime before he showed up at the front door. Then he was all hers!

So talk with your wife and come up with some practical and creative solutions.

One couple I know established a great tradition when their children were young—and they're still doing it 15 years later. At the end of the day, when the kids are tucked into bed, they sit across from each other at the kitchen table with a cup of coffee, and for 20 minutes they talk about *them*. Not the kids. Not what's happening the next day. But *their relationship*. What's going on in their hearts. They've taken to heart the wise admonition to not let the sun go down on your anger. So they talk about everything. And I mean *everything*. And their marriage—including their sizzling sex life—is the better for it.

Q: Both of us grew up in homes where we just didn't talk about sex. It's really uncomfortable for us. How can we get past this issue?

A: You're not alone. Many men and women, especially those from conservative backgrounds, are embarrassed to talk about sex. And yes, that has something to do with your upbringing for sure. But for the sake of your marriage, you need to move past this embarrassment. I dare you to read Proverbs 5:19 in the Bible. You tell me what that little puppy has to say to you. The fact of the matter is that you are like a delicate rose that needs to open each petal to your husband, who wants to love you and be part of your life. If this is an issue that continues to separate the two of you, find someone you can talk to. No, not a girlfriend—a professional. And take your husband with you. Together you can overcome this embarrassing situation. It's too important not to.

Q: My wife said the other day that she doesn't think we communicate well. I don't get it. We have sex a couple times a month, and I tell her I love her, but she says sex isn't satisfying to her—that she needs more from our relationship. So we tried sex once a week, but that didn't work either. She says we never talk anymore. I don't get it. We talk about things all the time—about how our kids are doing in school, where we want to go on vacation, etc. Isn't that communication?

A: Sure, you're communicating, but it sounds like, from your wife's dissatisfaction, you're not communicating on all levels. What your wife is longing for is intimate communication, not just the act of sex, and in that, it's clear you're falling short.

In one of the best books I've ever read about communication—*Why Am I Afraid to Tell You Who I Am?*—author John Powell talks about the five levels of communication, which I want to discuss briefly.[1]

The fifth level—cliché conversation. The following catchphrases are examples of this level of conversation: "Say, you're looking good." "You been keeping busy?" "How's the family?"

The fourth level—reporting facts about others. Ah, this is easy! These are words and conversations that are designed to keep us aloof and removed from other people. We talk about others but avoid getting ourselves involved in the conversation in any personal way.

The third level—ideas and judgments. Here we begin to approach an area of real communication. At this level we are beginning to share our ideas, thoughts, and opinions. We still tend to be somewhat apprehensive and guarded, and if we meet with disapproval, we may modify our opinions so that they are more to other people's liking. At this level we are most anxious to avoid conflict and criticism.

The second level—feelings and emotions. As husband and wife we begin to share the feelings that are underneath the ideas and opinions we've expressed. And far too many couples rarely get to this level. For example, think of the husband who leaves the dinner table every night without saying anything to his wife about the meal or about his appreciation for her efforts in fixing it.

The first level—complete emotional and personal truthfulness in communication. For us to survive in marriage, this is a must. We have to develop an openness and honesty within our relationship that says, "I can tell you how I really feel without you judging me." This level of communication is very difficult because of the possibility of being rejected.

But it is also at this level that couples crave time together— where they long to know each other in every way and can't get enough of each other sexually. By going to this level, you're saying, "You fascinate me. I want to know you. I can't imagine my life without you. Your heart is one with my heart."

That's the level at which your wife lies in bed with you thinking, *This is the most amazing guy. And he chose me. Wow. I can't wait until our next sexual interlude. I have some surprises to show him. . . .*

See what a little communication can do?

Q: My spouse has a problem with anger. It's hard to talk to her about anything because she blows a gasket about everything. If I make a mistake or forget to do something she's asked me to do, she gets really angry. (And she knows how to take it out on a

---

5 Qs to Ask to Heighten Your Emotional Closeness

1. If you had a magic wand and could change anything about our relationship, what would it be?
2. What are three things you'd like me to consider doing differently in the bedroom?
3. Are there some things in your life you've never told anyone? Would you feel comfortable telling me one of them?
4. What do you think are the three most important things in life?
5. What would your life be like if I weren't in it? What things would you have done or not done?

---

guy.) Sex is definitely not happening anymore because there's no way I could please her. I know, because I've tried. But I never do anything right, according to her, so I've stopped even trying.

I can't imagine living another month, much less a year or years, like this. For the first time ever, I'm starting to think of divorcing her. (And I can't believe I'm even writing that, but there it is.) Can you help me? Can you help us?

A: It sounds like your wife's anger is holding you hostage—and in more than just the sexual area of your relationship. High on the list of people you don't want to marry are: (1) an ax murderer, (2) an angry, critical person. Your wife's anger will affect everything about your life, and unless it's dealt with, it will continue to develop in your relationship and will eventually destroy your love for each other.

You and your wife are at that critical point right now. Your wife needs some help . . . but so do you. And you need it quickly, since your relationship is strained enough that the thought of divorce has now entered your head.

Both men and women can get angry. But there's a way to be good and angry—without ripping other people. Here's what I mean. (I'll use the illustration of a balloon.)

1. Your spouse does something to tick you off. You say to yourself, *Never mind. It's going to go away. She's going to stop.* But the anger begins to build. (You blow air into the balloon.)
2. She continues in that behavior, so finally you say something. But she ignores you. (You blow more air into the balloon.)
3. You get angrier and angrier. (You blow more air into the balloon.) By now your veins are bulging. (You blow more air into the balloon.)
4. What happens next? *Pow!* There's an explosion. It's sort of like being sick with the flu and saying, "Oh, I wish I could hurl! If I could just throw up, I know I'd feel better."

Sure, you might feel better if you throw up, but look at the mess you'd make. Yeah, you'd feel better, but then you'd still have to live with the people you just vomited all over—psychologically, emotionally, even physically. And what would it gain you in the long run?

Anger is a very natural emotion. We all have anger. Even Jesus Christ was angry when he walked this earth. Notice that when he saw the money changers in the temple, he didn't say, "Oh, hi, fellas. Have a nice day." He threw them out. He used action, not words.[2]

Do you remember that terrible sound you used to make when you slowly let the air out of a balloon—*squeak, squeak*? It drove your brother, your sister, and your parents up the wall. (Fun, huh?)

What happens when you do that with your balloon now? The balloon gets softer, more malleable, doesn't it? Is it likely to explode? No.

Here's the analogy: If your wife has feelings of anger, the best thing you can do for her is to help her learn how to articulate that anger. Even better, help her learn to articulate her disappointment and annoyances *before* they become anger. Address the issues as they build. And although you might not think things will change, they will—slowly, one squeak at a time.

Will it happen overnight? Rome wasn't built in a day, and neither was your marriage. If your wife doesn't respond when you gently say to her, "Honey, I love you, but this is an issue we need to work on together," you may need to insist that both of you get help from a professional counselor to talk through the issues. Something is provoking your wife's anger, whether it is built up from issues in her past, or is a result of something you've actually done or that she believes you've done. Isn't it time to find out where that anger is coming from so you can do something about it? That's the only way to help her start letting the air out of her balloon. And it's the only way to begin rebuilding trust and love in your marriage.

Q: Whenever we get into a fight, my spouse retreats when I want to talk it out. And I get the icy backside for a week in bed. Might as well hang a sign: *No sex here.* How can we learn how to fight—and accomplish something?

A: A good question, and one many couples ask. Because you marry someone different from you (good thing too), often your styles of fighting are completely opposite. One wants to talk; one wants to retreat. But if you are going to fight, you have to do it fairly.

Playing hide-and-seek in the midst of a fight never works, because eventually your spouse will have to come out of hiding. But is your spouse hiding to give you time to cool off so you're reasonable? Is your spouse hiding because then you'll come after him or her in that hiding place and try to make things right? Or is he (guys are often the ones who get silent and retreat) hiding in order to regroup and think? What's the motive for hiding?

Maybe it's time to consider the way you respond in a fight. Is there any way you can respond differently so your spouse won't go into a turtle shell?

And what's the purpose of your fight in the first place? To air your opinion that you won't change no matter what? Or to state what you think and hear what the other person says—even if you don't agree? If neither side is willing to listen to the other, there can't be any resolution.

When you fight, it's important not only to hear what the other person is saying but to really listen. That means seeing beyond the emotions to the heart of the issue. Even if you don't agree, you have to validate what the other person is saying and consider it as important as what you are thinking and feeling.

Don't let your emotions drive the train. Don't ever go to bed mad. That will build a wall that's not easily torn down, especially when layers build up and weather into hard cement. So talk through the issue before you sleep—whether it takes 20 minutes, 30 minutes, or 2 hours. Sometimes you can't entirely resolve the issue. But you need to at least come to a resolution where you say, "We know we haven't solved the problem yet. So let's set a time and a place to address it again." That way, you have an action plan.

After a fight, it's very important to reconnect both lives and hearts. Sex is the greatest of glues for married couples. Both of you need to know that everything's okay, that life can go on. In fights, you have to fight fairly. If there is a winner and a loser, then as far as your marriage goes, you both lost. Marriage is a team event, not a solo one.

Ground Rules for Fighting Fair

1. Hold hands. Never let go.
2. Look the other person in the eyes.
3. Let one person talk at a time. Don't interrupt. When one person is done, the other person can ask for clarification. Continue the cycle until both sides understand the problem and can come to a mutual solution.
4. Don't use the words *always* and *never*.
5. Don't use *you*; use *I*. (For example, "When that happens, I feel . . ." instead of "You make me so angry when . . .")
6. No bone digging allowed (don't go back and unearth problems that have been dealt with earlier).

Q: I heard you say once that sex is more about relationship and communication than technique. Is that really true? I admit, my spouse and I are struggling in the area of communication. Our sex life isn't doing so well either. Any advice?

A: Sex isn't really about the G-spot, the I-spot, the X-spot, or any other spot. It's about a relationship. And communication is an integral part of that relationship. If you suffer in your sex life, chances are it's because there are unsettled issues, past hurts, between you and your spouse. It would indeed be rare for a couple to have a great sex life but lousy communication and a lousy relationship. The two simply don't go together.

If you and your spouse struggle in this area, why don't you take off the masks? Why don't you bare your hearts to each other? Marriage is too precious a union to let go of and not fight for. If your car isn't hitting all eight cylinders, you'd take it to a mechanic, wouldn't you? If your marriage isn't hitting all eight cylinders, you may need to get some outside help. If you need to do that, look for someone who's married and appreciates what marriage is all about. Or find a professional counselor who wants to provide several sessions to get to the heart of the matter—not one who wants to sit down with you for two years.

At the heart of the marriage relationship is the ability to communicate in love, with what's best for both of you in mind. Sure, some topics may be more difficult to talk about than others, but what have you got to lose? You're in this relationship for a lifetime. Why not make it the best it can be?

Straight Talk

Communication has to be a priority in your marriage, but you can be creative and smart with how you go about it.

If you're a woman: You converse naturally, so no problem there. But if you want to converse with your man, pick your time wisely. You don't want to pick Sunday afternoon, during the fourth quarter of his beloved Bears game, to try to launch a conversation.

Want to get dear hubby's attention? Try these top two ways:

1. Watch something he's in the midst of doing (like building something out of wood in the garage) and say, "Wow, that looks interesting. Tell me more about that." Now you have his attention. You've shown interest in one of his projects, and all boys—little and big—*love* that. He'll be more than happy to talk with you. Plus he'll share his heart along the way and be willing to listen to your sharing too.

2. Touch him. Touch is so powerful to guys, and it can open up wonderful communication lanes between you. As you're touching him, say, "Honey, I have a really important question to ask you. You seem to be deep in thought, so now may not be the best time. If so, just let me know, and I'll wait until the time is right." But by touching him, you already got his

attention. By addressing him with respect, you secured his attention. And by letting him know you're willing to wait to talk, you're almost guaranteed to have a captive listener!

If you're a man: The most important thing you can do is conserve some energy (and word count!) during the day so you aren't running on empty for your wife at night. Maybe this means making phone calls and doing appointments earlier in the day, and scheduling quieter, nonverbal activities later in the day.

Also, when you leave the office, turn your thoughts toward home. Shrug off your work and the pressures of the day. Think about your wife and why you married her—all the things you love about her. Put her in the front of your mind.

Remember the three most important things to a woman are (1) affection (that means closeness but *not* sex), (2) communication, and (3) commitment to family. If you major on these three, you'll have a happy bride.

13

Not Now, Honey, We'll
Wake the Children . . .

(But We Don't Have Any Children Yet!)

What those excuses really mean . . . and what to do about them.

I'm really tired tonight. I just don't feel like it."
"What if someone hears us?"
"Okay, if you really feel we have to."

Excuses can mean many things. And most of them are not good. Sure, you can honestly be tired. But even tired spouses have been known to give their eager spouses quickies.

Usually underlying those excuses are one or more of these real meanings:

1. I've been hurt by life and have a hard time being intimate with anyone, even you. (More on that in chapters 20, 21, and 23.)

2. You're such a lousy lover that sex simply isn't pleasurable. No wonder I'm not motivated.
3. I've never been successful in this area, and I don't want to fail again.
4. You're so predictable—you start at A, go to B, and end at C.
5. I'm mad at you about something, and this is payback time.

Do you know who most often (85 percent of the time) offers the excuses? The woman. "Now why is that, Dr. Leman?" you're asking. "Surely you're stereotyping." Notice that I did say 85 percent. And that's because men only need a place. Women need a reason, an environment, in order to want to be part of a sexual symphony.

Many men struggle with foreplay. It's an art that doesn't come easily to men. After all, they shouldn't rub a clitoris like a major league pitcher would rub a baseball before the first pitch of a game. Men would make love in a garbage can if that was the only place around. *Ambience* isn't a word they use—or even know.

But to a woman, foreplay is much different. It's taking out the garbage; taking the kids to the park for a couple hours in the afternoon; gathering up the newspapers and the crumbs on the kitchen floor; and vacuuming the family room, which the kids have trashed. And here's the important point: without her asking you. Got that, gentlemen? Foreplay to her means that you noticed her world and you helped out. When you enter her world, see it through her eyes, and meet her needs, you'll be amazed at how the excuses melt away.

And, ladies, the same is true of the gentleman in your life. Don't reject your guy when he's asking for sex with you. He'll take that personally—and he'll take it out on you. (Even if you married a "nice guy," sexual rejection hits at the heart of a man.) So find a way . . . use your creativity. I know you've got it. You're a woman, after all.

I've learned a lot from my Sande about creativity. That woman is amazing. Bet your husband will say the same of you too. So set the excuses aside and enter your man's world. You'll be glad you did.

Q: My husband and I have been using the natural family-planning method. Up to this point, it's worked well for us. We have three kids under the age of nine. But after our last daughter was born six months ago, Rob stopped having sex with me. He's found ways to sidestep any time in the bedroom with me by working late and coming home when I'm already asleep. I finally had the courage to ask about this yesterday, and he just barked out, "Well, sex equals kids, and one look around here tells you we don't need any more!" How do I get around that one?

A: Your husband's right. There isn't any way around that one. Your three kids are proof. You might want to talk to an ob-gyn and consider your options—soon.

Q: My husband thinks that I don't work because I'm a stay-at-home mom. I take care of the dishes, the trash, and everything else around here. . . . I'm tired. Ya think that after all that I'd be interested in sex? Are you kidding me? How can I get him to help?

A: You should be ticked off. Your husband is an idiot, and I'd be the first one to tell him so. If you've made that tough decision to stay at home and take care of the ankle biters, your husband is one lucky guy. He is being very disrespectful, not to mention chauvinistic, in treating you like his personal servant and vending machine. You feel offended, and rightfully so. Stand up for yourself. Write him a letter or an email and lay it on the line. Get yourself engaged in some activities on Saturday when he's home. Then tell him, "Well, honey, I'm not going to be here.

Good luck with the kids. I'll be back in two hours. Remember, the baby needs to be in bed for a nap by 1:00." Then leave for another activity—just you, no kids! And let's just see how he does, shall we?

I'll never forget the time my wife went to a weekend conference with a bunch of women from our church. I heard her making arrangements for her mom to come over and babysit our kids. Our girls were 3 and 18 months at the time. So I, being the wonderful husband I am, said, "Oh, honey, call your mother back. I don't want you to worry about it. Listen, I'll take care of the kids. Don't worry about a thing. You just go and have a great time."

Even now, all these years later, I remember every moment of that day. When Sande got home at 5 p.m. on Saturday, I, bleary-eyed, watched her coming through the door and thought, *Praise God!*

I said, "You're home! How many days have you been gone?"

She looked at me like I was crazy. "Days? What are you talking about?" (She'd only been gone since the morning.) Then she looked around the family room. "What happened in here?" she asked in that shocked Sande tone.

I said, "Don't give me that 'what happened' bit. I cleaned this room three times today!"

I'm telling you, a kid came through the back door on a little tricycle with muddy wheels, and I didn't even know who the kid was! I don't think our kids even knew who he was! He just zoomed in the back door and out the front door. It was a zoo trying to keep on top of those little kids the whole afternoon.

Your guy needs a little reality discipline. He needs to walk awhile in your shoes to get a firm appreciation for the job you do. Once he does, things will turn around in your house. Suddenly you'll find you have a helping husband . . . and you'll be more willing to have that bedroom fling.

Q: What is it with guys anyway? My husband thinks he can give me grunt responses to my questions at dinner, ask me to get the oil changed in the car during dessert, and then, as soon as it's bedtime, give me that knowing eyebrow wiggle that's supposed to lure me into the bedroom for a fling. Right. Grunts and oil changes are certainly romantic talk. Then he wonders why I suddenly find a book intensely interesting. This is the same guy who *always* brought me flowers or chocolate to start every date. It's like he got the "marriage job" done, then checked me off his to-do list . . . and I guess sex is at the end of his nightly checklist now that we're married. What gives?

A: Let's just say that the way a man *thinks* he's communicating love and kindness sometimes isn't the way it's perceived. That's why communication between a husband and wife is so important.

Women are wired to desire a heart connection. They have to be intimate emotionally before they can feel comfortable being intimate physically. If your husband isn't communicating (other than giving you grunts—which mean nothing to you but everything to the male species—and a to-do list for the next day), why would you feel close enough to him to want to share your body with him? And if he doesn't recognize the work you do,

---

First Words

"Holy moley, would you look at that!"
—*Adam's first words when he saw Eve*
"Sorry, I'll pass. I have a headache."
—*Eve's first words to Adam*

---

he's plain dumb. (Sorry—guys are just dumb as mud sometimes.)

You need to shoot straight with your thickheaded guy. Tell him frankly that you feel used when he treats you like that, and it doesn't make you very interested in having sex with him. What *would* make you very interested, however, is if he showed he cared about your day, and if he did something to show he thought of you and had your best interests in mind.

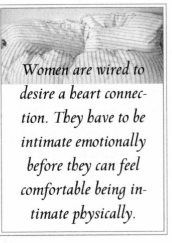

Women are wired to desire a heart connection. They have to be intimate emotionally before they can feel comfortable being intimate physically.

Good luck. Guys can be dumb, but if you "edumacate" them (as an old Iowa grandpa once told me), they can learn quick.

Q: My wife seems so tired and overwhelmed lately. We haven't had sex much, and I can't blame her. She has a lot on her plate. But I sure miss the sex. Any suggestions to help us until life settles down?

A: I'm glad you asked. Ever heard of the phrase, "Sex begins in the kitchen"? That's one I coined years ago in my book by the same name. I bet you'd find its ideas right up your alley.

In that book I talk about the fact that a man is wise to make love to his wife *outside* the bedroom. What does that mean? It means he's a helper. He changes diapers, he does laundry, he helps with homework, and he tucks the kids into bed. He knows all the women in the carpool, and he sometimes even drives the kids to school. He's a good daddy and an attentive husband. He listens to his wife talk about her day, because he knows it's important to her and because they share one heart.

155

He shares with her details about his day, because he knows she needs to know to stay close to his heart. He uses his authority to protect, serve, and pleasure his wife.

You see, every day your wife is taking emotional and mental notes on how you are treating her and your children (if you have them). Those feelings have everything to do with how available and willing she'll be to meet you in the bedroom, even for a quickie.

How are you doing in the area of sex outside the bedroom? Are there ways in which you could take some of the burden from your wife so she could reserve some time for you?

That's what love, partnership—marriage—is all about.

Q: We have three kids—all teens. My wife just can't seem to relax at night to have sex. She always wonders what they're up to. So, any ideas? Other than waiting until the kids are in college?

A: Does your wife have a reason to be worried about your children? If so, that's another issue! And one you'd best immediately address. But you're right—waiting until they're in college isn't an option.

Kids of any age can be great interrupters of sex. After all, they are concerned only about themselves. I always call them "hedonistic little suckers," and they most often prove that to be true. So it's time to create some basic rules and safeguards.

Lock your bedroom door so you don't have to worry about getting caught in the raw.

Take the bull by the horns and get a babysitter if you're worried. Yes, your kids will hate it, but maybe if they hate it enough they'll learn how to behave themselves.

Take your spouse out to dinner and then out for a stress-free fling.

Make a reservation at a hotel. Ask a neighbor to stay over, then return the favor another time.

Do something creative that surprises her enough to take the edge off having those kids constantly in the mix.

Someday those kids are going to go to college, get jobs, and move out (hopefully). Then who's left? The two of you.

Ah, now that puts everything in perspective.

Q: My wife says she doesn't have "the urge" to have sex anymore. When I hear that, I almost panic. I can't imagine living the rest of my life without sex. Is there some kind of Viagra that women can take?

A: Sure there is. But women don't take it. You give it. Viagra for a woman is you holding her tenderly and gently, listening, communicating, sharing your feelings, and helping her win arguments while she helps you win arguments so you live in harmony. Now that's Viagra to a woman. That's what will really make your wife respond to you in the bedroom. How are you doing in those departments?

And here's the flip side. If you strive to serve her and please her, then she will want to please you back in all ways. She will become your best friend and confidante. She will turn on, and she'll turn you on.

Also, it's time to romance your wife again. To get yourself in the mood, make a list of 40 of her best qualities. Post it where you can see it every day. Write her short notes. Kiss her (without it leading to sex). Treat her with kindness and gentleness. Think

---

Sex Tonight, Anyone?

Two lovebirds are sitting on a wire.

One says to the other, "I don't care if we are lovebirds. I still have a headache."

Romance 101 at Home (for Guys)

1. Build a fire (uh, only if you have a fireplace).
2. Have dinner ready when she arrives home (something other than pizza).
3. Set the table and use real napkins and goblets.
4. Clean the bathroom.
5. Turn off the TV and put on her favorite CD.
6. UPS the kids to Grandma's house.

---

about her day and night. As you do this, your own attitude and emotions will change (funny thing is, they follow what you're thinking about). Then watch what happens to your sex life. It may take some time, but it's the Viagra your wife needs.

If your wife continues to struggle with lack of interest in sex, she ought to see her doctor. She might be struggling in other areas as well.

Straight Talk

What do excuses really mean?

In short, they mean: "I don't feel loved." "I don't feel connected to you." "I don't feel like you really care about me. All you care about is what I can do for you."

Sex is too important to let it go. I've always said, "The state of sex in your marriage will reflect the state of your marriage," and every word of it is true.

Making time for each other is about priorities, respecting each other, and giving yourself fully to each other in order to become one. Your marriage is too important—don't shortchange yourself.

14

Ms. Boring Meets Mr. Predictable in the Bedroom

Breaking out of the predictability rut.

There are people who eat the same way, brush their teeth the same way, and do life the same way all the time. Many of these are firstborns, perfectionists, achieving people. It's who they are. I ought to know, because I'm married to one.

But what happens when two of these people get married to each other? It's "Ms. Boring Meets Mr. Predictable," and the results are (yawn) boring and predictable. If that's you and your spouse, no wonder you don't find yourself in the sack. You've bored each other to death.

But what if things could be different? What if you, as a wife, physically took your husband's hand and put it where you wanted it to go? Would the earth shake? Would the world end? No, but maybe your marriage bed would have a little earthquake of its own. And guess what? It would be fun.

So why not try to make things a little more exciting? Why not say, "Honey, would you be willing to try something? Just lay on your back. I want to show you something." If your spouse isn't willing to break out of the rut, why don't you initiate it? Literally take his or her body into your hands.

What if you got rid of the kids and met him at the front door after work in something very unlike you—just to show him things can be done differently? I guarantee that man would drop his jaw—and his laptop—right at the door. And you wouldn't have to worry a whole lot about the rest of the sexual interlude. He'd be in shock, so you could lead him anywhere.

Why not try it sometime? You might just like it . . . and your spouse might just love it.

Q: The first time we had sex, the sex just happened. It was beautiful. After that, it's like my husband turned into a sex robot who went from step to step to step, doing the same things all the time. I hate it, but I don't want to hurt his feelings. What feels good one day doesn't feel good the next. But I know he won't get that.

A: Are you sure he won't get that? Have you tried talking to him? You know, husbands aren't mind readers. In order to understand what you're thinking and feeling, most men need to have clear, direct information in short sentences.

Like this: "Honey, I need to talk to you about something. You know, last Saturday when we had sex, it was delightful. I felt special and so close to you. It was unbelievable. Then the following time when we had sex, it seemed like you tried to repeat what happened on Saturday. I don't know if it's just the way I am or if every woman is like this, but what I really like is when you change things up and do things differently."

And then walk your husband through what you do like. "Surprise me. Don't always start here. What would happen if you started there?" (Give him a wink.) "And while you're at it, what things would you like *me* to do differently for you? I'd sure love to please you."

That way, when you're approaching your husband, you aren't criticizing him. Most men who are criticized won't get angry outwardly, they'll just get quiet and shut down. Men are like submarines. If you hurt them, they'll go underwater and they won't come out. "Run silent, run deep," as the old war movie said.

So be careful of your guy's feelings. There's a little boy's heart hidden inside there. A heart that loves you very much, even if he's not good at verbalizing it.

> *Be careful of your guy's feelings. There's a little boy's heart hidden inside there. A heart that loves you very much, even if he's not good at verbalizing it.*

Q: I admit it: our sex life is so routine and boring, we nearly fall asleep during sex. Any suggestions to zip it up?

A: If you're so bored, what have *you* done to liven things up? It's easy to sandbag, to lay back and say that your sex life is boring. But finger-pointing never works. You have to own up to your part of the equation. A marriage takes two, and you are one of those two.

So why not try something fun? Email a photo of yourself in enticing wear to your husband at work. Go camping and bring extra towels to have wild sex in the wild. Be creative. I know you can do it!

The most important thing is your attitude about sex and that it becomes a priority in your life as a couple. It's too easy for sex to get shoved to the back of the bus, so to speak. Kids and jobs become too important and take over. Don't let this happen to you.

Q: It takes so much energy to think up creative ideas to keep my husband happy. Sometimes I have to wonder, *Is it really worth it? Would he miss it if I just kinda forgot about sex?*

A: I'll be blunt. If you aren't interested in your husband sexually, he'll take that personally.

Sure, there may be times where you aren't interested at all—like when you're a day away from your period and you feel crampy and bloated. But your guy still has needs. Would taking three minutes of your time for the man you love be too much to ask? This is where a quickie comes into play—a well-timed handjob. You can please your husband in a jiffy without the effort of going the whole nine yards. And who knows? Maybe watching him get happy might just put you in the mood too.

Certain women will read that and write me off as Hitler incarnate for suggesting that you as a woman please your husband in such a way, without getting anything out of it yourself. But if you want to function well as a team, you need to realize that the differing physiology of men and women requires that kind of thinking.

Some of you have the mind-set that everything in marriage has to be 50/50. Well, the goal is for everything to be 100/100, but practically speaking, there are times when it isn't, for various reasons. During those times, it's your job to get creative. Within three to ten minutes, you can have one happy dude on your hands. And a happy dude will perform in many other ways as well. Just you wait and see.

Q: I'm really struggling in my marriage sexually. My husband is so . . . *predictable.* I could fall asleep for five minutes and still give a role play of what happened because it's like he has his script memorized. My best girlfriend says, "Hey, he's not going to change. Remember the time when you told me he said, 'Well, you used to like it that way; what's changed?' Girl, that man is clueless. . . ." Any hope for me?

A: How would you like it if your husband broadcast to his co-workers your weight, the size of your breasts and thighs, and your dress size?

Well, that's exactly what you're doing to him. You're talking to your *girlfriend* about your sex life? That's a violation of your marriage vows. As your guy would say, "Hey, honey, what happens between you and me in this marriage is, you know, between you and me." And that's where it should stay, unless the two of you are in professional counseling.

There's a difference between talking to a trusted mentor or counselor together and gossiping with a girlfriend about your guy. If you want to chase your husband away and make him turn against you, that's a great way to do it. But is that really what you want?

I want you to try something. Count the number of girlfriends you have. Now count on one hand the intimate friends your husband has. I said "one hand" as a joke. You don't even need one hand. Just your index finger will do it. If he's representative of a lot of us men, he has no friends he can talk to. You thrive on relationships, but he, by nature, holds people at arm's length. That means you are the conduit for all your husband's emotional relationships. That says a lot about you and his trust in you, doesn't it?

You were fortunate enough to get closer to your husband and to become his #1 priority. So show him that respect now. Talk to him gently, not demandingly. Tell him how much you love and appreciate him. Tell him that you'd like to try something new . . . and that you're in the mood right now. Complete that statement with a suggestive look, and it ought to get your red-blooded male willing to try something a little different. Have fun!

Q: Now that we've settled into being married longer, we're running out of fun ideas. Help!

A: If you're a man, when was the last time you surprised your wife and made all the arrangements to take her someplace special? When was the last time you sent her a little Shoebox card with a tender note in it, from your heart to hers? When was the last time you took a bar of soap and made a big heart on the mirror near where she gets dressed in the morning, with just a little love note about how much you appreciate what she does in your family?

Think about it this way: in life, you get what you pay for. In the area of sex and your spouse, it's the same thing. You get what you pay for (in time, money, and energy). If there's one thing that ought to be a priority in your life, it's sex. So why not do something exciting? Treat your bride as a bride all over again. If you do, then your woman, who functions like a Crock-Pot (slow to warm up) may just turn into a microwave. And watch out: she's coming after you.

If you're a woman, how about a little message tucked into your husband's briefcase or lunch that says, "Great news! The

---

5 Ways to Break the Predictability Rut

1. Make love to your spouse's feet (everyone loves a good massage).
2. Rub your spouse's head (ahh . . .).
3. Shower together.
4. Come to bed fully dressed, with the expectation that your spouse will know how to get those clothes off.
5. Rub each other's bodies with scented oil (and I'm not talking Valvoline).

---

kids are gone tonight. They're going to Grandma and Grandpa's. I have some hors d'oeuvres that I plan on wearing. I'll see you right after work."

Now, if you're a man, and you get that message at 10 in the morning, what are you going to be thinking about all day? Your engines are going to be running hot, I'll tell you. That woman of yours is going to be on your mind no matter what deadlines you have. It doesn't matter if you have a jerk for a boss or you're in a dead-end job that you hate or you have a migraine. All those things will suddenly disappear in the golden glow of your anticipation. And boy, will you want to please that wife!

As my best friend, Moonhead, says, "If you don't have to take a shower after sex, you haven't had great sex."

With just a little thought and a little planning, you'll be surprised how happy Mr. Happy and Little Miss Delightful can get—and how long the memory will last.

Q: Since the first year or so of our marriage, our sex life has gone down the drain. My wife never initiates sex and barely kisses me. I'm tired of feeling rejected. The thought of the next 50 years like this totally depresses me.

A: Then it's time to go where you're not comfortable. Otherwise you'll tend to repeat the same relational pattern you're living with now. There are a lot of things you can do to make your marriage more exciting—to make your sex life more important. But you know it all gets down to relationships and what kind of sacrifices you're willing to make for each other. So start with an area that's uncomfortable for you. What do you have to lose if not much is happening in your life anyway?

Let me give you an example from personal experience. Let's just say that my wife is modest, okay? When we're in a hotel room and she gets out of the shower, do I see her? No, I see a towel with Holiday Inn embossed across it. It's just the way the woman is. She dresses in her walk-in closet. She's about as conservative as they come.

Now, we've always celebrated our anniversaries well. (I think a marriage is worth celebrating.) Once a year, on August 5, I make an extra-special effort to make sure Sande understands just how pleased and happy I am to call her my bride.

In the summertime, we live in western New York state, which is not far from Toronto, Canada. Toronto is an exciting place to visit. And, again, my wife loves those five-fork restaurants. The real nice ones. I hate them with a passion. But you know what? I want to please her, so where do I take her? To the five-forker!

One year I arranged to take her to see *Phantom of the Opera* at the Pantages Theatre. The next night I made dinner reservations for 7:30 at a five-forker. (I like to eat at 5:00, and the fewer utensils, the better. Do you get the picture? It was all to make my bride happy.)

Flash back to that night. It's 7:30, the time we're supposed to be at the restaurant, and Sande is still in the bathroom getting ready. So I yell, "Hey, honey, come out! They're not going to hold the reservation for us."

"I'll be right there, sweetheart."

Yeah, right. I know Sande better than that.

Ten minutes later, I'm still pacing up and down, with a sport coat and tie on. (Note that the only other time you'll see me in a sport coat and tie is at funerals.)

Finally she comes out . . . in a negligee—a see-through negligee. My wife! The Baptist!

I stare at her and mumble, "I don't under . . . stand."

All of a sudden there's a knock on the door. Sande goes back in the bathroom and slams the door. I'm standing there like a deer stuck in the headlights. Somehow I must have managed to make my way over to the door to open it.

A guy was standing there. I don't know what he said at first. From the look on my face, maybe he thought I was sick or something. Finally his words made it through to my befuddled brain.

"Sir, I have your dinner. Can I bring it in?"

"Sure."

So he brings it in. Still shell-shocked, I sign a little leather thing.

When he leaves, Sande comes back out . . . again in that see-through nightie . . . and she's holding two little candles.

She comes over to me. "Leemie, Leemie, it's okay. . . . I just thought we'd eat in tonight."

I said, "Okay."

And those are all the details you're going to get. (I do have some scruples in the stories I tell.) But, I'm telling you, it was great.

Want to make a 40-year-old man, a 50-year-old man, or a 60-year-old man smile for a few days? Step out of the bathroom in a see-through nightie. Why was that night especially exciting for me? Because I know that's not who Sande is. She did that just for me, her husband, to surprise me. And it was a surprise I'll never forget.

I have news for you. I do all kinds of things for her as well. That's what marriage is all about—knowing what your wife's needs are, knowing what your husband's needs are, and meeting them with a happy face.

And a few surprises too.

Straight Talk

Why are you putting up with what's boring and predictable? You deserve so much more.

It's the smart man who surprises his wife with flowers and a new nightie. It's the smart woman who emails her husband on their anniversary (or any day of the year) and says, "Hey, I have an idea. I have 60 dollars. If you have 60 dollars, I'll meet you at the Red Roof Inn. Believe me, I have something to show you. And guess what? Whoever gets there first doesn't have to pay."

> *Want to make a 40-year-old man, a 50-year-old man, or a 60-year-old man smile for a few days? Step out of the bathroom in a see-through nightie.*

I can guarantee you that guy will be logging off his computer and racing out the door of his office as fast as his feet can carry him. Who would want to miss that?

So have fun. Kidnap your spouse. Act like you did when you were dating. Renew the spark of your intimacy, and you can enjoy a sweeter, sexier, more satisfying marriage than you ever dreamed possible.

168

15

Love Handles Can Be Sexy!

Why not cut yourself some slack?

I'll never forget one particular morning show at *Good Morning America*. I was there as a guest to talk about marriage and family issues, and they were doing a spot on Barbie dolls. "Look how perfect they all are," I said. Interesting, isn't it, what Madison Avenue focuses on? And what unrealistic standards we fall for as the ideal, and try to meet? Someone once quipped that if you met a person in real life with a Barbie doll figure, she'd never be able to walk upright with such tiny feet, rounded hips, and a top-heavy bosom.

I dare you to go to the mall, sit on a bench, and look at all the people who go by. How many model-looking, good-looking, less-than-125-pound women do you see? How many handsome, sculpted, well-built, 6-pack-ab men do you see? How many people are dressed to kill, with no extra poundage and long legs that actually look good in miniskirts? How many people stop you in your tracks and make you say, "Wow, look at *that!*" One in 500? One in 1,000? One in 2,000? You tell me.

The reality is, most of us are average at best. Now, it may not please you to admit that to yourself. No one wants to be called average, but that's what most of us are. We fall within the wonderful, huge category of being pretty average.

And still we compare ourselves to others: *I'm too old. I have fat thighs. My breasts should be bigger. . . .* The list continues.

Because the nature of sex is so intimate, one of the first places the comparison game shows up is in a person's sex life. *Why would he want to have sex with me? I've gained twenty pounds since college, and my thighs now look like tree trunks.*

But I can guarantee, ladies, when your guy has you in the sack, he's not thinking about those little love handles. He's thinking about your breasts, which are now fuller, and another little area that's even more intriguing to him than your thighs, which have their own beauty and enticement for him. If he's thinking about your love handles, then he needs a male engine check because something is wrong with that man.

Fact is, as we mature, we spread. Or is it that the same weight just jiggles itself around and down a little? Either way, you can't take life so seriously. Could it be time to cut yourself some slack? To accept the love handles you have and move on?

Q: My wife has a beautiful size 14 body, and I love every inch of it. But when we're getting ready to have sex, she always turns the lights out and pulls the covers up to her chin. I want to *see* her. I like to look at her; it turns me on. She's a gorgeous woman, and God gave her to me nine years ago. How can I help her understand that *she* is the one I love, and that to me, she only gets sexier each year?

Why Models Look So Good: Tricks of the Trade

1. They have their picture taken a zillion times to get the best shot.
2. They have a makeup artist and a hair stylist.
3. Their clothes are picked carefully by a stylist to be the most flattering to them and are pinned in all the right places to hug their bodies.
4. They wear high heels with everything to make themselves look taller and distribute the weight over longer lines.
5. All their flaws are fixed in Photoshop.

A: Good for you! You have the right attitude. About 99 percent of women are clapping and cheering you on too. They all want *you* for a husband. You have your priorities straight.

How can you get your wife to understand how beautiful she is? Caress her. Whisper sweet nothings in her ear. Call her gorgeous. Bring her flowers. Romance her like crazy. If she's bothered by her weight, tell her that you love her just the way she is. Offer to take her shopping for a hot new dress—something she can wear just for you. Gradually your wife will become more comfortable with her body (at least with you). And then, oh, the fun you'll have.

Keep on doing exactly what you're doing. I'm rooting you on from the sidelines.

Q: When my husband and I have sex, I always fall into the rut of comparing myself to his gorgeous ex. I know there's no way I can measure up to her (Miss Blonde 36-26-36), and I feel really ugly. I can see the disappointment in my husband's eyes when I back off in our sexual play and get shy, but I can't seem to help myself. How can I get over feeling inadequate?

A: Has your husband ever said anything to you about how beautiful his ex was? Or how good in bed she was? If so, I'll take him out and thunk him on the head myself. Chances are, he

171

probably hasn't. You just met her or saw her picture sometime, and you're making assumptions on their sex life as a result. If Miss Blonde 36-26-36 was so gorgeous and so perfect, why is your guy with you? There must have been some flaw in her character or in their relationship. So why are you letting her hold your sex life hostage?

Concentrate on the reality that your husband chose you. He's done with his ex. Evidently she has nothing on you, because you're the one who won the prize: him. So go after that man like the prize he is. Make some new sexual memories with him to dim any he has with the blonde miss. Now that sounds like a fun assignment . . . for both of you.

Q: My wife's had two children, so she's not quite as curvy as she used to be. Because my mom was such a slob when I grew up (she always wore sweatpants to the store, and it drove my dad nuts), it's important to me to have a wife who keeps herself looking good. But any time I say anything to her about her weight or a diet, she freezes me out of the bedroom for two weeks. How can I show her that I love her as her, but I also want her to look her best?

A: Who do you really have in mind here with your question—your wife, or you? Do you have your wife's best in mind, or do you just not want to be embarrassed by a wife who's a "slob" (like your mother was)? Before we deal with the issue of your wife, you need to delve a little deeper into your own background and how your dad treated your mom. Was your mom a slob because your dad was critical of her? Did your mom perhaps even gain weight and wear sweatpants to keep your dad disinterested in sex with her? What was their relationship like? And how did that influence you, both in your childhood and now that you're married?

Could it be possible that your wife has gained and kept her weight because you're critical of her? And that she's freezing you out of the bedroom to hide from your criticism?

Remember that when you point the finger at your wife, three fingers are pointing back at you. So deal with your own issues first. If you have actively criticized your wife, now is the time to ask for her forgiveness and to change your ways (so your children won't fall into the same relational patterns down the road).

I'm also fairly confident that one of the reasons her weight gain bothers you is because it's not sexy to you, is it? When you married, she was probably thinner. And for certain men—not all—it's more exciting if the woman is thinner and "sexy." If you want your wife to lose weight, the first thing you need to do—*right now*—is to stop criticizing her. Don't suggest that she eat differently; don't bug her if you see her eating chocolate. And apologize for the way you've been acting toward her—as if she's not valuable to you anymore, you're not committed anymore, you don't love her anymore—all because she gained a few pounds. That's not forever love; that's conditional love (probably something you saw in your parents' relationship—and do you want to be like them?). Your wife will never want to change if she feels like she can never perform to your satisfaction, if she can never be good enough for you anymore.

Your wife's weight gain has nothing to do with your sexual satisfaction. It has everything to do with your past, your parents,

---

Why Real Women Like You Are Sexier

1. You're the real deal. No Photoshop there.
2. You've earned every wrinkle; be proud of them.
3. Your body has borne the children of the man you love.
4. Your husband loves you, needs you, and wants you—just the way you are.

the beliefs and rule book you've carried since childhood, and the relationship you've formed with your wife.

Commit yourself to loving your wife, and let her take care of the rest.

Straight Talk

When you're tempted to bemoan that there's a little more of you to love than there used to be, just say it out loud. "Okay, so I weigh more than I used to. And I do have love handles that jiggle." There now, you said it. Wasn't so bad, was it? Now you can move on with life.

But what's more important to your husband, who loves you and wants to be with you? He longs for a willing partner in bed, for that's the essence of two becoming one. Chances are good that if you've gained some weight, so has he. Should you spend your time swapping stories about how many pounds you've gained? Or should you focus on eating healthy together and keeping your relationship healthy in all other ways, including sex?

That sure sounds like a lot more fun to me. How about you?

16

Help! I Married Judge Judy

Tackling the biggest sex killer—criticism.

If there's something that can kill a sex life faster than anything else, it's a critical-eyed person. That's why I'm including a separate chapter on criticism, because I get questions about dealing with it all the time. The very nature of sex in a healthy marriage is about spontaneity and giving unconditional love, warmth, and closeness to each other. As soon as criticism enters a marriage, the entire atmosphere changes. Husband and wife become guarded and defensive, and their relationship reeks of conditional love.

"He's a great guy," the wife says, "until you cross him."

"She's a great woman," the husband says, "as long as she gets her own way."

People who dish out criticism are hedonistic, caring only about themselves; they have a tough time thinking about how another person might take their criticism. Oftentimes the critical spouse in a marriage is the firstborn spouse, who "just knows how things oughta be"—meaning their way or the highway.

What happens to the spouse on the receiving end? They feel as if there's a trap door underneath them at all times . . . and at any moment, it might just spring open. So they're continually on guard.

No one likes criticism. It undercuts the very foundation of a marriage: love and respect. If a woman is criticized by her husband at the dinner table, it's highly doubtful she's going to be a willing, loving sexual partner after the 10:00 news. That's just not going to happen, because the criticism has ruined the atmosphere—the mood that she needs in order to engage fully and joyfully in sex. She can't enjoy sex if she's waiting for the other shoe to drop.

As big and tough as men appear on the outside, they're really little boys on the inside. The entire male species is extremely susceptible to criticism. Your guy may not show his anger outwardly, but oh, boy, he'll be angry on the inside. He will get long in the jaws and go right into his turtle shell . . . and he ain't comin' out. No sirree. You could read *Oprah* magazine cover to cover—in fact, a whole year's supply—and you won't get him to come out from his turtle shell. That is, until you say the words, "I'm sorry. I was wrong. Will you forgive me?"

It's true that you attract more flies with honey than with vinegar. Maybe some of your aunt Martha's admonitions way back then were worth their weight in gold.

Q: As soon as my husband walks in the door at night, he finds something to criticize: I haven't cleaned the kitchen enough. His favorite shirt is in the laundry. The kids are too noisy. How can I explain to him how awful that makes me feel, when I've worked hard all day? I've lost all interest in sex with him but do it just because I have to. I'm finding myself wishing these days that he wouldn't come home until after the kids are in bed and I've had a chance to relax . . . or could at least pretend I'm asleep.

A: You're feeling attacked, and rightfully so. It's like your husband walks through the door every night and launches a bunch of missiles your direction, and you have to duck. Your home should be a place of refuge, yet you're being attacked there. And the missiles are coming from the one who should be supporting you the most.

Let me tell you what criticism is really rooted in: insecurity, fear, and anger or control. It's aimed at a *person* instead of a behavior. Your husband is busily hammering away at your sense of self-worth.

But what is love supposed to be? Affirming, tenderhearted, kind. That doesn't sound like what your husband is launching in your direction.

When one wife I know got fed up with her husband's criticism one night, she made a swift decision. When he criticized the way she was cleaning up the kitchen after dinner, she just smiled and said, "Well, since you know so much about how it should be done, I'll just leave it in your capable hands. The kids and I are going out for ice cream. We should be back about the time you're done." She gathered the kids into their van, and off they went! When I talked to her recently, it had

---

5 Ways to Crush Love

1. Fire off a volley of cheap shots, barbs, and innuendos.
2. Use the bullets to build up a wall over time.
3. Never talk about it.
4. Go to bed angry.
5. Decide it's not worth it and give up.

---

been three months since she'd done the ice cream run. Her husband had never since criticized the way she cleaned the kitchen.

Ah, so men *are* capable of learning. Sometimes they just need a little nudge.

Maybe that's what your husband needs . . . tonight.

Q: I grew up in a home where my parents were extremely critical. They held me to high standards (higher even than the other kids, since I'm the firstborn). Sometimes I find myself falling into the trap of criticizing my husband—about how he changes our son's diaper, the way he folds the laundry, how messy the garage is. I know I need to stop because I can see it hurts him (he gets really quiet and goes downstairs to watch TV instead of snuggling with me when the baby's finally asleep), but I can't seem to quit. Can you help me?

A: If you grew up with intense criticism, it's not surprising you're having a hard time breaking out of the mold.

But let me give you a challenge. Since you're a negative thinker who can spot a flaw at 50 paces, before you open your mouth, stop and think, *What do I normally say in this situation? What's the new me going to say in this situation?* In other words, look for ways to get the information across by being encouraging rather than discouraging.

Pastor and inspirational speaker Joel Osteen is tremendously popular today. If you listen to his messages, do you know what you'll find? Messages about encouraging one another, lifting up each other, and being positive rather than negative. That's what people are dying to hear!

What is your husband dying to hear from you? I guarantee the fastest way to get him back into your bed—and to keep him there—is to say the magic words, "Honey, I'm sorry. I was wrong. Would you forgive me?"

Every day make sure you share with your husband at least two things that you love and appreciate about him. When you open your mouth to criticize him for not folding the laundry correctly, think through your words carefully. Is correct laundry folding really a hill to die on? If it is to you, then you may need more help than I can give you.

Q: Every time I ask my husband to do something differently, he gets defensive and says I'm criticizing him. How can I get around this? It's affecting everything in our relationship—especially our sex life (or, shall I say, lack thereof).

A: My best guess is that your husband is balking because you are too controlling of his life and actions. (Or he has memories of his mother controlling his life and actions and is projecting that onto you.) Every man wants to be a man. Does that mean he won't listen to you? No, your guy has ears. And he'll be all ears if you approach him in a respectful manner. What your man wants is to be valued as a man, not treated like a little kid who has to be told everything. If you devalue him, it will show up in his attitude toward you and in every aspect of your relationship.

What can you do? You need to make sure that you separate the act or behavior from the person. If your husband grew up in a critical home, with a critical mother or a critical father (or, even worse, both), he will be even more touchy about this issue.

Let's face it. Our society, from the ground up, is built on negativity. A fourth grader takes a spelling test and misses two questions, and what's at the top of the paper? "Minus 2." What's wrong with "Plus 23," I wonder? But we don't think in those terms; we think in negative terms.

When you translate this propensity to be negative to marriage, it's no wonder that defenses go up and walls now separate the two of you. With each criticism, you add another brick to the wall. You "stonewall" each other. But over a period of time, the wall becomes so high you can't see over it, and so thick you can't reach through it. Then there's no longer a relationship.

Couples *will* disagree. But when you do, it's important to separate the person from the behavior. You may not like what your spouse does, but you still must show him that you love him. Your relationship must be more important than the issue at hand.

Q: My husband and I are in our late 50s. Four months ago, Frank decided to take early retirement from his management job. But now that he's home, he's still "managing." He constantly suggests "better" ways to do things like grocery shopping, laundry—all things I've done in our marriage for over 30 years—and even insists we should change the schedule for walking the dog. (Why does it matter to him since I'm the one who's done it all these years anyway?)

Then, a week ago, he posted a schedule on our bedroom door for when we should have sex. That was the last straw. Let's just say that ever since then, I've been sleeping in our spare bedroom, and he's not welcome, even on the scheduled

---

No Parking

I knew I was in trouble when I walked into the bedroom and saw a sign above the bed:

Don't even THINK of parking here.

---

sex nights. And this is the retirement we looked forward to? All I want is for him to go back to the office. Right about now, a flight to a Pacific island somewhere . . . *by myself* . . . is sounding very nice. Any hope for us?

A: A football coach's wife told me once, "Hey, Kevin! I just figured out how my husband and I get along so well. It's because he's always gone."

Does that ring a bell? Sometimes when a man retires and comes home, he has a hard time retiring. Keep in mind that he was a manager, the guy who called the shots . . . and a natural flaw picker.

Well, the one thing women need least in the world is flaw pickers. After all, you're hard enough on yourself. And you've run your house for X number of years—mostly by yourself—and done well, thank you very much. Now Mr. Manager comes home and decides he's going to rearrange everything you've handled capably all these years . . . without all the extra schedules, thank you very much.

You definitely need to have a talk with that man, especially about the sex schedule on the bedroom door. That's simply over the top, even for a manager personality (unless, of course, you both have manager, Type A personalities, and you had come up with the schedule together).

You need a good role definition for who does what in your family. He's been a busy, successful person, and I'm betting role definition is still important to him. Busy hands make light work—and tighter lips— so I'd give him the job of paying all the bills for the family, if he doesn't

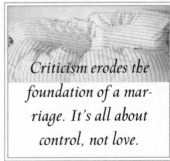

Criticism erodes the foundation of a marriage. It's all about control, not love.

already do it. Let him do any online research for the family. Suggest that he do some things with his buddies.

Think of what's happening in your home this way: You've both been rowing your individual canoes down the river of life. Now one canoe has floated down the river, so you have to get into the other canoe together and figure out who is going to paddle where.

What you're experiencing is very common. You've spent all your lives being away from each other most of the time, and now you're around each other, stepping on each other. You know what usually happens with retirees? One or both of them finds a different kind of work, because they find it hard to be constantly under each other's feet.

We're creatures of habit, and we don't like interference. But this is the time for some straight talk. You need to figure out a division of labor. Allow your husband to help with some things—now that he has the time and availability that he didn't have during his working years—and you do others. Then each of you manage your own particular responsibilities, without treading on each other's territory.

Now that you have your husband helping, give yourself a break. Find some things you can do with your girlfriends *and* with your husband. Take a photography course at a community college; take Spanish lessons; swim at the local Y.

Discover something completely new—together. Now that you have more time, take your time when you make love. Throw out that schedule. Let the phone ring. Be spontaneous. Try new positions. Be creative. Laugh.

Such experiences will give you the kind of bonding you need at this stage in your life. Good luck.

Q: I've lost respect for my husband because he's so critical. I can't do anything right, and he says I should do everything differently, but why should I even try? He'll only criticize my efforts more. The last time we made love (let's just say it was a long time ago), I couldn't do anything right. My nightshirt wasn't sexy enough. I didn't try hard enough to climax or I would have. It's not that he always *says* these things outright, but I can read them in his body language and in his impatience. He's always been the kind of guy that likes to move from one thing to the next at lightning speed. I used to admire that, but now I feel left in the dust.

A: It sounds like you've been through some rough experiences with your husband. From what you've said, you don't feel important to him anymore. Let me ask you something: Why did you marry that man? What were his positive qualities? Are you focusing right now on merely his negative qualities? Could he be focusing on *your* negative qualities rather than the qualities that caused him to fall in love with you?

Let me challenge you to do something. Each day over the next week, write down five positive qualities your husband has. Post them nonchalantly on the refrigerator. If he asks you what you're doing, just say, "Listing the things I like about you." Then just walk away. That ought to get his attention. As he sees the list grow day by day, you'll find him sneaking over to check it out when he doesn't think you're around to see. He might even begin to ask some questions that will prepare both of you for the discussion that will inevitably come. If he asks why you're making the list, state simply that you are struggling right now because everything you do doesn't seem right or good enough. You feel you'll never be able to please him, so you're trying hard to remember the good things.

If your man has any brains at all, he'll begin to get the picture. Hopefully that knowledge (and his competitive nature)

An Adage to Live By

For ages 4 to 104

If you can't say something nice, don't say anything at all.

will kick-start a list of his own on *your* positive qualities and will help to tame his critical tongue.

And as you go over the list of positive things about your mate—every day for a while—the list will begin to make its way back into your heart. If you act upon your love for him promised in your marital vows, then feelings you thought would never return may just surprise you.

Straight Talk

I once asked basketball coach Lute Olson what to do about criticism: Should you believe it? Do anything about it? Or shrug it off? He thought for a minute. "Kevin, it depends on who's doing the criticizing."

Bingo. Do you trust the person who is criticizing you? Is there a reason he or she is criticizing you? Do you have something to learn from his or her words—any improvement you could make? Or is the criticism off base or something you can't change?

If you're the one with the critical eye, does your criticism really need to be stated? Will it improve anything in your relationship—or will it cause harm?

Criticism erodes the foundation of a marriage. It's all about control, not love. But can you disagree with something your spouse does? Of course. And you can voice that disagreement. But disagreement is aimed toward the action or event, not the person. Criticism is aimed at the person and erodes the relationship.

And, ladies and gentlemen, you do not want to go there. It's wise to cut off the flow of criticism.

17

Too Pooped to Whoop?

What to do when your spouse is giving you that Bullwinkle the Moose look . . . and you're already in hyperdrive.

When I speak at 10 in the morning and I ask women, "Ladies, what are you having for dinner tonight?" do you know what? Most ladies know! In fact, they can give at least three to four details about dinner: "We're having chicken, broccoli, rice . . . oh, and ice cream for dessert." Interestingly, whether the woman works mainly in the home, has a career outside the home, or works part-time or full-time doesn't seem to change that fact. Women, in general, just know. Even if they're picking up Chinese takeout, they know what's on the menu. They're planners. They've got the to-do list down.

Now the men? When I ask, "Men, what are you having for dinner tonight?" they just shrug—the universal symbol of "I have no clue."

You see what I'm getting at here?

When I say to my wife, "Honey, can we have So-and-So over?" she immediately begins to think, *Oh my goodness. What is he talking about? I'd have to go to the store, clean the house, make something really great for lunch. . . .* All I'm thinking is, *I just want him to come over and go fishing with me on the lake.* But she automatically starts a mental list of the things that will need to be done. Now, my buddy and me? We wouldn't care what we ate. Sandwiches are okay by us. And I can guarantee you my buddy isn't doing the dust test on our house. But, you see, it matters to my wife, and because I love my wife, I have to pay attention to what she's thinking behind the scenes.

With all these to-do lists flooding into a woman's mind and all the activities she somehow manages to cram into a day—enough activities to choke a horse—it's no wonder that sometimes she gets to the end of her day and says, "An interlude in the bedroom? Are you kidding? I'm too pooped to whoop."

Gentlemen, that's where you have to get smart. You have to wear the pants in the family . . . but it may be in a very different way than you think.

Q: I can tell my wife is really tired . . . *all* the time lately. She's so good at what she does, though, that I'm not sure how I could help lighten her load. I know I wouldn't do things as well as she does. I wish she didn't have to work part-time, but with me getting a salary cut this year (it was sure better than a layoff), she had to. I want to be a good husband to her, and a good daddy, but sometimes I just feel, well, inept.

A: Buddy, join the club. Our wives could run circles around us any day of the week, even on our good days. But don't let your feelings of ineptness stop you from trying to help. I bet that woman of yours would be thrilled with *any* help. You see, what your wife needs most of all is a willing husband who says, "You tell me what I can help with, and I'll do it. Just say the word!"

This is especially important to a woman since her day revolves around her family, whether she is a stay-at-home mom or works part-time or full-time outside the home. (Case in point: how many working *moms* pick up their children from school and day care compared to how many *dads* do? I rest my case.) Even the woman who is a business executive is thinking, *Let's see, what can we have for dinner? I'll have to help Timmy with math tonight, pick up my dress at the dry cleaner. . . .*

Women are multitaskers, and they're brilliant at it. But multitasking is also exhausting. So take a careful look at your own schedule. If there are things you could take on—such as the grocery shopping, or picking up your daughter from day care three days a week, so your wife can finish her work in the office during the day instead of having to go back at night—then go after it. Discuss your ideas with your wife first, though. Some things may be more helpful to her than others. Use your days off to tackle anything you can on her to-do list—and take care of the kids too.

Don't worry about doing things perfectly. Just step in and help. I wish more guys had your kind of attitude.

And you know what? As you plunge in to lighten her load, you'll be amazed at how much more intensely attracted your wife will be to you physically, emotionally, and sexually.

Q: I've been married for seven years, and sex just isn't that important to me. I started a new job six months ago, and by the time I get home at the end of the day, I'm exhausted. Sometimes I can tell my husband's in the mood, but it's too much work for

---

8 Ways to Make Love to Your Wife . . . Outside the Bedroom

1. Set up a shopping date for her—and provide the cash or credit card.
2. Clean the basement and the garage.
3. Pick up your own, hers, *and* the kids' messes.
4. Wash the dishes. (Do you know how sexy you look to your wife with a dish towel over your shoulder? It's a turn-on for a woman.)
5. Don't pee on the toilet seat or leave the lid up so she falls in at 3 a.m.
6. Always ask her for her opinion.
7. Take the kids to their dentist and doctor appointments. In fact, just take the kids anywhere. . . .
8. Hire a limo to pick her up for her birthday dinner.

---

me to drum up the energy. I'd rather put on my comfy clothes and just watch TV.

Lately, sex hasn't seemed that important to my husband either. He doesn't even ask for it anymore. We'd rather just spend the night curled up on the couch, watching a good flick. No muss, no fuss, no exhaustion. I think sex is overrated. Because we see it all the time in movies and on TV, we think we have to do it or we're nerds. What's the big deal about sex anyway? It's just sex, isn't it?

A: Well, either your husband is undergoing depression or a male testosterone problem, or he's simply given up because you're not interested. But let me ask you: is that man of yours worth keeping in your bed? If so, you'd better willingly offer him some action, and soon. For a man, having his sexual advances rejected (for any reason) is paramount to emasculating him. No wonder your husband just wants to lay on the couch. Mr. Happy knows it ain't gonna happen, so he's not even going to think about rising to the challenge. But neither should you do it just because you feel you have to. That will make you feel demeaned and used.

What's the solution? A change of attitude. Sex is not something you use. It's not something you pull out of your pocket and look at when you feel like it. It's a gift from God to be enjoyed by both husband and wife. It's the crux of "the two shall become one" vows you took way back when.

Is it easy? No, but it's sure worth the effort.

A healthy sexual relationship fulfills both a man's and a woman's deepest desires, the way the Creator intended them to be.

Now that's worth getting off the couch for. Or, on second thought, maybe that couch could come in handy. . . .

Q: I know that as a young wife I'm supposed to give myself first to my husband, that the kids come second in line. But that seems so unrealistic. My kids, after all, can't feed themselves, can't reach the refrigerator, and have to be watched so they don't kill each other. And I'm supposed to save time and energy to have sex with my husband? Who'd want to have sex with me when I smell like baby cereal, drool, and Kool-Aid anyway? Don't we moms ever get a break from our responsibilities?

A: I have two words for you: time out. You have to make time for yourself. We're all given the same amount of time: 24 hours a day. It's how you manage that time that counts. I know you're busy and there seems no way out. For your own sake, your husband's sake, and your children's sake, you need to take time out. It might mean going to the gym and working out (if that's your bent), or maybe taking a walk each week with a girlfriend. Maybe it's setting a time when your husband can keep the kids and you get a Starbucks break after grocery shopping. Maybe it's a day at home when your neighbor watches your kids so you can do laundry and read a book in peace, and then you return the favor.

Do yourself a favor. Find a friend or two and form a co-op. You'll see a difference in your attitude not only in your patience level toward your children but also toward that guy you married.

Q: Is there a "guy code" out there, or something that says romance has to equal sex? Every time my husband gives me flowers or offers to drive our kids to a friend's for the evening, I get suspicious he has "getting in the sack" in mind. (That meets his track record for the past four years. . . .)

I have two words for you: time out. You have to make time for yourself.

I wish, just once, that he'd give me flowers just because he loves me, or offer to drive the kids to a friend's for the evening, then come back, put on romantic music, and let me sit in a soothing, aromatic bath all by myself. (Bringing me Perrier and chocolates would be a bonus.) Are guys so completely clueless? We've been married 15 years, so you'd think he'd get it by now.

A: Go back and read what you just wrote. I'll wait a minute. Do you hear what I hear? A lot of anger and bitterness against that guy you used to think was your knight in shining armor. You're feeling used, and maybe rightfully so. Your needs for intimacy and connection are not getting met (but evidently his are—probably with you being very grudging about it).

But here's the important question: do you know for sure your guy is doing this on purpose, or is it simply because he's doing the one-track guy thing? Have you ever talked with him about it (without being ticked off)? "Honey, I love you very much. I'm so glad you chose me to be your wife. There are times, though, when I don't feel very important to you or valued. I miss feeling special to you. I miss the days when you surprised me by putting a flower in the windshield wiper of my car at work. I want to feel special again. Can we talk about it?"

What are you asking for? A time to connect that isn't sexual and that meets your needs. If your husband can't get his head around that, then he's a pretty dumb lug. Setting up such a discussion should defuse any defensiveness he might feel, and it also defuses your own anger. But the key is having your attitude right before you talk to him. (Think about why you married your guy in the first place. What drew you to him?) Approach him with a smile, then talk straight to him—be blunt but kind.

Q: I love my two children, and so does my husband. But I have to admit that they are really, really draining. It's hard for me to save any time for intimacy. Any tips for me—for us? (My husband is behind me as I'm typing this, nodding.)

A: Kids are immature young people who largely care only about themselves. And when they're born, all they care about is what? Being fed, being dry, being held, and any kind of tactile stimulation that keeps them happy (or distracted). Well, put a couple of kids in the mix—especially young ones—and oh my goodness, you're exhausted. You're too pooped to whoop.

But here's a little tip: sooner or later, those little nippers will grow up to be big nippers, and they're going to leave your cozy little nest to fly on their own. Who's going to be left in the nest together? Mama and Papa Bird.

With that in mind, you have to take time for yourselves. You need time to be a couple. If you're lucky enough to have

> *Sooner or later, those little nippers will grow up to be big nippers, and they're going to leave your cozy little nest to fly on their own. Who's going to be left in the nest together? Mama and Papa Bird.*

Grandma and Grandpa or an aunt nearby, terrific. If not, you're going to have to fork out the pesos to get a babysitter you trust.

Here's another idea: Find three or four families who have children, whom you enjoy spending time with, and who have values similar to yours. (Even *one* other family would help!) Form a babysitting co-op and say, "Listen, if you take our kids on Tuesday nights, we'll take yours on Friday nights." The kids will think it's great to have playmates, and you'll get some needed couple times.

Straight Talk

When I first wrote my book *Sex Begins in the Kitchen*, I added a subtitle: *Because There's Company in the Living Room.* But somehow the publisher wouldn't go for it.

Sex doesn't begin in the bedroom. It begins in the kitchen and in the living room (and other places too). Let's say you have a group of couples over at your house. If you as a woman had to simultaneously entertain your guests and get the meal or dessert ready by yourself, that would be hard, wouldn't it? But, boy, wouldn't it be nice to have your husband by your side, saying, "What can I do to help?"

Think of a wife who drives home after a long day at work, thinks of the terrible mess from the previous night that didn't get cleaned up, and dreads doing it when she arrives home. Let's look at two scenarios.

Scenario 1: The husband arrives home when the wife does and proceeds to complain that the kitchen is a mess. While she cleans up the kitchen, he changes clothes, lounges in front of the TV, and then comes in to complain that there isn't any dinner ready. Then after dinner, he expects her to be ready for sex.

Scenario 2: When the wife arrives home, she discovers that her husband has beat her home by half an hour and is already finished cleaning up most of the mess. Because he saw a job that needed doing, he rolled up his sleeves and began taking care of it. He didn't wait around for her to do it; he took the lead and tackled the project himself.

Now think: which scenario would make that wife the happiest and the friskiest? You figure it out. And you know that smart husband? He knew his wife so well that he knew what she was thinking, and he went ahead and plunged in to help.

Today is a great day to be a woman. Unlike prior generations, a woman can do anything she wants to in life. What wonderful opportunities she has! She could be a surgeon or the captain of an aircraft. But the hard thing about all of these opportunities is that she becomes even more of a Velcro Woman. She already has many things tugging at her, and adding a career, especially with young children, adds a new strip of Velcro to her already jumbled schedule.

Contrast that to the husband, who doesn't have a lot of people piling on him. Most husbands leave work at the door. The other person or persons in his schedule are his wife and children (if they have any). His life is much simpler. That's why husbands have to understand all the things tugging at their wives.

Don't forget that your brain is probably the best sex organ you have. It's the ability of you and your spouse to share from your hearts, to grow together as one, that forms the center of your relationship. That's what brings you together as a couple. That heart closeness is what will turn up the heat on your passion—and make it burn like a raging fire. It's what will make a husband take a bullet for his wife. It's what will make a wife say to her girlfriends, "He's the most incredible guy I could ever imagine. Boy, do I know how to pick 'em, right?"

18

Romancing the Stone

How to turn up the heat without getting burned.

Women always get the rap for being cold, or "frigid," in bed. But did you know that 15 percent of the time it's the husband who is?

These are the people who say they're too tired, they're too stressed out, they just don't feel like it. They can be men and women who perform very well in the business world—folks who look like they have their act together. But underneath all the success on the surface, something is happening deep inside that person. It seems the "stones" come in two categories:

1. Those who have been abused sexually and have negative associations with sex, and therefore go out of their way to avoid any sexual intimacy.
2. Those who are naive, who are from conservative backgrounds, and who are predisposed to believe that sex is dirty and nasty even in marriage.

These stones are the ones who say by their attitudes, "Okay, I know we have to do it, so let's just get it over with."

If it's the female who is cold and unresponsive, it doesn't take rocket science or a PhD to understand that her guy will sooner or later wander into or fantasize about being in someone else's arms.

If it's the male who is cold and unresponsive, the woman is likely to fall into at least an emotional affair (which, of course, will soon bring sex into the picture).

Soon there's a great divide in the marriage that you could drive a semitruck through. Without the adhesive of sex—the great release of sexual tension, the intimacy of becoming one over and over again—before long it's "Have your attorney call my attorney." Is that really the direction you want to head?

Whatever gender the stone might be, if it's a cold one, it usually spells big trouble for your marriage. And now is the time to find a competent counselor. That would be the next best step.

Q: My husband always wins our marital fights . . . mainly because I give up. It's not worth it. I know I'll be the loser, so why try? It never fails that as soon as the fight is over (because I quit), an hour later he wants sex. When I give in to his demands, I feel like the loser once again. When I don't give in (I tell him I'm sick or tired), I lose too. Either way, I never win. What's worse, I'm a pastor's wife, so I have no one I dare talk to for advice. Is there any help for me? Or am I stuck this way for life? (There is no way my husband would allow me to get a divorce.)

A: It might surprise you to know that many pastors' wives feel the same way, and they're afraid to speak out too. What your husband is doing has nothing to do with love—certainly not the love he probably preaches about in 1 Corinthians 13. It has everything to do with control—controlling *you* through sex.

A man can control overtly, as your husband is doing, or covertly. A guy who is controlling may have an overly voracious need for sex. He may even want it more than once a day. He might want it twelve times a week and on demand. He'll just come up to his wife and start the sexual process without even asking if it's all right with her. If she says no, in all probability he'll dismiss that and continue anyway (if he's in a good mood, he might cajole her to go along; otherwise he'll just demand it as his right as a husband).

What is such a man doing? He's affirming his masculinity through dominance—not through a loving, caring, sharing relationship, which a marriage should be. He tells himself that as long as he can have sex when he wants, he's in control.

Your husband is in a very dangerous position. You cannot allow yourself to be used or dominated any longer. If your husband will not listen to reason and will not back off in his dominance and manipulation, you need to take the next step. Tell him that you insist he go to a counselor to deal with his control issues. You could look for a counselor from out of town. That might make it easier for your husband to seek the counsel that he so desperately needs. If he resists, tell him that you will need to notify the chairman of your church board that your husband is dealing with some personal issues and that the two of you will need time off to work through them. If he cannot get his striving for domination under control, he has no business being the head of a church.

Such straight talk ought to bring him up short. You need to show a backbone. Do not allow yourself to be abused further, because that's exactly what's happening.

Q: We barely have sex because my wife says "it hurts." Is she just avoiding sex, or does it really hurt? I thought sex was supposed to be a natural thing. Am I doing something wrong?

A: Many women have pain with intercourse for a wide range of reasons—everything from vaginal dryness to a yeast infection to something else going on. Yes, it could be an avoidance of sex for emotional reasons, but it also could be that she needs to visit a specialist in vaginal pain. Pain is a sign from our bodies that there's a problem and that we need to take care of it. Ask the doctor to explore the potential causes of vaginal pain and to pursue treatment.

This is really important. Don't let it go. You don't want your wife to associate sex with pain. Take the time to find out why she's having pain. If there are no physical issues causing it, then explore any potential emotional causes—both in her relationship with you and in her past relationships and her childhood.

Good for you for having the courage to ask the question. Now use that courage to help your wife figure out what's going on—for both your sakes.

Q: When we have sex, it's okay, but I feel empty inside when it's over. Is this normal?

A: Your feelings have everything to do with the closeness and stability of your relationship. Sex is supposed to bring you closer together as a couple, not leave you feeling empty. If you are feeling empty in your sexual relationship, something is missing in other areas of your relationship with your spouse as well. Take a look at your relationship outside the bedroom. How does your spouse treat you? How do you treat your spouse? Are there any unresolved issues that you're struggling with that might influence your feelings during and after sex?

Think of your sex life as a thermometer of your relationship. If there is too much conflict outside the bedroom, you won't be turning up the heat inside the bedroom. You'll be two stones trying to romance each other. Your emptiness is a wake-up call for something in your relationship with your spouse that needs to be addressed.

It could also have to do with your prior sexual relationships (whether with your spouse or with others). If you had sex before you were married, you gave your sexual partner(s) a big piece of your heart and body—pieces that you will never get back. Memories of those sexual liaisons tend to pop up at the most inconvenient times.

> *Think of your sex life as a thermometer of your relationship. If there is too much conflict outside the bedroom, you won't be turning up the heat inside the bedroom.*

No matter the cause of your emptiness, I suggest you pay attention—today.

Q: My wife never initiates sex and seems to barely tolerate it when we have it. Even her kisses are like little pecks, but there's no emotion behind them. She seemed so warm before we got married; now she's guarded. What gives?

A: Ah, there are two options.

Option 1: You have a controlling woman on your hands—a woman who withholds or gives sex to manipulate you. If she wants to buy something for herself or the house, does she appear more eager? Does she use sex as a tool to loosen you up before she makes her request? If you're not a "good boy," does she withhold sex? Is she showing her anger or discontent with you by becoming a stone?

If this is the case, you need to tell your wife (gently) how it makes you feel when she withholds sex—like you're a little boy begging for a prize that you used to get all the time. You also don't understand why she is responding to you the way she is now. Is it something you're doing that she would like to see change? If so, isn't now the time to know?

Option 2: She's struggling with something in her life. It could be a prior relationship or something that happened to her as a child. Here's what I mean. One woman I'll call Elaine was sexually abused by her stepdad for several years, beginning when she was 9. Yet somehow she was able to overcome all that abuse and marry a wonderful man who loved her dearly, and to give herself freely in sex to him.

Then, one day, everything changed . . . on her daughter's ninth birthday. She withdrew from her husband, became very cold and suspicious, and wouldn't allow her daughter to be alone with him. What was going on? The abuse she'd thought she was "done with" had circled back around, and now she was seeing the husband she loved as a potential abuser to *her* 9-year-old daughter.

The marriage that had been so stable for 13 years became extremely rocky for two years, until finally the couple went to counseling together and figured out what was going on. Once they did, they were able to talk about some solutions together—to put some safeguards in place to make her more comfortable and still allow him to spend time with his daughter.

For those two years, that couple wondered if they were headed for the divorce court. But today their marriage is stronger than ever. Why? Because they decided to work through the issues together. Was it a lot of work? Yes. Was it worth it? The smiles on their faces in their recent family portrait say it all. You see, miracles can happen.

They can happen for you too. If your wife is struggling with a prior relationship or childhood sexual abuse, she needs your help, your understanding, and a professional counselor, because that past experience has everything to do with how she views life and how she views you, her husband.

Q: It seems like everyone talks about the woman as the one who loses interest in sex. That annoys me. My husband and I have been married for 17 years. But my husband is the one who seems to have no interest in sex. *At all.* Frankly, I'm sick and tired of being blown off and pushed away. Is there anything you can suggest? Other than divorce, which I don't consider an option?

A: Your guy needs to go to his general practitioner for a checkup. Could he be depressed? Is he facing major stress (a job loss, a death in the family, or something else that rates high on the stress scale)? Could he be struggling with guilt over a past sexual experience? Is it a recent thing that he's showing no interest in sex—or has it been that way throughout your marriage? If it has been that way, take a look at his relationship with his parents. What kind of temperament does his dad have? His mom? Did your husband feel like he never measured up? Is he afraid to fail? Or does he just need some help with his male libido?

Here's another option: your husband could be subtly controlling you by withholding sex. Perhaps he feels criticized or emasculated by you. The only way he can get back at you is by withholding something you want—sex. So is there something in your relationship that is making him feel like you don't care about him as a man?

Talk to your husband. Touch him first (that's how you open a man's ears). Tell him how you feel about the lack of a sexual relationship. Ask him to go to the doctor. If he doesn't want to go, then tell him you're going to make an appointment for him. Tell him this is important for the longevity of your marriage. Also, you need to evaluate how you are treating him. Are you being respectful of him as your husband in all areas of your life? Does he feel wanted? Needed?

Things can't continue as they are. It's time for a change—for both of you.

Q: I am not fat or ugly as far as I know. I've never asked my wife to do anything that's not "appropriate" for a married couple. Yet she presents any request for sex as a task she must simply endure. She has absolutely no imagination for anything other than the basic missionary position. She will allow herself to be unclothed only as long as it takes for the sexual act to complete, then she gets up, takes a shower, puts on long flannel pajamas, and goes to bed. Is she that repulsed by me that she doesn't even want to cuddle?

We've been married for 40 years, and I feel so unfulfilled in the areas of love and sex that I don't even know where to start. We've often gone eight months at a time with no sex. And when we have sex, the excitement is definitely only on my side. I've always been the helper, the patient supporter, the worker, the nurturer. I have always been loving and faithful to my wife and have been married only to her, yet I am still unfulfilled after all this time. What am I doing wrong? I feel so alone and ignored.

A: Let me make a guess. Your wife is a firstborn in her family and grew up in an extremely conservative environment. She had a lot of expectations heaped on her about what was right and what was wrong. About what women did and what women didn't do. What people of the faith did and what people of the faith didn't do. So for many years she was schooled to behave a certain way as a woman, and those early impressions have stuck with her. Most likely she's the type of woman who also has trouble exposing her body to a doctor. She's not going to be the "Me Jane, you Tarzan," swinging-on-a-chandelier type.

For the sake of your relationship (I'm amazed that you've been able to keep your marriage together for 40 years without the glue of sex), you need to step out of your comfort zone. Talk to your wife. Assure her of your love. Explain how lonely you feel. (If she doesn't respond to your feelings of loneliness, there is more trouble in your marriage than just sex, and those problems also need to be rooted out.) Tell her that being one with her is very important to you, that you chose her all those years ago and would choose her again. But you don't want to live the rest of your married lives this way.

Ask her to *consider* being a little adventuresome. Assure her that you won't judge her if she's not "good at" something, but you just want to try. If you are gentle, soft-spoken, and loving, that wife of yours might actually take a risk. But if you are critical of any of her attempts, she'll crawl right back into those flannel pj's and under the covers . . . and she won't come out.

It took 40 years for your relationship to get to this point. It's not going to change overnight. But you can gently romance that stone.

Q: I've done the lingerie, teddies, garter belts, panties, slinky nightie thing . . . much to my dismay (none of these things look good on me). I've given my husband oral sex; I've tried different

---

Way Back Before Doctor Ruth . . .

King Solomon—generations before Doctor Ruth—was a great marriage counselor and sex therapist. And he had the right idea. From gazelles to goblets, that guy knew what he was talking about. Go ahead and take a look. In fact, read the whole book of Song of Solomon. I guarantee you won't be disappointed.

> I belong to my lover,
> and his desire is for me.
> Come, my lover, let us go to the countryside,
> let us spend the night.

—*King Solomon, in Song of Solomon 7:10–11*

---

positions, trying to please him. I like watching him in "prone" position . . . or any position. I like it slow; I like it quick. If it was my choice, I'd like sex once a day, but my husband is a twice-a-month (if that) kind of guy. Is something wrong with him? He's only in his late twenties, and we've been married for four and a half years. When we have sex, it's really good. But a guy's libido drops when he gets older, right? So then what am I supposed to do when I'm in the mood and he's not? According to him, since he's the guy, he gets the say on when we have sex.

A: Clearly you have a higher sex drive than your husband. That doesn't make one of you wrong and the other right; you're just different. But if you're doing all those things to keep your guy happy and still not getting much of a response, there might be something else going on.

Is your husband depressed or unhappy about life? Is he on medication for depression? Is he taking Propecia, a drug used to regenerate hair? (One of Propecia's side effects can be limited sexual desire. It doesn't happen in all cases, but it's significant enough that it's on the warning label.) Is your husband physically challenged in some way? (However, even physically challenged men who can't perform with their penis can get creative in other ways.) When there's a will, there's a way, and when there isn't a will, there's a reason. And that reason is rarely "I'm tired" or "I just don't feel like it."

There are also other possibilities.

Was your husband brought up in a Puritan-like environment where he learned that sex was nasty and filthy, so he brings a prejudice to it? Does he believe that sex isn't something to be enjoyed, so he avoids it whenever he can?

Has your husband experienced sexual abuse in his past? By a father, uncle, brother, or (more rare) a trusted woman in his life?

Or could it be possible that you married someone who is gay?

Before you write me an angry letter back about that one, take a step back. I want you to think about it. Is it possible that your husband is gay and that he's hiding under the cloak of the respectability of being a married man? Trust me, there are thousands who do exactly that, because they don't want to face the question of their sexual orientation. Thousands of others who are married are secretly engaging in homosexual practices (and that's why they are so tired and don't have time for you). Yes, he could have fathered children with you; he could be a great father; and he could be sweet, kind, and loving in a lot of other ways, but when it comes to showing up in the bedroom and being intimate with you, it's a no go.

So let me ask you: Do you have any reason to think your husband might be gay? Can you think of any occurrences in marriage where you really wondered where he was? Any phone calls or emails you found suspect? Have you ever sat down and asked him if he has ambivalent feelings about sex? About the way he looks at and thinks about other males?

It's time you got to the bottom of the excuses.

Q: My wife complains that I don't show her enough "interest" outside the bedroom. I don't really understand what she means, but I do understand the results: no sex for this husband until I figure it out. Can you help me?

A: Sure can! Your wife is telling you (not in a very good way, by withholding sex from you until you perform to her expectations) that she wants to be romanced. So turn on the charm, Don Juan, outside the bedroom. Do I mean you should make love in every room in the house? Well, that sounds like fun! But no, that's not what I mean.

A woman longs to be affirmed for who she is and what she does *outside of* the sexual relationship. She needs to be told how beautiful she is (yes, even if she's resembling raisin status more than she used to, 30 years ago when you first got married—it's a wise husband who doesn't bring up that part). She needs to be reminded (and not just once—when you were first married—but often) that she is the one and only woman in your life. That you long to meet her needs and she is still attractive to you.

A woman loves nonsensual touch. By that, I mean touch that doesn't lead to something else (the full sexual monty). And that's where we guys often get confused. We might start off with good intentions, but our engines get running, and before we know it, we're in the mode of sexual foreplay. As one woman told me, "When I really want to relax, I go to a professional masseuse. My husband loves to give me a massage, but it always leads to something else . . . you know what I mean."

Yes, I do know what you mean.

But a guy who understands that his wife just wants a back or a foot massage after a long day—and he holds back his own desire for sex because not having sex that day is in her best interests—is filling up her love reservoir.

Every day your wife wants to know that she is the one woman for you. That you have eyes and ears only for her. That you have hands only for her. And that you want to be close to her.

If she knows these things, she'll feel secure both inside and outside the bedroom. And then inside the bedroom, just watch the temperature soar!

Q: I heard what you said when you spoke to our women's group about a woman getting more aggressive and assertive in her sexual life. I've read several of your books, and I respect what you have to say. However, I grew up in a very conservative home where "that topic" wasn't even addressed, or anything having to do with "that area down there" (you know what I mean). I understand what you're saying about being assertive and aggressive, but that's just not who I am. Why do I have to be something I'm not?

A: I noticed you couldn't say the words *genital area*. You used *that area down there* instead. But let me assure you I understand where you're coming from. I've talked with a lot of women who come from conservative backgrounds. In fact, I live with one. But let's not take my word for it. Let's see what St. Paul has to say about it:

> The man should give his wife all that is her right as a married woman, and the wife should do the same for her husband: for a girl who marries no longer has full right to her own body, for her husband then has his rights to it, too; and in the same way the husband no longer has full right to his own body, for

it belongs also to his wife. So do not refuse these rights to each other. The only exception to this rule would be the agreement of both husband and wife to refrain from the rights of marriage for a limited time, so that they can give themselves more completely to prayer. Afterwards, they should come together again so that Satan won't be able to tempt them because of their lack of self-control.[3]

Now, let me "Lemanize" the Scripture for you. What St. Paul is telling us is that he wants us to do it. And if you want to stop for prayer, that's okay. But what I love about this great saint of the church is that he says, "After prayer, I want you to do it again." Now that's my kind of saint. (And look at all the churches and schools named after him in the world!)

Why did I pull that particular Scripture? To prove that God's Word has something to say about the importance of sex. Sex isn't something created by Satan. It's a great gift to husbands and wives. It's to be engaged in on a frequent basis—*without embarrassment*—and enjoyed.

Does this mean that you have to rip off your clothes and your husband's the instant you see him each night? That you have to make wild, passionate love on the kitchen floor, like what you see in the movies? No. (Though those might be fun ideas to consider.) What it means is that you show an open, ready attitude toward sex, and that you consider your husband and his needs to be important enough for you to step outside your comfort zone and the way things have always been in your relationship.

Also, I noted that you said, "That's just not who I am. Why do I have to be something I'm not?" Did you happen to notice how many times you used the word "I" in those two sentences?

Marriage is about two people—and coming together for the common good in all areas of the relationship. Perhaps it's time to stop thinking about what's best for "I" and start thinking about what's best for "we"—if you want your marriage to last in the long run.

Straight Talk

I already stated this once, but it's worth repeating: when there's a will, there's a way, and when there isn't a will, there's a reason. And that reason is rarely "I'm tired" or "I just don't feel like it." Your job as a married couple is to figure out why one (or both) of you is acting like a stone. You might need a third party to help you through it. But trust me, whatever time and money you spend will be worth it.

19

Yesterday, When I Was Young . . .

> What happened to you in the past has everything to do with how much you enjoy sex.

Kendra was 7 when she first discovered what sex is (or, should I say, sexual abuse)—from her father, who had been sexually abused by an uncle when he was young. The abuse continued until she was 13, when she and her little sister, who was 9 at the time, ran away from home. That was the night she discovered that her father was also abusing her little sister. She had thought that by "keeping quiet," she could keep her sister safe.

Walt, handsome and well-built, has always wondered if he's gay. Otherwise, why would his uncle have found him "interesting" as a sex toy when Walt was 9? He thought, *There has to be something about me that isn't right, and my uncle was attracted to that. . . .*

Lana planned to graduate from college in a month when she went out on what she thought would be a fun date with a new guy.

After drinking a Coke, she passed out. She woke up hours later, half-clothed and alone in a forest. She'd been raped and left alone miles from town.

All throughout her childhood Keri watched while her continually drunk stepfather used her mother for sex. He even made Keri and her brother watch once when they were teenagers, so they'd know how to "make love."

All of these individuals are understandably struggling today with the concept of sex in marriage, and they're not alone. Experts tell us that as many as 40 percent of women have been abused. The percentage of men who report abuse is lower (but it's also more difficult for males to admit they've been sexually abused, since it's so emasculating).

Children are born with a natural trust in their parents. They will jump into a parent's arms from ten feet high, because they trust that parent to always catch them.

But there are also a lot of children who grew up trusting uncles, fathers, brothers, and even mothers and aunts, only to be violated by them. Those children don't know love because they never got a chance to see what it is. They've only seen control, dominance, degradation, and abuse in the name of "love."

So, ladies, along comes a healthy person who is not sexually addicted and not a pervert. That person's only "sin" is falling in love with you. He wants to marry you, wants to make love to you, and has a natural sex drive. What is going to happen? You as a woman are going to struggle with that man. Why? Because you don't see yourself as worth loving. So what do you do? You avoid sex, because of your past negative experiences with it. And your husband may have no clue why.

If you're a man who has experienced abuse, you could be the best husband and father in the world. You might always be smiling and put on a great show. You might hug people and be warm and welcoming to them. But underneath it all, you've learned that if you truly let others get close to you, then you'll get hurt. So you paint a happy face on your mask, and you deal with the stress of living in two worlds.

This kind of abuse is very difficult to get over, because it will crop up at different times in your life. You can forgive those who abused you so that you can move on with life. You can confront the problems and the relational patterns. But those who have experienced abuse say that a residue of their experience is always with them.

If this is your story, you're in for a rough journey. Will you need a professional to walk you through it? Most likely. Will some scars remain? Yes. Is there a price to pay? Yes. If I told you otherwise, I'd be lying.

But that doesn't mean you can't learn to enjoy sex—as God originally intended it to be—with the one you love.

Q: I had been so excited about having sex on our honeymoon and getting to dress provocatively, for the first time in my life, for the man I love. I was stunned, upon coming out in the see-through nightie I'd spent days looking for, that Andrew barely gave me a second look. He just caressed my cheek, said it was pretty, and then took my hand to go look out the deck at the ocean. We didn't even have sex until the fifth night of our honeymoon (if you call having sex just brushing each other naked, because he never did enter me). I guess it shouldn't have been any surprise to me when, four years later, Andrew admitted he had struggled with homosexuality since his early teen years. In seventh grade the kids in his class had branded him "gay" because he was a band geek, he wasn't developing much physically, and he liked to read books.

After he went to college, Andrew found acceptance at gay bars and clubs, but he assured me he had never acted on any homosexual feelings. He did love me deeply, he said, but he just couldn't drum up a passion for me, even though he had been trying. He had thought that by marrying me, he could "cure" himself, but it didn't work. Neither of us are ready to give up our marriage (we now have a daughter), but we're both feeling hurt and confused, especially in the area of our sexual life. Can you help?

A: Thanks for your honesty. You and your spouse are dealing with a tough situation. There are thousands of couples like you in the same position because many men (and women) have tried to do the same thing as Andrew did—"cure" themselves with marriage as the panacea.

Any kind of sexual deviation has a profound effect on a person's personality. Let me explain it this way. Take a look at a piece of wood. The grain runs one way. If you try to reverse the grain that's already been set, you can't. You can cut it, chop it, lacquer it, paint it, and float it in water, but that grain of wood still won't change. The experiences of your husband in his early years will influence his behavior as an adult. So if your husband was brought up with the whole concept of sex in a setting where it was disruptive, negative, unhealthy, or abusive, can you expect him to snap his fingers and change his view to a mutual satisfaction between two people who love each other for a lifetime? Your husband will need some help—professional help—in this instance.

If this is the case for your husband, I'm sorry for his stolen innocence. But that is something that can't be changed. In reality, there is no *Back to the Future*, where you can change an event and relive life so it turns out differently.

That means the two of you will need to deal with this together with a lot of time, patience, understanding, and professional help.

Q: For over 20 years, I've held myself back from my husband because of horrific abuse I suffered as a child. There was no way I was going to put myself in a position to be hurt again sexually. I didn't want to talk about sex, and I didn't want to have sex (except where I was forced to, in order to have our son and daughter). But as I read *Sheet Music*, I realized how wrong I've been in not giving all of myself to my husband, who has loved me all these years in spite of myself and my background. But how do I start now? And how do I explain to Rick, who has been so loving to me, why I withheld myself for so long?

A: I applaud your courage in deciding *now* to make some changes in your life. Because of the horrific circumstances you've endured in your past, you're one gutsy lady for being willing to face them again. I can see why your husband loves and admires you.

Where do you start in explaining to Rick? You start by asking him to set aside some time—to take a walk together, to go to a quiet place, maybe even have a weekend retreat. You tell him up front before you leave (so he isn't nervous and can relax and hear what you have to say) that you love him so much and feel like you've been very unjust to him over the years, and that you want to make some changes. Then look at him, touch his hand, and say, "And, honey, I need *your* help."

Then tell him everything. Start at the beginning. Tell him that the story might be a little long, but it's important to you to say it all in one sitting so he understands. End the story by saying, "This is why I've treated you the way I have all these years—

because I was afraid. I was so afraid of getting hurt again. I was afraid to trust. I've wronged you. Will you forgive me?"

That time spent together, that openness and honesty, will bring that man right into your court. What self-respecting man doesn't want to help his wife? Especially when she tells him she wronged him and asks for forgiveness?

That's how you start. And then you just take it one day at a time. Ask your husband for help. I'm sure he'll jump at the chance.

Q: I grew up in an abusive home—physically, verbally, and sexually. Yeah. It was not a nice place to live. When I was 10, my mom got remarried, and my 19-year-old stepbrother came to live with us. I was used to being yelled at and slapped around; now I was cajoled into my stepbrother's bedroom with the promise that he'd take me to the movies (which he never did). By then, I figured, what did it matter? What did anything matter?

In my early twenties I put my old life behind me. I'd cut off contact with my entire family by that point. I'm now turning 30 and have been married for a year to a wonderful guy named Jared. I love my husband and want to give love to him, but as much as I try, I find it really hard to have sex. I can't seem to shut out the images of what happened to me as a child. I start feeling really nauseated, and then I throw up. (Really sexy, huh? I have no idea how my husband puts up with me.) Help!

A: You've been through a lot, and no wonder your past is still following you around. Just because your life is now going in a different direction doesn't mean you won't remember what happened. In reality, you were so dominated as a child that you were trained to be anything but aggressive and assertive (that

Moving Past Abuse

1. Realize that, no matter what has happened to you earlier in life, the spouse you have is not the perpetrator of any abuse. Many times people pay for the sins of their fathers and their fathers-in-law. Especially women. So a little reminder here to those of you women who have experienced abuse: remember that this isn't your dad or stepdad who sexually and verbally abused you. This is your husband—the man who loves you.

2. What you say to yourself is extremely important in your self-perception. People who are abused tend to turn that abuse inward, becoming abusers of themselves. They deny themselves relationships or things that they would enjoy, all because they don't see themselves as worthy of love or pleasure. So keep telling yourself every day, *I'm loved. God the Father loves me, my husband loves me, my kids love me. I'm worthy of being loved. My husband values me for who I am. He respects me for who I am. Lord, help me to love myself as you love me.* You may even want to try praying while facing a mirror with your eyes wide open, to gain a new glimpse of yourself.

3. Realize that you are on a journey. Things that happened to you that shouldn't have happened and that aren't your fault will circle back into your life and thoughts at different points. As a result of what happened to you as a child, there is some scarring in your life. Your attitudes and emotions that arise when certain events happen today are a reminder of what happened all those years ago. Does that mean life won't go on? No, not at all. You simply need to be aware that there may be some emotional residue in your life.

4. Choose to say no to negativity. I once counseled a woman who continually journaled. That was important to her. The problem was, she only journaled the negative experiences in her life. It wasn't until she threw away that journal and bought a new one to record positive steps that she began her journey of healing. For you, as negative thoughts arise, replace them with positive things. Make a list of all you've accomplished and keep it where you can see it every day. What you see and what goes into your head is what will come out.

shows in your comment, "I have no idea how my husband puts up with me"). Changing that mind-set and reclaiming a healthy view of worth will take some doing. It will be a time-consuming and emotion-consuming process.

I applaud you for your courage in addressing this issue. What happened to you was not your fault. You didn't cause it to happen. It occurred because there are evil and sick people in the world who abuse children. Although your abuse may have seemed all about sex, it actually had nothing to do

Now is the time to reclaim your sexuality.

with it (at least sex as God intended it to be). Rather, it had everything to do with power and control. I am so glad you've married a man you love and that you love him enough to address the issues of your past in order to move into a healthy, satisfying sexual relationship for both of you.

Now is the time to reclaim your sexuality. Talk to your husband. Tell him how much you love him and why it is so difficult for you to have sex. Ask for his help and patience as you heal from your experience. Work with a supportive therapist to help you reshape your view of sex. Sometimes that may mean no sexual interaction for a period of time, such as a year, to give you time to heal and enjoy a sensual touch that is not demanding or painful—in order to begin the process of really enjoying sex with your husband down the road.

The important thing is that you and your husband go for the goal *together*. Wading through past memories can be time consuming and extremely emotional. This is a time for both of you to be gentle and patient with each other as you move beyond your sexual history to an understanding of sex as the Creator intended.

Will you ever forget that abuse? No. Such traumatic experiences are imprinted deeply on the human brain. But you can recover and reclaim your sexuality.

Straight Talk

A supportive spouse makes all the difference in the world for someone who has suffered abuse in the past, especially since those who have been abused need to reorient their entire view of the opposite sex. And that takes an extremely understanding mate to work through the issues with you. It also takes a commitment to make the healing process and communication your top priorities as a couple.

I want to end this chapter by telling you the real-life story of Libby and Mark. They're now in their late thirties and have two "miracle" children, ages 12 and 14. (You'll see why they're miracles in a moment.)

Libby was 5 when her stepuncle sexually abused her for the first time. Then when she was 7, that uncle moved into her home, and he, along with her stepdad, continued the abuse on a weekly basis. When she was 11, she told a teacher she trusted about what was happening. That day Libby was taken to the Department of Child and Family Services (DCFS) office, and her brothers and sisters were also removed from the home. After that, Libby spent her teen years going from one foster home to another until she reached high school and found a "permanent" home with a couple who loved her and helped her work through the issues of her abuse.

In college, Libby met Mark, and they fell in love. But she was terrified to tell him of her previous sexual experience because she worried that she was "damaged goods" and not pure enough to

218

marry him, since he was a virgin. When she finally told him, you know what that man said to her?

"Libby, I am so sorry that happened to you. It was not your fault. Not in any way your fault. I love you so much. You are beautiful, and you are pure to me." And the next night he fell on his knees, sang "You Are So Beautiful," and asked her to marry him. She cried. . . . Wouldn't you?

Libby was overwhelmed with joy to know that her honesty about her past did not change Mark's love for her. That's when she knew her husband-to-be *unconditionally* loved her. During the months of their engagement, he did considerable research about sexually abused women. Together they went to extensive marriage counseling. They also visited the ob-gyn together, and they wept together when they heard the news that she would never be able to bear children since her body was so scarred inside from the sexual abuse.

Fast forward five years. Libby was pregnant, and they danced together in joy under the stars. Their daughter was born. Three years later, she was pregnant again, with their son.

But the journey is far from being over. Two years after their son was born, Libby became extremely fearful. Through talking with a close friend, she at last realized she was fearful that her husband would change—that he would somehow abuse their daughter. Why did this fear come up all of a sudden in a "stable" marriage? Because their daughter had just turned 5—the same age Libby was when she was sexually abused. It was another thing that the couple had to work through.

For Further Reading

The Wounded Heart: Hope for Adult Victims of Childhood Sexual Abuse by Dr. Dan B. Allender

This very helpful book covers issues of shame, sin, powerlessness, betrayal, ambivalence, false memory issues, and much more.

There have been times during their marriage when they have had to cut back on activities because Libby was feeling overwhelmed and wondering if Mark still loved her. Has their marriage been easy? No. But together, step by step, they're choosing to live each day and love each day.

Yes, you too can make it. But you need to be determined to stand strong . . . together.

20

Why Jack or Jill
Is Still on Your Mind

You can't change your past relationships. But you can choose to move on.

R emember the movie *Lady and the Tramp*, where the two dogs fall in love; share some loving glances, a night on the town, a plate of spaghetti, and a last meatball; and stay up late watching the moon and being lovey-dovey? When you were young (or not-so-young), did you fall in love—or get the tinglies (an immature love based on physical attraction)?

When I was a kid, I fell in love several times in one month. One relationship ended in disaster, I must say. My "true love" in seventh grade, Pat, stuck the friendship ring I had given her into her jeans pocket, and her mama did the laundry that night. The ring came out all mangled . . . kind of like our relationship after a week.

These teen years, continuing into the early twenties, are called "the critical years" for a reason. These are the years when the mistakes you make can influence you for a lifetime. One mistake at the wheel and you could be dead in an auto accident; one experiment with meth because you're curious and you could be dead of an overdose; one night of hooking up and you could be pregnant. . . . Fast forward a couple years, and that guy who married you because he had to (or your dad would have gone after him with a shotgun) will be going out with other girls at night and leaving you home with an 18-month-old. That might have happened to some of you reading this book—and you're now on your second marriage.

These are the years when hormones run so high that often people make decisions they regret—like dating, marrying, or having sex with multiple partners before finding their "true love."

But you might be wondering, *If I'm happily married now, why should my past make any difference?* Because you could be 23 years into your marriage and all of a sudden your first boyfriend's face will pop into your lovemaking session with your husband. Or you'll start thinking how Jill, your ex, looked in that negligee and say her name instead of your wife's when you're ready to ejaculate. Does this mean you don't love your spouse? Not at all. It just means that any sexual experience is deeply imprinted on your mind. That's because the nature of sexual experiences has everything to do with intimacy, with connection, with knowing someone in the most personal of ways. Those experiences have everything to do with not only your body but also your mind and who you are.

Whether you realize it or not, the hurts and wounds of previous relationships (including verbal, sexual, or physical abuse by others) have already influenced you—and the person you've chosen to marry. That's because the brain is a great memory keeper.

You have a great spouse now, and you're settled into marriage. You have two wonderful children. Life is looking rosy. You're having passionate sex with your spouse. But all of a sudden a thought of a past relationship starts to haunt you. . . .

Q: Before I got married, I had sex with nine other men. How do I know the exact number? Because I remember every single one . . . but I wish now I could forget. I feel horrible and unclean every time my husband and I even start into sexual foreplay. I was his first. I wish I could say that about him. Talk about stupid. Yup, that was me. Any hope for me? Or will I feel this way forever?

A: You'd make a great poster child for a "Got Guilt?" campaign, because guilt is pouring from you. And yes, you have a reason to feel guilty. You chose not to wait for sex, and you're reaping the consequences. There's no magical eraser that will make your previous sexual experiences go away. Based on research from the Guttmacher Institute on teen sex, if you've had nine sexual experiences, and the man you had sex with the ninth time had nine sexual experiences, then whether you realize it or not, you've been exposed to 511 sexual partners![4] So the bed is much more crowded than you think.

But it's your choice whether you want to bemoan your fate and continue to call yourself stupid or you want to take charge of your thought life. If you want to take charge, here's some advice. Every time one of those old boyfriends comes to mind, say your husband's name with passion. Begin dreaming of him. Don't allow your mind to dwell on any previous guys. Work on pleasing your guy, and take the focus off yourself. No woman is attractive if she's berating herself. Your guy deserves an eager lover who will give everything she has to the man who *really* loves her. Don't punish him for your past.

Q: This is so embarrassing to admit, but I've really, really blown it. Before I met Marissa and we got married, I had a live-in girlfriend for about three years. I thought I'd totally forgotten about her. But yesterday, when Marissa and I were heavily into it, I goofed and said my live-in girlfriend's name instead of my wife's. All action stopped. Marissa got up, left the bedroom, and hasn't talked to me since. Have I ruined everything?

A: I always say guys are dumb as mud, and you just proved me right. Your wife has every right to be mad. Your saying the name of your ex-girlfriend violated the trust of your marital vows. Here you're "heavily" into sex with your wife, and you forget who she is? No wonder she's not speaking to you.

Before you even apologize to your wife (which you'd better do soon, buster), you need to think about why that came out of your mouth. Did you honestly forget who you were with? Is your old girlfriend still important to you and still in your life? Was it an honest slip out of habit? You need to carefully think through your words since words can be extremely damaging to a relationship. For a woman, it's difficult enough to reveal all of herself in the act of sex—way more difficult than it is for a man because of the way a woman thinks about body image—much less to be called some other woman's name.

So go apologize quickly, admit that you were really dumb, say that you love her, explain how the other woman's name came out of your mouth, and try to make things right. (A whole box of Godiva chocolates won't undo this one; only time, your loyalty, and love will.) Assure her that she—and she alone—is the only woman for you, and that you are sorry you hurt her with your thoughtlessness. Think of her continually during the day, and put love notes in her car. Guard your thoughts. If images of prior lovers crop up in your mind, think instead of your wife's face and body.

In the marriage bed, develop your own sexual rhythms that are uniquely yours as a couple. These little steps will help to direct your thoughts toward purity and the wife who chose you for a lifetime.

And one more thing: don't be surprised or offended if your wife checks up on your emails and phone calls for a while either. Or if she calls work to see if you're really there. She has every right to do so. She's only protecting her territory.

Q: I lost my virginity shortly after my fifteenth birthday to a guy who was in college, only to have him boast to everyone he knew of his "conquest." I was so embarrassed and ashamed that I shut my feelings down and pretended I didn't care. After that, I slept with guys to make them *my* conquests, rather than me being the victim.

I've finally found a guy who seems to love me for me (and I don't know why), but I can't seem to help it—I'm always wondering when the dream is going to end, when my husband is going to turn into that college guy and talk about me behind my back. I'm having a really hard time trusting him; I can't seem to break through the emotional shell I've built around myself.

A: Previous experiences tend to color your perception of the here-and-now reality of life. In the here-and-now, you have a loving, kind, thoughtful guy, yet because of your past experiences, you're sitting there waiting for the trap door to spring shut on your heart. *It's happened before*, you tell yourself.

But do you have any reason to feel that way about your current relationship, based on the way your husband treats you now? Is there anything in his behavior or demeanor that suggests he is anything other than who you think he is? If not, then cut him some slack! Be grateful for what you have now, and express your thankful heart to him.

Don't fall into the trap of sabotaging the relationship based on a jerk who entered your life when you were 15 years old and somewhat naive. That jerk doesn't deserve another moment of your brain cells. You've given him too much playtime already.

But your husband? Ah, now there's someone worth trusting.

Q: My husband had sex with other women before we married. I've seen pictures of some of them, and I can't even come close to measuring up. That makes me feel shy and inadequate when we have sex. How can I tell him how I feel without looking like some catty woman who just doesn't like any competition for her man? That just sounds so . . . high school.

A: You two need to talk about this. Is the feeling of inadequacy all from you, or has your husband said something—or indicated it in thought or attitude—to make you feel that way? If he has, he's dumb and insensitive and needs to be brought up short. (Just give me ten minutes with that guy, and I'll set him straight.)

Now's the time to ask him directly, "Am I pleasing you when we have sex?" If he looks startled and says, "Uh, sure. Why

---

How to Get Rid of Jack or Jill

1. Focus on what you have. Be thankful every day.
2. Tell your spouse how much you appreciate and love him or her. And that you don't take for granted a man or woman who loves you just the way you are.
3. Build your relationship on mutual respect.
4. Deal with issues as they come up.
5. Acknowledge the past but don't mire yourselves in it. Think present, and focus on your future together.

do you ask?" then go on to explain how you don't feel like you're measuring up. If you are the one making the comparison (because of your own past experiences where you've felt inadequate), at least you'll find that out. You might be a little embarrassed and feel a little silly, but you'll find out the truth.

If something is bothering him, and he is comparing you with another woman, you'll find that out too. If you have great trust in each other, a high degree of vulnerability, and an extraordinary amount of maturity, you just might be able to discuss this. But we're talking powder keg here. There are some things that are really worth resolving and others that are better left buried. A wife doesn't need to know everything about a former lover, nor does a husband. Details like that are awfully hard to shake from a memory bank.

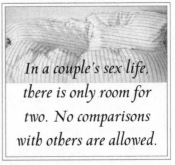

In a couple's sex life, there is only room for two. No comparisons with others are allowed.

In a couple's sex life, there is only room for two. No comparisons with others are allowed. That's a violation of the marriage bed. If you're feeling inadequate because your husband had previous sexual experience and you didn't, consider how long you've been married. After three years of marriage, sexual experience shouldn't be an issue anymore.

Women especially tend to be great comparers—body, hair, even shoes. But they certainly don't want their guys comparing them to other women. Every woman longs, wants, and needs to be the center of her man's attention.

And that includes you. Stay on this one. It's too important to let go, because it has everything to do with the security and stability of your union.

Q: Before I got married, I had two boyfriends, and I had sex with both of them. Then, nine years ago, I met Michael, who was so different from the guys I was used to. He seemed to really care about *me*. Ever since we married seven years ago, I've felt guilty for my promiscuous past, especially since Michael was a virgin. (I wish that would have been me.) Michael is such a wonderful guy, but every time we make love, I see images of my old boyfriends. What is wrong with me? I know my past is in my past. So why does it keep popping up in the present?

A: I wish there was a pill that could be prescribed to wipe anything out of your mind that you don't want there. But the mind is the most sophisticated of computers ever made. It records not only the images but also the feelings regarding past experiences, making it more difficult for you to realistically enjoy your marriage with your husband.

Don't allow guilt to rule. Instead, admit your mistakes, ask for forgiveness, and move on.

You can try not to think about it, but that doesn't really work, does it? If you believe in the power of prayer and the power of forgiveness, I suggest you go down that lane in life. You have to understand that if you ask (and truly want to do life differently), God will forgive you for any transgression that's occurred in life. Even more, he'll wipe the slate clean in heaven—as if it never happened. That's how good the Almighty's forgiveness is.

The problem is with us mere mortals. We're not God. We're not as good at burying our transgressions. We remember them over and over again, and the memories are extremely painful.

But the same loving God who forgives you for your transgressions can also help you in your daily battle so you can freely enjoy the love you've found with your mate.

If you're not a person of faith and don't believe in God at all, forgiveness probably isn't a consideration for you. But if you've been brought up in the church and taught right from wrong, the guilt factor from your past transgressions can run high. That guilt is the propellant for many of the lousy decisions you have made and might make now or in the future.

Don't allow guilt to rule. Instead, admit your mistakes, ask for forgiveness, and move on.

Straight Talk

How can you get Jack or Jill out of your mind?

You have to realize that what's happened in your past is past, but it does affect the present. However, it's your choice as to whether you will allow it to affect your future. And that choice starts now. Either you allow yourself to dwell on the past and miss the joys of the present, or you make an active decision to replace those images of the past, one by one, with other images. Images of you and your spouse, and your most sizzling moments of intimacy.

The person who said, "What you think, you become" was wise indeed.

21

Starving for Sex!

How to know if your spouse is a sex addict—or just has a high sex drive.

We love to put labels on people, don't we? Labels are easy. Slap one on, and a person is neatly categorized. Sexual desire disorder. Orgasmic disorder. Pain disorder. Arousal disorder. All courtesy of the American Psychiatric Association, thank you very much. But does the label really fix the problem or address a solution? And does a label make that person right or wrong, or simply different?

Let's say one third grader is a voracious reader. Another third grader would much rather read people than books. Does that make one right and one wrong, or are they simply different?

"Of course they're different," you say. "There's nothing wrong with that."

So why do we put such a different label on people who merely have a higher sex drive than their spouse? Just because they're different, does that make them wrong? Does that make them sex addicts? And, by the way, what is a sex addict anyway?

Let's say you have a need for sex twice a week, and your spouse has a need four times a week. Does that make your spouse a sex addict? Or does it simply make the two of you work together to come up with a solution? Perhaps you'll have intercourse two times a week, and your higher-sex-drive partner will get a handjob the other two times. That's what marriage is all about—negotiation for your mutual good as a couple.

But I also don't want to underplay the dangers of sexual addiction. Yes, there are sex addicts in real life. People who misuse the great gift of sex and pervert God's intention of one man and one woman for a lifetime. People who use sex as a means of control in their relationships. People who use pornography and visit prostitutes to take care of their sexual urges.

Many wives are shocked to find out that their husbands are viewing pornography. Pornography is as addictive psychologically as crack cocaine is physically. It's difficult for a man to dismiss sexual images in his mind once he has viewed pornography. For many boys, viewing pornography starts early in life (via magazines or the Internet) and becomes more addictive as time goes on.

Why is pornography so destructive to a marriage? Because the person using pornography gets to the point where his physical pleasure is met through erotic pictures (which need to get more and more intense and degrading to satiate his sexual appetite), not in the marital bed with his wife. The user of pornography needs help, and he needs it immediately.

Pornography can also lead to a lust for prostitutes. Even the mighty have fallen because of this (like the governor of New York, who lost his job over his involvement with prostitutes). This directly and physically impacts not only the husband connecting with the prostitute but also the wife, who deals with both emotional and physical fallout as a third party.

If your husband (or your wife—women are not immune to the lures of pornography or prostitutes, although this is far less common for them than for men) uses pornography or prostitutes, then you are facing serious issues, because both of these things tear down your marriage. Any woman would feel violated—and rightfully so. *Guess I'm not good enough to please him, huh?* As a woman, you will beat yourself up over it and take it to heart. But you need to understand this very important concept: you didn't make that choice to visit the porn shops or to get it on with a prostitute. It was his decision, so he's the one who needs to be held accountable for it.

Are you or your spouse starving for sex? Does one of you have a higher sex drive? If so, how are you dealing with it? In a way that will bring you together as a couple and improve your heart connection and communication, or in a way that divides your home and lets shame and guilt in the door?

Q: Here's my secret: I really, really love sex. And I'm a woman. (If the other Sunday school teachers could hear me now, I'd be the talk of the church for a year.) I'm a passionate kind of gal, and I've been married for seven years to a passive kind of guy. He often doesn't have much "umption in his gumption," as my old grandpa used to say. How can I encourage him to romp with me? Lately, I've found myself looking—just looking, mind you—at a bunch of other guys. I love my husband, but it's getting harder to believe I'm ever going to find passion with him.

A: Thank you for your honesty. If honesty is the best policy, you win. As I've said before, women are great teachers. You need to take this man—gently—and show him what it means to be adventurous, without making him feel like he's being overpowered. Show him in your rich, full, alluring way how wonderful a sex life with great variety can be.

Let me point out something else. He may be more predictable, pedantic, and laid-back than you'd like him to be, but again, these differences are what make you a couple. He's the gentle breeze and you're the tornado. Believe it or not, those two can coexist. Quite frankly, if there are two tornadoes in a marriage, I'd worry about that more.

But is your situation workable? Yes. Is your husband teachable?

Here's my secret: I really, really love sex. And I'm a woman. (If the other Sunday school teachers could hear me now, I'd be the talk of the church for a year.)

Yes, he is. And you sound like a good teacher: a Sunday school teacher who likes sex. You're my kind of woman.

I wish you the best in this kind of assignment. Have fun, and don't wear the boy out in the first lesson.

Q: You know, we were like two bunnies in a field the first two months of our marriage. And then our sex life went in the dumpster. What happened?

A: When the two of you were dating, you both put your best foot forward. Everything was new and exciting. Your guy was doing what males do naturally: focusing on one goal, which was winning your love. Then you married and started having to make bucks for your own expenses, rather than counting on Ma and Pa. Some years down the road you might have had one or more hedonistic little suckers—not to mention those never-ending projects and activities—that sapped your time and energy. When you were dating and first married, you could enjoy candlelit dinners, long walks, and starry nights spent gazing into each other's eyes and lying in each other's arms, with nothing else trying to claim your attention but each other. But those days became faint memories in the realities of making a buck and changing diapers.

Since a guy is so singly focused and wired to provide for his family, he figures, *Hey, I accomplished the love goal. Got the marriage job done, right? Now on to the next thing on the list . . . like providing for my family financially and putting up drywall in the basement.*

But every day a woman is asking, "Do you really love me? Do you really care?" If your husband had the faintest clue you were asking that question, he'd probably say, "Sure I love you. I said I loved you when I married you, didn't I?"

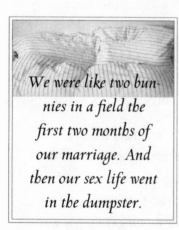

We were like two bunnies in a field the first two months of our marriage. And then our sex life went in the dumpster.

See the difference in thinking? You two need to talk. You need to cut your guy some slack, and he needs to rearrange his priorities. Love isn't just a onetime feeling; it's a continual action. If he's overly busy, see if you can take something off his to-do list (you probably put it there in the first place). Send the children to Grandma's for the night, make his favorite dinner, put on a nightie he can't resist, and wait for the fireworks to start. . . .

Q: My new husband is just about ready to wear me out with his constant need for sex. How much sex does a guy really need anyway? We've been married for a year, and I can't seem to get anything done except for in the bedroom. Could he be a sex addict?

A: First things first. There's something about your question that makes me think your husband is using sex as a means of controlling you. If he needs constant reassurance through sex that he is loved, respected, and wanted, it might be an indication that he's a control freak—which has little to do with your sex life and much more to do with your basic relationship.

All couples have different sexual appetites, but most couples engage in some type of sexual behavior a couple times a week. If your husband is demanding sex every day (and the key word is *demanding*), then yes, you're dealing with sexual addiction.

There is a definite difference between sexual addiction and a high sex drive. A person may have a greater than average interest in sexuality, in intercourse, and in a sexual relationship. But it always has to be *managed*. That means the person is relationally sensitive to his or her partner and concerned about that person in a way that's reasonable—in a way that treats the spouse with dignity, thoughtfulness, affection, and care. If that's the case, a high sex drive is perfectly fine.

But sexual addiction always ends up damaging relationships and damaging self. It demeans the spouse.

Which characteristics do you see in your husband? How are they affecting your relationship with him? Is he sensitive toward you and your needs? Does he treat you with dignity? If he is demanding (there's that word again), you may have a sex addict on your hands. If so, he needs more help than I can give here. Encourage him to see a trusted counselor. If he doesn't think he has a problem and refuses to get help, go to counseling yourself to get advice on how to deal with the situation.

Q: My husband has been arriving home quite late from work each night for the past two weeks. It's unusual behavior for him. Yesterday I was doing the laundry, and a slip of paper fell out of one of his pockets. I didn't recognize the number and thought, *That's funny.* So I called it. It was a call girl service! I drove straight to my husband's work, walked into his office, shut the door, and confronted him about it. He shrugged, admitted it—like it was no big deal!—and said I'd been busy with the kids and didn't have any time for him, and he needed some sex. You've got to be kidding me! This is not the man I married! Where can we go from here?

A: I'm so sorry for your discovery because of the betrayal of trust that it represents and the physical and emotional fallout both you and your husband will feel as a result. Your husband's callous attitude—thinking it's no big deal—is a big concern, since it shows a lack of respect for you. (Or perhaps being nonemotional is a way to assuage his guilt.) It's a very big deal, because he just betrayed your marriage vows. Pointing the finger at you because you've been busy is a pass-the-blame game. Sure, maybe he needed more attention than you were giving him (and that's something you'll need to work on, should your marriage continue), but that's no excuse for his behavior.

> *A person may have a greater than average interest in sexuality, in intercourse, and in a sexual relationship. But it always has to be* managed.

You need to ask your husband immediately, "How long has this been going on?" This is crucial for you to know because of the high risk of sexually transmitted diseases with prostitutes.

All genital contact between the two of you needs to stop immediately (as if you'd feel like it now anyway—but you'd be amazed at the stories I've heard from women who are desperate to hold on to their husbands). You must insist that he gets himself checked out by a doctor for STDs and that you are going along for the appointment. (He may be embarrassed to tell the doctor why he's *really* there, but too much is at stake for you to risk him not telling the truth.) If you have had sex with him during the time he's been with call girls, you should get yourself checked out too. STDs (including HIV) are nothing to mess with. The doctor can tell you how to proceed next based on the results you receive.

You must also insist that your husband goes to counseling. As things progress, you may wish to have some couple appointments too, but just remember, you were not the one in the arms of the call girl. He needs to be the one held responsible.

Trust, once betrayed, takes a long time to be rebuilt. It will take a lot of forgiveness on your part, a working out of your anger, and a deeply felt and acted upon repentance from your husband. And quite frankly, I think your chances are less than 50/50. I wouldn't be surprised to see you walk. You certainly have a reason. But the fact that you have children will be a huge factor in your decision to really make an effort to make your marriage work or to walk south quickly.

Q: My husband wants to rent a porn flick to get us "in the mood." But I'm uncomfortable with the idea of watching anyone else have sex . . . or even the idea of bringing pornography into our home. But my husband says that such ideas come from my overprotective parents. I have no clue what to do. I want to make my husband happy and honor his wishes, but watching a porn flick makes me feel a little sick, to be honest. What should I do?

A: Oftentimes, guys think pornography is just a picture on a screen or on a piece of paper. Here's the problem with that. Say a guy is relaxing in his office, and some pretty young thing comes in the front door. Well, because of the way guys are wired, the first thing that guy will notice is how attractive this sweet young thing is. But to be a healthy guy who has a proper respect for women, he has to take his thoughts of *Ooh-la-la* a step further to, *That good-looking woman isn't just a sexual object. She's a person created by God almighty himself. Someone to talk to, empathize with, have compassion on.*

In the same way, the female person on the paper or the screen represents a human being. She's a person who has parents. A person with hopes, desires, problems, and struggles. And the probable reason she allowed herself to be in the porn flick? Simply because she's desperate for financial stability and a better kind of life.

Pornography is, at its heart, degrading and debasing to human beings, whom God created. It should have no part in your life, your husband's life, or your home. You have to hold firm on this one. The answer is a definite no.

Q: I find myself having sexual fantasies all the time. Is that normal, or do I need some psychiatric help?

A: First of all, the last thing you need is psychiatric help. I've been a practicing psychologist for over 40 years, and my basic advice is to avoid people like me at all costs. Go only when absolutely necessary. So for starters, let's keep you out of the shrink's office.

Having sexual fantasies is a very common occurrence for both men and women. Although men might be more apt to admit to it, my sense tells me women aren't too far behind. I mean, think about it: it's private, it's safe, no one gets pregnant, and characters in a sexual fantasy will do exactly what you want them to. (It's a little different in real life, with real people.)

Is fantasizing a problem? Here's where things get dicey.

First, how much are you fantasizing? Fantasizing can begin to encompass more and more of your thought time, relational time, and work time. In other words, you're at home with your mate, sitting on the living room couch, and you're fantasizing about sex (instead of doing it with your spouse).

And second, about whom are you fantasizing? If it's about someone else, you have a problem. Your sexual needs are definitely not being fulfilled by your sexual relationship with your spouse, and things have to change—for both your sakes. If it's about your spouse and a new position or technique you'd like to try with her, well then, great! As long as your spouse agrees, why not try it out?

But if you are using the fantasizing as a replacement for communicating with and working on your sexual relationship with your spouse, that's unhealthy. There will be an increasing disparity between what is reflected in your sex life with your wife and your fantasy images.

Simply stated, fantasizing is the result of unmet needs in marriage. Why not talk to your mate about your fantasies? Why not work on them together? Fulfilling your fantasies with your spouse—now that's interesting. In fact, it's downright intriguing.

Words to Remember

Whatever is true, whatever is noble, whatever is right, whatever is pure, whatever is lovely, whatever is admirable—if anything is excellent or praiseworthy—think about such things.

Philippians 4:8

Q: I'm stunned. I just found a stack of pornographic magazines in the trunk of my husband's car. At first I thought it had to be a mistake. Why would my *husband* have those? Then I got suspicious. I checked the history button on our computer and was shocked to see the direct links to porn sites. I knew it had to be my husband, since our children are too young to use the computer, and I certainly didn't log on to those sites. I feel so betrayed . . . and sick at heart. How could he? I don't know whether to vomit or be mad or both. How can I respond to . . . *this*?

A: I'm so sorry you discovered porn in your husband's car and on your computer. Sorry for a couple of reasons, because those images of pornography will forever be indelibly imprinted on his brain—and yours—and subject to recall at any time. Now is the time to get tough, to fight for your marriage. Confront him with the facts, eyeball to eyeball, in a loving way. If you can't do it eye to eye, write him a note, mark it "personal," and hand it to him. Or put it on the dashboard of his car (or inside the top cover of one of the porn magazines—that would give him the idea very quickly) or somewhere else that's obvious.

Don't pull any punches. Tell him how hurt you are by his actions, that you feel violated and betrayed, and that you feel your relationship has been cheapened. Your husband may hear what you're saying, but he may not realize how it's going to affect your relationship from then on until . . .

You know that little feeling you get when you're in bed, when all of a sudden your husband touches you and you feel that sexual energy? Whatever that touch is, it's his way of saying, "Hey, I'm here, and I'm interested." So whenever that signal comes, turn and look him in the eye and say, "Honey, the farthest thing from my mind right now is having sex with you. I feel like our marriage is over. I can't compete with those hot bodies onscreen. I want you to get some help."

Give it to him straight. Because if you don't, he's going to ruin your marriage—or certainly ruin your sex life. He's going to continue to hurt you and himself by involving himself further in pornography. There is a reason that pornography is a huge, multibillion-dollar business in the United States alone—because it's addictive.

When a man is involved with sexual addiction—also called "living in the zone"—there are recognizable symptoms. If your husband's mind is preoccupied with sexually explicit pictures, he'll be more self-focused and less interested in "regular sex" with you, since that sex will no longer satisfy his sexual appetite. Because pornography depersonalizes people, he'll have more trouble relating to you and be less sensitive to others. He'll begin to isolate himself from activities he used to enjoy and engage in more secretive behaviors (such as late-night computer forays, closed doors, and unexplained errands). The fantasy world he's created for himself begins to become more enjoyable than real life.

When a man is involved with sexual addiction—also called "living in the zone"—there are recognizable symptoms.

That's why *now* is the time to fight for your marriage, to fight for your family. Insist that your husband get help from a professional counselor. Should you go into the counseling room with him? No. He needs to face the music himself. Don't be his rescuer.

Consider these very important differences between men and women. For women, pornography is about personal and relational betrayal. For men, it's a visual temptation. *It's just a picture,* your guy is thinking. *No big deal, right? After all, I don't know this woman. I just like to look.* But that picture can create havoc in your marriage, in your trust level, and in your husband's mind. It allows the man to focus even more so on what women look like instead of admiring the fact that they have brains, character, and intelligence. In other words, viewing pornography can skew a man's entire perspective on who a woman is and how she should be treated. And that directly affects *you.*

You can be compassionate toward your husband, but you cannot back down on this issue. Talk to him now and *insist* that he get help.

Q: When I heard you talk about the dangers of pornography, it really hit a chord with me. My dad introduced me to pornography when I was 11. He thought it would be a "male bonding" thing. I was shocked at first, then intrigued. I would wake up at night, wanting to see more. Now I'm a churchgoing kind of guy, and I'm married. I really love my wife, but I can't get the images out of my head. Trouble is, I work on the computer a lot. How can I keep myself from temptation?

A: Good for you for being on the front end of temptation before it drags you down. You'd be smart to put a safeguard on your computer that blocks any type of pornography. If you have a computer at home, move it to a room in the house that has constant foot traffic (such as the kitchen or the den, instead of your office). Angle your computer screen at work so co-workers can see it. These may sound like little steps, but they have everything to do with the will to resist. If you rearrange your life, you rearrange your heart.

You also need to make sure your wife is aware of your background and your struggle. Give her the permission to step into your privacy at any time and demand an account of your actions or any websites you've looked at. If you struggle with resisting Internet porn, perhaps you'll want to discontinue your Internet service and access email only at the local library once a week. (When you're in a public viewing area, the temptation to get into pornography decreases tremendously.)

You also need to talk about the issues that pull you toward pornography. For men, it's typically boredom and a craving for excitement. When you begin to feel boredom, rather than turning on the computer, find something else to do.

For women, it's typically loneliness. A good solution? Call or meet with a friend. And if worse comes to worst, turn on *Desperate Housewives.*

Q: I'm desperate for sex. And I'm a woman. (Are you shocked yet?) I'm a 26-year-old stay-at-home mom who has a 2-year-old toddler, and my sex life exists only in my head. I'd love to be ravaged by my husband some evening (or morning, or during naptime, or anytime!), but it seems he has no interest in me post-baby like he did pre-baby. I've never seen him have so many stomachaches or headaches that stop us from having sex. What, am I fat or something? Do I turn him off? I've gained only a few more pounds than I did pre-baby (and I must say, he's gained more than I have).

When we finally get around to sex, I wonder if I could be just any warm body next to him in bed, since everything is always the same old, same old. I have girlfriends who wish their husbands would ask for sex only once a week. I'd give anything right now for *any* man to find me attractive. I need a real lover, not just a man to share a last name with.

A: You know what would fix you two? An afternoon romp in the sack while that toddler is taking a nap.

But first you need to have a conversation after that toddler is in bed (or, even better, a night out for the two of you). "Honey, I notice that you just don't seem to be interested in sex anymore. Is there anything I can do differently to interest you?" Or, "Are there some things going on in your life that are bothering you?" That's much better than, "Hey, Bozo. I'm dying here. Ya think Mr. Happy could stand up and pay attention?"

Gently lead your husband through questions to figure out what's bothering him. Wade through his excuses (headache, stomachache) to find out what's really the crux of the issue. And then do what you can to set his fears to rest. Since you're thinking about sex a lot anyway, use that time to think creatively about how you can entice that man into your bed. Timing is everything, and your husband may be more sensitive to it than you think.

Straight Talk

"Dr. Leman, my husband wants sex all the time," one woman told me. "And when I say *all the time*, that's exactly what I mean," she whispered. "Like two to four times a day, every day, even on Sundays. I'm about worn out. What can I do?"

I already had that guy's number. "Here's what you do," I told her. "I want you to pursue him. You wake him up in the middle of the night every night for the next month and tell him *you* want sex."

She looked at me like I was crazy, then agreed (she wasn't sleeping anyway). Within a month, that guy was impotent. When she flipped the tables on him and pursued him, he didn't know what to do. That's because sex to him was about dominating his wife and controlling the process. In just 30 days' time, Mr. Happy couldn't stand up for a happy ending. But that woman? She was smiling. No longer was he using her in a demeaning way. She had his number too.

How can you tell if your spouse just has a higher sex drive or could be a sex addict? If your husband wants sex three to four times a week, he's not a sex addict. If he wants sex three times a day? Now, I'd say that's over the limits, and something else is going on (like he's using sex to dominate you and control everything about your day).

The answer has everything to do with your relationship. If your guy has to affirm his own masculinity through having sex and having it frequently—and always on his terms—you have a problem. If not, it's just that Mr. Happy needs more action than you're used to, and you can figure out other fun ways—together—to keep your guy smiling.

The key is this: if both of you aren't feeling prized and loved after sex, it's not good, healthy sex.

22

The Grass on the Other Side May Look Greener . . . But You Still Have to Mow It

How to handle life when it isn't quite what you expected.

Why is midlife the time that everyone talks about as a crisis? Could it be because that's the time when families are in transition? Although some families today have children later in life or adopt as older parents, many families with parents in midlife have children in high school, in college, getting married, or moving to their own homes. That changes family dynamics significantly.

For many women, whose lives have been so centered on their children, this is a time when they wonder what's next. *I haven't thought in years about what I'd like to do*, a wife thinks. *I don't even know where to start.* There can be uncertainty and yet joy in moving ahead on hobbies and such.

A husband also finds himself with more time on his hands now that there's less involvement with children (even if that involvement meant just showing up when and where his wife told him to). He has enough time to stop and think, *Hey, this job isn't really what I'd like to do. It's a dead end for me.* Then he takes a look downward and notices the flab settling like a spare tire around his middle. He's not quite as attractive as he used to be. . . .

Then the husband and wife look at each other and think, *And, you know, my spouse isn't quite what I expected either. In fact, life isn't quite what I thought it would be.* Such thoughts can lead to depression (I can't do or be anything right), affairs (I have to trade in my old wife model for a new one while I still have something left), and job switches (it has to be better at another company).

If the wife has become wrapped up in her children's lives, merely acquiescing to sex as a duty, her husband will feel that intensely and take her lack of pleasure as a failure on his part. And he'll be tempted to go elsewhere. The wife who may be involved in the sex act but doesn't have intimacy feels used, and sometimes without even realizing it, she begins to look elsewhere for her emotional fulfillment.

In short, the grass in someone else's lawn can start to look a lot greener. That's why you see a guy dump his wife to marry someone 20 years his junior.

A young mom has dreams that she and her husband will be among the most elite of society by their tenth year of marriage and have three kids by age 32. But the dream doesn't quite turn out the way she envisioned it. Her husband is still working, one level up, in the same job he had after-hours in college, and she's gone back to work full-time to help out with expenses. Because her schedule is so wildly busy now, she and her husband don't connect anymore.

One day a male co-worker comments, "Oh, I love your sweater." It's the first verbal affirmation she's heard about her looks in so long that she stands still and stares in shock. Within a week, the two are having a cup of coffee together in the employee cafeteria. They really hit it off. Fast-forward three months, and all of a sudden they're taking a day off work to secretly check into a motel.

How can such things happen? There are womanizers in the world who don't value marriage—who say, "Yeah, that's my wife, but I have four girlfriends on the side." That's the thrill seeker who doesn't understand what marriage and commitment are. Then there are those who just "fall in love"—or is it need?

During these years of adjustment—when bodies are sagging and broadening, when life perspectives are adjusting—it's extremely important for you as a married couple to work toward a satisfactory sex life for *both* of you. Sex and intimacy need to be an integral part of your life as a couple, driving you continually toward each other . . . rather than into someone else's arms.

Q: My wife and I have been married seven years. I love her, but things are just not very exciting anymore. I'm attracted to someone at work—we've had coffee once and met once to work out at the gym—but we're not involved. Is it so wrong to want a friendship with someone of the opposite sex?

---

6 Ways to Reinvent Your Relationship

1. Take a class together at a community college.
2. Do something you've never done before (for example, camping).
3. Take a bus to another town.
4. Stop asking questions.
5. Renew your marital vows. Write them yourself. Make it a ceremony if you want.
6. Take a short vacation without the kids.

A: You mentioned the word *friendship*, yet you said you were attracted to her. The two are not the same. You said you're not "involved." I take this to mean that you're not involved physically—at least not yet. But you *are* involved emotionally since you've met each other several times. That means you are very much at risk for taking things further, into the physical realm.

However, do you realize that you are already "cheating" on your mate, even though you're not involved physically yet? You're deriving comfort from someone outside your marriage and are cheating your spouse out of those intimate details. And do you know what your wife longs for the most from you? An emotional connection. Yet you've now made that emotional connection with another woman.

> *Sex and intimacy need to be an integral part of your life as a couple, driving you continually toward each other . . . rather than into someone else's arms.*

We all want to be flattered by someone else's attention. But flattery can take you farther than you want to go, and it can keep you there longer than you want to stay. Did you know that every physical affair starts off with an emotional connection?

You need to be wise about anyone who could risk your marriage relationship. One man I know always mentions his wife when he has to take women clients out to lunch, to establish an immediate boundary. He also keeps a picture of his family right on his desk to communicate the importance of his marriage and family to anyone who walks in the door.

This is your time to live up to your marriage vows to forsake all others and keep only to your wife. Instead of being flattered by some other woman's attention, you need to stir up the fires between you and your spouse. You need to immediately tell that other woman that you cannot have coffee or go to the gym with her any longer. You need to emphasize the fact that you are married—and that if you led her on to believe anything else, you are truly sorry and would ask for her forgiveness. And then you need to go home and tell your wife about the situation.

Will she be angry? Of course. What wife wouldn't be? But because you stepped up to the plate and told her, the breach in trust won't be nearly as wide as it would have been if she'd found out from someone who happened to see the two of you at the gym. Have your wife help you set up some parameters for your relationships with the opposite sex. (Believe me, women are very smart in knowing how other women will try to "hook" their men.)

All your years with your wife would be a terrible thing to waste. Don't let an attraction or an infatuation ruin what you've spent years building—a closeness in heart.

You need to be vigilant, intentional, and honest with your mate at all times. Share with her any temptation that comes up—*as it comes up.* You may have a bad day initially (like you will when you tell your wife about your coffee and gym times), but a heated discussion now is much better than a divorce court a year or more down the road. Wouldn't you agree?

Q: My husband has hurt me many times over the past two years by flirting with other women, and I've always forgiven him. But now he's stepped over the line. I found out last night that he met his former wife for dinner. He told me he had to work late at the office, but a co-worker of mine happened to see them at the restaurant and called me.

When I waited up for him (he got home at midnight—long dinner, huh?) and confronted him about it, he just snapped back at me for questioning him and made up some excuse that it was regarding his divorce settlement. But I happen to know that settlement was done more than three years ago, before we got married. And since they didn't have any kids, what could be left to talk about? He said he wouldn't do it again, but I don't trust him. I don't know if I can keep forgiving him. Why do I always have to be the one on the giving end? I'm worn out.

A: I can hear the discouragement through your letter. And I bet that when you confront your husband, he says, "I'll never do that again," and then it happens again. No wonder you're exhausted and wrung out. Such men (or women!) are not easy to live with. They can really wear on you emotionally. Trust is a huge issue in marriage, and it's clear you don't trust your husband . . . and you have reason to wonder.

Now is the time to talk to him—after you're done seeing red. Approaching him when you're angry won't do any good. Instead, go to him quietly and say, "You know, I don't think I'm different than any other woman. Every woman wants to be able to trust her husband. She doesn't want to worry about where he is or what he's doing . . . or that he's doing the right thing. But when I find out that you've gone to dinner with your ex-wife, that puts me in the position of not being able to trust you. What can we do about that in the future?" If you approach him in such a way, without anger, you'll have the best possibility for a loving response from him. If there really is something going on in his life or the beginnings of an affair, that may become clear too, and you can ask some follow-up questions.

And regarding forgiving him, let me share something from the flip side with you. If you are a person of faith, did you know that you don't have any choice regarding whether to forgive him? Even if he hurts you three times a day! (As awful as that sounds.) Forgive 70 times 7, Jesus says. That means 490 times. In the language the Bible was written in, that number meant "eternity." Forever.

Why would forgiveness be so important? Because a lack of forgiveness hurts *you*. It becomes a poison. If you don't forgive, it's like you're drinking poison and hoping your husband gets sick. But you're the one who's going to get sick. Buried anger is never buried dead; it's always buried alive. And the longer it stays buried, the worse it will be for you, your spouse, and your relationship.

So if staying angry isn't an option and we are commanded to forgive—for our own and for others' best interests—what can you do? Forgiving someone doesn't mean that you do nothing and just ignore that a problem exists. Instead, why not explore why your husband is doing what he's doing? Why would he be interested in going out to dinner with his ex-wife? Is something lacking in your marriage? In your communication? In your love life? Is he angry with you for some reason? Does he think you're angry with him? Do you diss him to your girlfriends? Is his boss giving him a hard time, and he doesn't think you'll understand or is concerned that you'll worry about his job, so he needs someone else to talk to about it?

Unless you get to the bottom of why he's behaving as he is, he will do this behavior again because there's already a pattern of it. That's why you need to talk to him about it now. And you also need to decide how you'll handle it when it happens the next time.

No, you haven't caused his uncertainty, flirting, and anger—everyone is responsible for his or her own choices—but you do have a decision to make. Don't let unforgiveness linger in your life. It can manifest itself in both physical and emotional symptoms such as stress, depression, and discouragement. If you don't react in anger but state calmly how you feel, it's amazing how things can change in your house.

Q: Man to man, I have to be honest. My spouse just doesn't turn me on the way she used to. I've tried, but I can't seem to drum up the old feelings. Is this just the way things are as people grow older in a marriage, or is there anything I can do about it?

A: Sure there is. You can stick your head in the real world. Most men enter marriage with this thought: *Oh, yeah! I just won the big one. I get to have sex all the time now. Anytime I want it. Any way I want it. As much as I want it. For the rest of my life. . . .* And you start soaking in the pleasure.

But notice all the "I's" in those statements? A little selfish, aren't they? Where does your wife fit into your "I" world? And what about her needs? Marriage is about giving and serving. Your wife's primary purpose isn't to fulfill all your sexual pleasures. It's to be your helpmate and soul mate in every way.

The same is true of you. You need to be your wife's helpmate too, and that means thinking of her, not simply yourself. What does a wife want? To be held tenderly, cherished, and listened to. To be thought of when it isn't her birthday or Christmas. For you to hear and share her feelings. If you do these things and look to your wife's needs, you'll begin to understand who she is. You'll see her beautiful heart, and she will become even more attractive to you.

I challenge you this week to make a list of all the things that you value about your wife. As you realize her worth, your own emotions will change. You may not have "the same old feelings," but you'll have something far better—a mature love that will last the rest of your lifetime. Then just watch what will happen to your sex life!

Q: I'm wondering if my husband could be involved in an affair. How can I know (other than, you know, catching him in the act)?

A: Here are a few telltale signs. (By the way, most of these are true for both males and females.) Has his lifestyle or highly predictable behavior drastically changed (for example, he's now wearing aftershave)? Is he usually home at 5:30, but now he says he's working late and doesn't come home until 10 or 12? Has he recently changed his style of clothing? Is there a huge drop in the frequency of sex? Does he have new undergarments? Do you see lipstick marks on his clothes, emails in coded language from people you don't know, notes, or receipts from restaurants? Is he meeting people who are "just some associates from work"?

Do you ever answer the phone and find that no one is there? Check out the calls he receives on his cell phone. Read his emails on the computer. Am I telling you to be a snoop? Right now, yes. You have to be street smart, because you're fighting for something important—your marriage. If you're asking this question (and women are so darned intuitive to begin with), you're probably right in suspecting that there's an affair going on.

You need to talk to your husband about your suspicions, should you see any of these (or similar) signs. But do you say, "Are you having an affair?" That's kind of like asking a kid who

> *What does a wife want? To be held tenderly, cherished, and listened to. To be thought of when it isn't her birthday or Christmas.*

you know stole something, "Did you take that?" That gives the kid time to wiggle out of the question and say, "Uh, of course not." Instead you'd say, "I know you took your sister's money. Please explain that."

A statement is much clearer: "I believe you're having an affair."

My advice to you is this: don't do anything in knee-jerk fashion. Buying an assault rifle would probably not be a good purchase right now . . . as satisfying as it might be. Getting some epoxy and bathing Mr. Happy in it would also not be a good idea. The feeling is real, but the solution is lacking. This is not the time to do anything drastic, such as picking up and leaving your home. In some states, you might actually lose some of your marital rights by leaving the home. If anyone is to leave the home as a means of separation, it ought to be the perpetrator of the affair, not the victim.

Obviously you are not going to have sex with this man again. I say "obviously," but you'd be surprised how many women, fully aware that their husband is having an affair, will continue to have sex with him to try to win him back. There is that feeling of competition—going head-to-head with the "other woman." Instead of having enough self-respect and the moxie to say, "Out!" she might decide to work out and lose weight to try to please him. There she is, like an adolescent 15-year-old, trying to win back the love of her life. But who's the one who should be doing the work in the relationship now, I ask you? The spouse who was involved in the affair!

Great Resources for Midlife Crisis

Women in Midlife Crisis by Jim and Sally Conway
Men in Midlife Crisis by Jim and Sally Conway

To get beyond the affair, a lot of work has to be done by a husband and wife individually and as a couple. If your husband leaves your home, it's wise to change the locks on your doors and get an unlisted phone number to physically and emotionally put distance between you and him. If he's choosing to go outside your marriage for his fulfillment, you need to make sure he doesn't have easy access to the home you're living in by yourself or with your children. Believe me when I say that you will not be attractive in his sight if you're too easy. This is the time to play hardball and to protect yourself and your kids both physically and emotionally.

You're also not going to pick up and move your kids three states away in the middle of school year, nor are you going to put a "For Sale" sign out in front of the house. You're going to keep life as normal as you possibly can for your children, as well as for yourself, during these trying circumstances.

Some couples make it. But they make it only with a lot of hard work on both their parts and with the help of almighty God.

Is this hard to hear? Undoubtedly, yes. But it's also realistic, and you need to be prepared for that.

Q: A male co-worker has been paying a lot of attention to me lately, since I lost—finally!—over 40 pounds. He seems to notice everything about me . . . unlike my husband. I swear he wouldn't notice for a month or two if I got my hair cut and dyed it purple. My husband's still the man of my dreams, but how can I get him to notice me? I'm tired of being ignored.

A: Stop right there. Your husband may be thickheaded and distracted, but you're on thin ice. You're already paying attention to the flirtations of another man, which screams that you feel like there is a void of male attention in your life.

You need to sit that husband of yours down. Take away his paper and his remote control, turn him away from his computer screen, and talk to him. Touch him, hold his hand, and look him in the eye. "Honey, I need to talk with you about something. I could be completely in left field about this, but there are days when I feel you couldn't care less if I'm even in your life. I don't get much affirmation from you even though I've worked really hard to lose all this weight. I don't expect you to give me false praise, but am I so wrong in thinking that, as your wife, I deserve some encouragement? Hearing that you're proud of me for having made the effort?" If your guy doesn't respond positively to this or you don't see a change in him, you may need to add (in this conversation or in a later one), "Frankly, I'm getting a little scared because I'm finding myself enjoying the attention that I'm getting from a male co-worker."

Now, that ought to get your man's attention. If it doesn't, let me have five minutes with him and straighten him out. Any man who can't affirm you for losing weight is simply dumb as mud. Is your guy one of those strong-as-an-island types who says, "I told you I loved you when I married you. Isn't that good enough for you?" If so, he needs a Marriage 101 class.

And let me talk straight to you too. Chances are that you had gained those 40 pounds because you were stressed and didn't feel appreciated. You're going to eat when you're stressed, so without some affirmation, you might just gain those 40 pounds back. After all that work, do you really want that to happen?

That ought to give you courage to talk to your man. Especially since you just bought that dress you really love in a smaller size.

Q: Before I got married, I had an affair with a married man. Now that Aaron and I have been married for three years, I'm having a really hard time trusting him. I can't help but check up on him (his pockets, computer, phone records). I guess I just wonder if he'll be unfaithful to me, just like the guy I had an affair with was unfaithful to his wife. How can I stop being so suspicious . . . or do you think I have grounds to be?

A: You're not giving Aaron (poor guy) a chance, because you're still wrapped up in the guilt of your past affair. But that was *your* choice back then, not Aaron's. Don't make him pay for your bad and immoral decision.

Yet that's the nature of sexual behavior. Because any sexual experience bonds not only bodies but also hearts, the sex act becomes such a part of your personality, thinking, and memories that you project your own fears onto other people as you move along in life. That won't go away, and you need to be aware of it.

Because of that situation, it's not unreasonable for you to have paranoid thoughts and feelings that your husband will cheat on you. But in reality, *you* were the one who cheated, not your husband. You are taking your feelings of guilt and placing them on Aaron out of fear that he'll do what you did earlier.

You have to let the guy off the hook. Accept him for who he is and stop looking at him through the lens of suspicion. When suspicious thoughts come, make a list of all your husband's wonderful, loyal qualities, and read it over and over again. Positive thoughts will help keep the negative thoughts at bay.

Q: My husband had a fling and didn't tell me about it. I just happened to find out because he and a co-worker were joking about her. He says it was no big deal and she didn't mean anything to him; it was just a one-night stand. But can I really believe that? What would make him do that? And what if he caught something from her? I have no idea who that woman is, and he's not going to tell me about her.

A: You must be angry, and I don't blame you. Fooling around on you is a joke to your husband? That's so disrespectful that I'd like a few minutes alone with him to set him straight.

But in the midst of your anger, here is some important advice.

First, keep your knees together until he's been checked out by a physician for STDs (including HIV).

Second, instead of attempting to murder him in cold blood (which the law would frown upon), have a heart-to-heart with him about what happened. You need—and *deserve*—an explanation. If his explanation is that he was at an office party, had a few too many glasses of wine, and pulled a very, very dumb maneuver, and you're convinced it indeed was a onetime thing, you MIGHT (note all caps) be able to continue this marriage.

I'm sure a few eyebrows just got raised as I used those words. *Throw out a marriage—all those years—for what he says is a one-night stand? Dr. Leman, you've got to be kidding.*

That isn't what I'm saying. What I am saying is that your husband has seriously breached your trust and broken his marriage vows. When you think about it that way, how are you going to deal with the repercussions of that?

First of all, if your husband isn't talking about it, do you *know* it was "just" a one-night stand? Can you trust him to be honest with you about that? And second, marriage is such a delicate union that even *one* violation of this degree has the potential to bring down the entire marriage. This is why I tell everyone I counsel to protect their marriage—to especially be careful of being alone with or flirting with people of the opposite sex. *Just one violation* means a serious betrayal of trust. Promising to "forsake all others" in your marriage means exactly that. You've chosen your spouse for a lifetime. Even one night in someone else's arms breaks that vow.

Yes, people are human. There will always be temptation. And if you think even *you* are above temptation, you're not. Just ask many of the "mighty" men and women who thought they were immune to temptation—and fell hard, then had to deal with the repercussions for years afterward.

Choosing to have the affair was his choice, and it wasn't a good one. Now you have a choice to make. You could choose to end your marriage right now, and no one would think ill of you.

Or you can choose to forgive this instance and move ahead, working with your husband to set some parameters for his actions as you rebuild the trust in your marriage. But for that to happen, there has to be an honest exchange of feelings on both sides, with certainly a heartfelt apology and a request for forgiveness from your husband. He will also have to work hard to regain your trust (which can take time and a lot of humility on his part—both of which he may or may not be willing to give).

You may also have an added element to deal with. As a result of his sexual liaison—if you didn't know about it for a while and you had sex with him after his affair—he may have passed to you the heebie-jeebies or another more technical-sounding venereal disease. The least he can do for you is get himself tested—with you in attendance at that doctor visit. Get yourself tested as well. And until then, do *not* have sex with him until you see those results for yourself and know exactly what you're getting into. If you did catch something, the good news is that treatment is available.

Here's the kicker: if you do decide to stay married, the memories of this affair won't disappear. Let's say you find out next January that he's on a business trip for ten days, and it's across the country. Are you telling me the thought won't enter your mind that he's fooling around on that trip?

Can you deal with it? Yes.

Will you deal with it? Yes.

Will it be difficult? Yes.

Restoring, renewing, and protecting your relationship is possible, but it will take a lot of work on *both* your parts. Is he willing? Are you willing? Before you make a decision you may later regret—especially if children are involved—look at the big picture.

You're in a tough spot, and you have a lot to think about. I applaud your courage in stepping forward to write me at such a difficult time.

Straight Talk

Joel and Lisa have been married for 23 years. They have two kids who are as beautiful as they are. They have a lovely home, and they have what others envision as the "perfect marriage." So why is it that all of a sudden Lisa found out that Joel has been having an affair with one of his company's secretaries?

Did you know that the biggest increase in divorce rate is in the group of couples who have been married more than 20 years? Why is that? Is it because these couples haven't solidified the foundations of their marriages before the "grass is greener" midlife quandaries hit?

The biggest increase in divorce rate is in the group of couples who have been married more than 20 years.

There are many games couples play. One of them is "Dump truck, dump truck, who's got the dump truck?" Let me explain it this way. In the Southwest, where I live, it's hard to get grass to grow. So folks here use Arizona steer manure to fertilize their grass in the springtime. It works great—but let's just say that when someone fertilizes the lawn next door, you know it.

Couples play the Dump Truck game. Each of you has your own individual dump truck, and when you feel like you've been hurt by your mate, you get in your dump truck, locate your mate, lift up your load in the air, and *wham!*—dump it on your mate. You do this over and over until you show up in my office and say, "We don't seem to have feelings for each other anymore."

Well, it's no wonder! You've dumped 20 cubic yards of steer manure on your relationship over time, and it stinks to high heaven!

It all goes back to the democratic society. If you have a right to put me down, I have a right to put you down.

Sad to say, males and females don't compliment each other in general. And with all the TV sitcoms, male bashing is in vogue. No one bats an eye anymore.

So we play all these games, like Dump Truck and another of my favorites, Spit in Your Mate's Soup. How is that one played? A wife sweetly asks her spouse what kind of soup he'd like. He says, "Chicken noodle." She gets the soup ready and brings it to him, and just before she serves it, she spits in it. Then she smiles and says, "I *really* hope you enjoy your soup."

It's like the woman who says to her husband, "Sure, you go ahead and play golf with the guys. I'll just stay here with your mom and your sister." Are the words hostile? No, but the meaning is. *I hope you break your 6 iron.*

You see, most couples don't deal with things up front. They deal with them through cheap shots (take that!), they get long in the jaws (anger), and they shut down (the silent treatment). When one spouse asks, "What's wrong?" the quiet reply is, "Oh, nothing."

Well, *obviously* something's wrong.

But let's put things in perspective. If you found out you had just one year of your life left, how would you live it? And how would that influence who you are today in your marriage? It's so easy to major in the minutiae of life rather than the most important thing: relationships. And your relationships with almighty God and your spouse are the two most important ones of all time.

Such a thought forces us to focus on what is really important in life.

A good sexual relationship is the glue for a marriage. It's a time for reaffirmation, for celebration of your oneness as a couple. It's a time to put all cares of the world aside and just enjoy each other.

For a man, a good sexual relationship reaffirms everything about who he is. There's not much more important in life to a man than his intimate relationship with his bride. Keep in mind that males don't have close personal relationships like women do. If he says he has one good buddy, he's lucky; if he says he has three, he's a lying dog. He has his wife. Yes, I know he has work, and yes, I know he loves golf, but what makes him really go is his wife. If he feels like she respects him, listens to him, and wants him, he is one happy man.

If Coke is the pause that refreshes, sex is the pause that energizes.

For a woman, sex is the time when she has her husband's undivided attention. It's a time to experience the height of sheer intimacy with the one she loves. A time to get away from the pressures of world, children, and job. To build a relationship with the man who chose her above all others, tenderly cares for her, and finds her *sexy*.

If Coke is the pause that refreshes, sex is the pause that energizes. But life is busy. It's hard to find time for the intimate side of life. Too many things seem to take precedence.

But a healthy sex life is worth the long-term investment in time and energy. Rarely will you hear a couple say, "We had a great sex life, but we got divorced." Those couples are as rare as albino tigers in Nebraska. If your sex life is healthy, your spouse will have no reason to look at anyone else's lawn. His will be sprouting up as green as green can be. And he'll be smiling as he watches it grow . . . even if he does have to mow it.

23

After an Affair

How to rebuild what's good after the carnage.

There is no sugarcoating it. Pursuing healing from an affair is one of the most difficult things in life anyone could ever experience. If you are the perpetrator, you will find waves of guilt continually crashing over your head for your dumb move—and all that it has cost you in your relationships (and perhaps even in your work, if it was with a co-worker). If you were on the other end of the affair, you understand the shock and the tumult of your spouse's betrayal of your trust and marriage vows.

Such a tear in your marriage needs spiritual intervention. For those of you who are interested, the Bible says, "Forgive as the Lord forgave you" (Col. 3:13). Translated, that means, from God almighty himself, "If you don't forgive others, I won't forgive you." And that can be a very tall order for a woman who feels violated, because she's brought three children into the world with this man, she's been a good mom and a devoted wife, and then she finds

265

out he's doing the mattress mambo with the check-in clerk at the health club. "How could he do that to me?" she says. "I've given that man everything he wanted—I washed his clothes, took care of the house, had his children—for over 15 years, and this is what I get in return?"

There is no way to get over such an experience in five days or less. That one will take a long time. When trust is violated, it can be repaired only little by little, over time, and with great patience and tenderness.

Q: My husband had an affair with his secretary. He says it was only emotional, not physical (but others in the office say differently), but it still hurts to think that someone else was more important to him than me. He doesn't seem remorseful. He doesn't understand why this "short relationship" (as he calls it) hurts me so much.

When he told me it was over, he expected us to pick up our sexual relationship right where we'd left off when I first found out about her. But I just can't. I told him he had to leave our home. I can't trust him with my heart—or my body—anymore. And I'm also embarrassed because it seems like everyone in the office knows about the affair too. I can't stand to look those people in the eye. There's only one good thing about the whole mess—the secretary decided to leave when he broke up with her.

A: I'm sorry for your pain. And I'm not surprised, frankly, that you kicked him out of the house. He is showing little or no respect for you as his wife. I'm sorry, too, that word has spread, because that only makes things more difficult for you.

So here's my question: are you writing me because (1) you want to know how to get over him and be done with him, or (2) you want to see if it's possible to restore your marriage?

In regard to the first question, you can pursue a divorce, and that would be understandable. But even if you get divorced, you'll never be done with him, because he will always have a piece of your heart (even as angry as you are with him right now). This is even more the case if you have children and will be showing up at the same events for their sake. So, yes, you can cut things off and go through proceedings, but you'll be left with the residue.

In regard to the second question, I know that thought is hard right now. And, frankly, both of you have to be willing to work on every aspect of your relationship.

For his part, he would need to acknowledge that what he did was very wrong, violated your marriage vows, and betrayed your trust in him. He needs to not only say he's sorry but also regain your trust and put safeguards into his life to keep the same situation from happening again. He needs to date you and win your heart all over again.

Sometimes when a husband and wife are separated, it gives both of them time to sort out the issues. Perhaps he'll come to you and say, "I'm so sorry. I never meant this to be anything, and I don't want to leave you. I'm sick about this. And the kids! I want to repair this if I can. . . . Would you be willing to?" It could happen, and if it did, would you be willing? Or have you walled off your heart?

Here are some good questions to ask each other as you sort through your feelings and the events. Asking such questions is a good jumping-off point to talk about the *issues* involved in your relationship, rather than pointing fingers at each other.

1. On a scale of 1 (worst) to 10 (best), how would you rate our relationship before the affair?

2. What would it take to move our relationship from where it is today (probably in the minus category) up to, say, 6 or 7 in a year?

As you ask these questions, it will help the two of you to find common goals—and solutions for the unmet needs that caused a division between you.

Q: I have a wonderful husband (dull, but wonderful), who loves me very much. But spending two weeks in L.A. on business and meeting Pierre was just too big of a lure for my romantic heart. I can't believe I was so stupid as to fall into that guy's arms (and I'm sure some other chick was in his arms as soon as I left). He emailed a couple of times the month after I left, but that's all. I threw away my 12-year marriage for nothing. Now I really want my guy back, but how?

A: Eat humble pie, that's how. Go immediately to your husband and admit you have done him wrong, wrong, wrong. Tell him how sorry you are for letting fantasy get in the way of the incredible guy you had already. Beg his forgiveness. Start romancing that guy of yours all over again (before some other lucky girl gets him . . . even if he is a little dull). You're going to have to work really hard to rebuild trust in your relationship.

Also, you need to cut off all ties with Pierre. No phone calls, no emails. Get rid of any gifts. If you have to go back to L.A. and he works for a company that's a client of yours, either take your husband to L.A. with you or say you can't go.

If your husband is willing to accept you back, ask him what boundaries he'd like to have in place. Go to a counselor together. Be truthful in all things, even in the "little" ones. (Remember all those nights when he phoned you to ask what you were doing for the evening, and *then* you headed out the door to meet Pierre?) No more deception. No more lies. And if you ever happen to see Pierre, even on the street corner, you have to report it to your husband.

Can you get to the other side? Absolutely. But both parties have to be willing. You have greatly injured your husband. It may take him some time to recuperate—if he can. Be gentle with him. After all, you're the one who got the two of you into this mess.

Q: My wife got really close emotionally to a guy in our neighborhood several years ago, when I had to move to Texas to start my new job six months before we sold our house. She's assured me over and over again that nothing physical happened and that she loves me. So why do I still feel so bad about it?

A: A penis doesn't have to enter a vagina for an affair to happen. An affair, simply stated, is a violation of marital vows. The major components of an affair are, in fact, emotional. Sex is part of it, but it's the emotions that act as the glue for the affair: "Here's a man or woman who understands me, listens to me, wants me, and makes me feel special."

Affairs don't make sense. They're irrational. But people like your wife have them in huge numbers. Why? Because there is a void of some kind in a person's marital relationship, and the affair fills that void somewhere along the line.

---

4 Top Ways to Rebuild Trust

1. Practice forgiveness.
2. Spend some time each day thinking about how imperfect you are.
3. Don't pretend like the affair never happened; act like it never happened. (Your feelings follow your actions.)
4. Tell your spouse, "I love you"—every day, in every way you can think of.

What do you think the void was in your wife's life? Could it be that she was lonely because you were in a different state and that she hardly ever got to see you? And when she did, you were mentally and emotionally absent since you were thinking about all the stresses of your new job, where to find a house in Texas for your family to live, etc.?

If you keep that void in mind, it will give you some empathy for your wife that may get you over the hurdle of forgiving her . . . and moving on.

Q: It's been two years since my husband had his affair, and we've put our family back together, but I still haven't been able to have sex with him. I keep thinking about "the other woman" and wonder what she had that I don't. I keep seeing images of the two of them together, making love. I want my marriage to work for my kids' sake . . . even if there's nothing in it for me. But how can I hold on until they're 18? The youngest is only 5 now!

A: That you've stayed together for two years shows you're not ready to give up on your marriage (as much as you may feel like it right now). But have you managed to stay together because you've just kept your mouth shut and not said anything? If so, you're going to pay a high emotional price. Don't sweep your feelings under the rug. They have a nasty habit of sneaking up on you when you least expect them. If you truly do love your husband, don't let your thoughts drift to him with another woman.

Be honest with your spouse and tell him how much it still bothers you—how hurt, betrayed, and angry you feel. Then tell him that you want to choose to move on, but you need his help. He needs to work hard to regain your trust.

Now is the time to speak to a trusted mentor or therapist about what happened. Talk about what happened that made the affair "attractive" to your spouse. Make time together a priority; build up your relationship again. Go on long walks; hold hands (even when you don't feel like it); get involved in a hobby; get to know each other all over again.

Your relationship can emerge stronger, if you're willing to make it a priority.

There is no room for bitterness, no room for planning ahead to get out of the relationship as soon as the kids are grown. As long as the root of bitterness is there, your relationship can't move forward, you can't work through the issues, and you can't begin to rebuild trust.

It takes work to get to the other side of an affair. You have to be willing to put everything on the table, where it'll be seen, discussed, and cried over. You'll need to find new methods of communication and resolving conflict. And ultimately you will both have to forgive—for both real and imagined wrongs—just as God almighty forgives us.

Q: I've always been a career kind of woman. I took off the years when my three kids were little, but other than that, I've worked full-time for over 20 years. My relationship with Marc, a co-worker, began very innocently over frappuccinos, when he complimented me on my shoes—something my husband would never even notice. My husband is one of those plodder types who's happy if he's in the black on his checking account. I always dreamed of more in life than that, but he never understood my drive to succeed; he thought having kids would "cure" me.

Marc and I had an affair for a year, until his job was transferred to another state. Recently I lost my job when my company merged with another company. Now that I'm home full-time, I realize how much my family means to me . . . and how patient my husband has been our entire marriage, letting me work late hours, go on business trips, etc. How can I repair what I've done? The guilt I feel when he hugs me every day is consuming me.

A: Come clean with your husband. If he doesn't know about Marc, it's time to tell him. If you don't, the news will slip out some way, someday, and perhaps in front of your children. Your husband seems like a well-balanced guy. Give him some credit. Will he be angry? I'd hope so, because that shows he's fighting for you and what you have together. Will he find it hard to trust you? That's a given. But if you're living under the shadow of "what if . . ." and "when he finds out . . ." you won't be able to develop your relationship from this point on.

> *If you're living under the shadow of "what if . . ." and "when he finds out . . ." you won't be able to develop your relationship.*

Regarding your job loss, that's traditionally a time when many people step back and reevaluate where they want to go in life. Are you suffering from a midlife crisis? There's a great book called *Women in Midlife Crisis* by Jim and Sally Conway that I'd recommend.

Affairs always start innocently, when people are at their weakest emotionally. Marriages have become "old hat," and you're looking for adventure. Sounds like you took your spouse for granted (and maybe he took you for granted too).

Here you've had three kids, and you're probably feeling a bit of that midlife spread (just add to it a little belly from three childbirths, and that clinches the deal). So when someone different and intriguing approaches you, the flames are fanned. It's the thrill of the forbidden life.

Only problem is, the forbidden life scorches everyone it touches . . . and the flames will hurt many others in their wake.

I urge you, right now, to begin taking notice of all the wonderful things your spouse does. Build him up. Tell him how much you love and appreciate him. If you don't, someone else will.

Q: My husband had an affair and admits that he "went all the way." I didn't know until three months afterwards, and we had sex during that time. Now I'm angry. What if I caught a sexually transmitted disease from him because of her? I'm absolutely furious, and I don't know who to talk to.

A: Don't talk to your sister. Not your best friend. But do talk to a professional. Your ob-gyn would be a great place to start. And do not have sex with your husband from this day forward, until both of you are checked out by a doctor for STDs and you are fully aware of the consequences of having sex. You have no idea who that woman was or how many sexual partners she's had.

If you and your husband were virgins when you got married, there was no probability of getting a sexual disease. You would have been exposed only to each other.

But, as a study from the Guttmacher Institute on teen sex shows, if you've had 3 sexual partners, you're actually exposed to 7 sexual partners. If you've had 7 sexual partners, you're actually exposed to 127 sexual partners. Let's say that you had a sexual experience with 12 partners. If that twelfth partner has had 12 partners in his sexual experience, then you've actually slept with 4,095 people at that moment![5] Scary, huh?

So this is a defining moment in the marriage—when your spouse needs to know how seriously you view what he did. He needs to take responsibility for his actions (and the subsequent physical damage to himself and you and any others) and to end the affair, if it isn't already over. But you'll have a lot of work to do as a couple—especially for the next 18 to 24 months. It will take time and a counselor to help you work through the issues.

Having an affair is like eating a pizza on a Saturday night and still being able to taste it three hours later. Except the aftertaste of an affair lasts a lot longer.

Maybe that's why I've always espoused a "hands-off, pants-on" policy with everyone—except a spouse. Song of Solomon 8:4 says: "Do not arouse or awaken love until it so desires."

You have every right to be angry, and you have every right to withhold sex from your husband, since not doing so could be extremely dangerous for you.

Life has changed; it can never be the same again. But it's up to you how you will write the next chapter in your family's life.

Straight Talk

People choose to have affairs; they don't just happen. There is a reason for them. And that reason is that some void in the person's marital relationship isn't being fulfilled.

Everyone is vulnerable. Everyone can be tempted—you and your spouse. Even the mighty King David of Israel, one of the greatest

---

What Love Really Is

Getting a picture of the two of you, all wrinkly like raisins, in the paper for your fiftieth wedding anniversary.

An action, not just a feeling.

A choice to honor, respect, understand, and commit . . . every day.

---

kings known to humankind, chose to have an affair. You can read the story in 2 Samuel 11–12, but here's the Leman version.

One evening King David is out walking around the rooftop of his castle, catching some rays and relaxing. (He didn't really need Coppertone SPF 30 because he had rather dark skin.) He peers over the wall, to the next rooftop, and sees this woman. He runs in and gets his binoculars to scope her out. "Wow, *that* is a woman!"

Well, you know the rest of the story. The beautiful Bathsheba is bathing, and King David continues to get an eyeful. He can't stop thinking about her, so he sends a messenger to find out about her. She's married—the wife of Uriah the Hittite, the messenger says. But does the fact that she's married stop David from his pursuit? No, he's hot to trot. So he sends for Bathsheba, and they end up sleeping together.

Some time later David finds out that Bathsheba is pregnant. Uh-oh. Problem is, everyone will know that Uriah isn't the father, since good ol' Uriah is out doing his duty as a soldier on the battlefield. So King David has Uriah brought home to sleep with his wife. But Uriah is such a respectable soldier that he refuses to take comfort from his wife because the other soldiers are still in battle.

David, desperate to save his reputation, comes up with a wild, last-ditch idea. He tells Joab, the commander of his army, to put Uriah in the front of the battle so he'll be killed. Then, after Uriah is killed, David marries Bathsheba. But their child dies.

See all the consequences of David's lust, which led to an affair, a pregnancy, a murder, and the death of a child? Yet I've always taken heart in this story because God called David "a man after my own heart." And David was a pretty imperfect dude. So you tell me: what have you done in your life that is so terrible that God can't forgive you for it?

Now is the time to come clean with your spouse (if you've been the perpetrator) or to allow your spouse to tell his or her side of the story and to ask forgiveness.

You can forgive, but you can't forget. In fact, you *must* remember—remember where you were. There will be times when tears will roll, and you will think you cannot forgive your spouse or yourself . . . when you feel like you cannot go on as you are now.

But keep this in mind: if *you* don't have a love affair with your spouse, someone else will. Work on being thoroughly married.

24

There's No Such Thing as Over the Hill . . . Unless You Act Like It

How to combat the sexual effects of job loss, depression, and aging.

Two men meet each other at a forced social gathering, and the stimulating conversation goes something like this:

MAN 1: (Nods)
MAN 2: (Nods)
MAN 1: So, how about those Bulls?
MAN 2: (Nods, pauses). So, what do you do for a living?

Two women pass each other in the mall, and their conversation goes something like this:

WOMAN 1: Oh, I just love that sweater you have on. Would you mind telling me where you got that?

WOMAN 2: Sure. At J. Crew. The store's just around the corner. I shop there all the time. They have it in black and green too.

WOMAN 1: I love it. Green's my favorite. I was telling my girlfriend the other day . . .

And the two women are off talking twin stream for the next 20 minutes, then take a coffee break together to finish off the conversation.

Here's the interesting thing. In those 35 minutes, the two women never once mentioned what they do for a living—even though one is a podiatrist and the other a CEO, and this is the first day they've both had off in months.

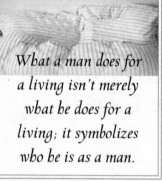

What a man does for a living isn't merely what he does for a living; it symbolizes who he is as a man.

See the difference?

What a man does for a living isn't merely what he does for a living; it symbolizes who he is as a man. For most women, a job is one of the many things she does during her day, but it doesn't define her. (Even top executive women make out their grocery lists over their lunch breaks and order ballet costumes for their daughters online. Now we guys? That would be way too much multitasking.)

That's why when a man loses his job, he tells himself internally, *I've lost my usefulness.* And he feels even worse if that means his stay-at-home wife has to go back to work to make up for his no longer bringing home the bacon. So that man receives two hits: (1) he's failed in his job, and (2) he's failed to provide for his family.

Those are bitter pills for many men to swallow. On the scale of top stressors in life, a man would list: job loss, loss of child, and loss of wife, respectively. No wonder so many men today, with our changing economy, are suffering from depression. By that I don't just mean, *I'm feeling blue*. I'm talking about the clinical depression that's sparked by something physiological in a person's body, that makes him feel like he doesn't even want to get up to face the day. He couldn't care less, since his world is a black hole with no hope.

Add to that the signs of aging, where a body is beginning to droop and not be as sexy as it used to be, and you have a very discouraged man who has no interest in being intimate with his wife.

Although job loss is not a big stressor for most women—since they don't identify themselves with a particular job or career as much as men do—women are greatly influenced by depression and aging. A woman is so intricately wired emotionally and hormonally that depression can hit her hard. And because of the fact she was raised from babyhood on to "look good," aging can hit her particularly hard. She can feel like she's no longer attractive to her mate, so why would he want to have sex with her?

Job loss, depression, and aging are all facts of life. They'll happen. The question is, how will you and your spouse handle them when they do?

Q: My husband lost his job last year. Life hasn't been the same around our house since. My husband worked hard for 20 years at the same company and enjoyed his work, but the company went out of business. Jake hasn't been the same since. He just sits around the house in the dark and mopes. It seems like he lost his sex drive with his job. How can I get across to him that I love him *with or without* that job? That I desire him physically?

A: There's something you need to understand about men. Men identify themselves primarily through their work. Women may work outside the home—as airline pilots, surgeons, or librarians—but they don't identify themselves with their jobs like men do. To men, they *are* their work.

That means when your husband lost his job, he lost his identity. He's probably beating himself up big time—telling himself he's not a man and he can't even provide for his own family. The fact that you have a job (as helpful as that is financially for your family) may even make him feel worse—like you're wearing the pants in the family. What he's saying by sitting around is, "I'm not really worth anything. You don't need me." He internalizes all his failure, and that comes out in his depressive mood and inability to function physically, emotionally, and sexually. He may even end up with ED (erectile dysfunction).

What your man needs is for you to *need* him. Let it be your challenge as a woman to make things happen sexually, even though there might be some initial resistance on his part. This is the time to be creative. Giving him time to become more withdrawn and more depressed certainly isn't going to be the answer to anything.

The words you choose to use with your husband are really important during this difficult time. He needs to hear you say, "Honey, you are #1 with me. And we're going to get through this together. You and me. I believe in you."

Your man needs to hear every day that you love him for *who he is*. That you need him in your life. That he makes all the difference in your life. And that, even though his armor is a little dinged at the moment, he's still your hero.

If the depressed mood continues for a couple of weeks, it's possible your husband may be clinically depressed. If so, your physician is capable of prescribing medication that could help elevate his mood. This therapy, along with your sympathy, encouragement, and understanding, will help that dark hole of depression lift over time. Although your husband may not seem to appreciate it at the moment, be close with him physically as well as emotionally. He has just lost a big portion of his world, and he's reeling from it. This is your time to focus on your husband and let go of other less important things in your world.

Q: My husband has always had a healthy sexual appetite. When he hit his fifties last year, it slowed way, way down. He seems to act "normally" other than that. Should I be concerned? Do you think he might be having an affair or something?

A: A lot of folks ask that question. Many of us men slow down as we get older. It happens to the best of us. My guess is that's what's happening to your husband too. Why don't you ask him?

As far as an affair goes, do you have any evidence of your suspicion? Is your husband staying out later than usual? Coming home from work late? Is he meeting people who don't seem to have names, at least ones that he'll give you? Has he just lost a lot of weight? Has he just bought a new wardrobe?

Those are simple clues that a man might be having an affair. If you're seeing some of these signs, you might want to check out his computer. The history button will show you websites he goes to, and you might want to check his emails too. Look at his cell phone—calls received, calls made.

Am I telling you to snoop? In this case, yes, because we're talking about your marriage, and you have every right to know. If enough of the other signs have come together to make you wonder, "Hey, is something going on?" then use your street smarts. Use your God-given woman's intuition to figure it out. If you find records that seem to confirm your suspicions, you need to talk to your husband immediately.

Don't say, "Are you having an affair?" because if he is, he can just deny it. Instead, say, "I found these emails and these hotel receipts in your pocket. Why don't you tell me about these?" You're smart to try that option rather than wonder.

Chances are, he's just growing old like the rest of us.

Q: After going through two rounds of chemotherapy and radiation, my husband is impotent. This really bothers him because he says he can't participate fully in sex like before. But crazy as this sounds, I don't mind. For the first time in our marriage, I feel like I'm getting the attention I need. Is it okay for me to feel that way? Are there ways I can still bring him pleasure?

A: Okay? It's perfectly understood. That's because 97 percent of women say that, for them, sex is about the closeness. They far prefer the loving, holding, and cuddling over orgasms or penetration. That's because what women desire most is that heart connection. They want to know that their husband is focused on them. That's the way women are wired. If they aren't connected emotionally first, they'll have difficulty being connected physically.

Because your husband is impotent, he's aware that he can no longer penetrate or ejaculate. This will give the two of you time to focus on other things. Help him understand that you are delighted with what you do still have together, and that you are excited about exploring new ways to be creative together. You

---

You Know You're Over the Hill When . . .
- you realize you can live without sex . . . but not your bifocals.
- you find yourself singing along with the elevator music.
- your bursitis—not the weather forecaster—tells you when it's going to rain.
- you ask what day it is every day.
- you eat dinner at 4:30 p.m.

---

might want to check out my book *Sheet Music* for some ideas too.

Tell him every day, "The smartest thing I did was marry you. You are the man for me. The man of my dreams."

Then touch him ever so gently on his penis. Just because he's impotent doesn't mean he won't like being touched there. There are not many men walking this earth who don't like the idea of having the one they love using her very soft, feminine, delicate fingers to caress Mr. Happy.

> *Ninety-seven percent of women say that, for them, sex is about the closeness. They far prefer the loving, holding, and cuddling over orgasms or penetration.*

Then caress his body all over, from head to toe. I can guarantee your man will be shivering with delight and grinning like a little boy who just got the last cookie out of the cookie jar.

Q: I used to love sex. Ever since I went through menopause, though, I've struggled with depression and have lost my urge for sex. I'm too young for this! What can I do to get my sex drive back?

A: Are you on an antidepressant? Antidepressants can also depress your sexual drive. But if you and your husband are aware of that, you can come up with solutions for it. Also, talk to your doctor to see if he or she might have some solutions.

Make sure you get several doses of bright sunlight every day. Sit in front of a sunny window when you have breakfast (or outside if it's warm enough). Go for a walk. Exercise helps to get your blood moving and clear the fog out of your head. It'll energize you and make you feel better about yourself. Remember how sex used to be for you and your husband. Relive some of your most passionate moments. And a big key: get enough sleep.

One in ten Americans experience some form of depression, and women are particularly susceptible because of the delicate way their hormones and emotions are wired.

There will be better days. Believe it and act on it, and they will come to pass.

Straight Talk

Ladies, this one's for you. Although men identify themselves with their work—promotions, raises, back slaps for a job well done—where your man really wants to succeed is at home. Underneath all his bravado, his grunts, his noncommunication at times, your man needs to be your hero.

You may be making a six-figure salary. You may be in charge of an entire day care. You may be running the lives of all four of your children ages 5 through 18. You may feel like you're doing quite admirably on your own. At least most days.

But beware of being too independent, because then the message you're subtly giving the guy you love is *I don't really need you*. And what red-blooded guy wants to stick around when it's clear that he's not needed? Or that his contribution to the family—as a provider, a husband, a father—is not appreciated?

Men are a strange breed, I'll admit. But here's the secret: if you treat us right and stroke us, we'll do everything to make you happy.

Men are a strange breed, I'll admit. But here's the secret: if you treat us right and stroke us, we'll do everything to make you happy.

284

Gentlemen, this one's for you. Your wife is a complex being of hormones and emotions, so help guard her from overwork and too much stress. If you see her slipping into depression, talk with her immediately about it and step forward to get help for her. There are many medicines today that will help a woman's depression lift so she can walk out of the fog and into the sunlight of enjoying life again. But sometimes she needs your help to put the pieces together.

Also, tell her how beautiful she is—how you love her body. She needs to hear these words from you as she looks around at all the Madison Avenue models and realizes she doesn't look anything like them.

Laugh together about the funny things that happen as you age. It's true: laughter is the best medicine. For job loss, for depression, for aging—and for all of life in general.

I'm now in my sixties, but if you asked my five kids, "Do you think your dad acts old?" I think they'd say, "No. Dad has fun. Dad's an optimist. Dad likes to have a good time."

You are what you choose to be. You can choose to be over the hill . . . or you can choose to enjoy climbing that mountain.

25

If Mick Jagger Can Still Sing, We Can Still Do the You-Know-What

> There's many a tune in an old viola, and it's some of the best music around.

Everyone pause for a second and, just for the heck of it, think about Mom and Dad having sex.

Eek! That ought to put a chill up your spine.

I can hear what some of you just said. "My mom wouldn't *think* of doing that." (Uh, wrong. How do you think you got on the planet?)

Now think for a minute of Grandma and Grandpa having sex. Oh my goodness, so close to the dinner hour!

Truth is, God made us sexual beings. There's no reason that even someone shuffling around in a walker can't enjoy sex with the person he or she loves.

I'm past 60, and there have been times when I've asked myself, "When will this come to an end for me?" And since I have the privilege of answering myself, I always say, "Never."

For some of you reading this book, *old* by definition means 40; for others of you it means 50; for others it means 60; and for people like me, it's way later than 60! But let me tell you something, you young whippersnappers: when you get old, you don't feel differently on the inside.

When you're 60, your wife can still make you feel like the frisky young colt you were at age 23. Your husband can still make you feel like the frolicking filly you were at age 22.

> *Everyone pause for a second and, just for the heck of it, think about Mom and Dad having sex. Eek! That ought to put a chill up your spine.*

I know some of you youngsters are shaking your heads, saying, "You gotta be kidding me. That can't be true."

But it is. Even more, research shows that the couples who may have the *most* satisfaction with their relationship (including their sex life) are couples in their fifties and sixties. For a senior couple, that means it's like Christmas—"the most wonderful time of the year," as the old song says—*every day* of the year!

How can that be? Well, the best sex organ is your brain. It's the words you choose to use, gentlemen, that can turn your woman on—even if she's facing the realities of vaginal dryness through a decline of estrogen. The right words said at the right time, in the right way, and with the right gentle touch can unleash a sexual fury in Grandma that would impress even Billy Crystal in *When Harry Met Sally*.

With the years come certain physical infirmities and hormone changes that might make traditional sex a challenge, but never fear.

It just takes some ingenuity, understanding, careful planning, and a sense of humor.

Q: I've noticed that my wife is more "touchy" about where I stroke her than she used to be. Are there normal sexual changes that I can expect as my wife ages? And what can I do about them—if anything—to help?

A: Yes, a woman's body changes. The most common change is a lowering of estrogen once a woman is past menopause. With the lowering of estrogen, a woman doesn't have as much ability to be self-lubricating. Her skin becomes drier—her shoulders, her legs, her vagina. She may need a much gentler touch, without as much rubbing. You may need to use products like K-Y Jelly to help her be more comfortable for entry. Ask her for clues as to what feels good to her and what doesn't. She'll be glad you asked.

But here's the great news: many women report that post menopause they have greater freedom in their sexual experience. They have more time; they're less rushed. And there's no more worry about creating a baby (therefore no birth control pills, no natural family planning counting, no condoms, etc.).

The most important thing to remember is that your minds are the most important sex organs you have. So use them wisely.

Q: When my wife turned 60 this year, everything that she used to like in sex over the past 25 years greatly changed. It's like I have to find the road map all over again. Help! I'm not as young or creative as I used to be. And do I need to back off on the frequency now that we're older?

A: Ah, but now you have more time to explore, don't you? Why not take full advantage of it in one of the most exciting adventures you could have in life?

We all change as we grow older—a good thing for most of us. It can be either a divisive time as a couple, or a new and fun season of love, like you're exploring on a second honeymoon. (Now, there's a thought—why not take one?)

The fact of the matter is, men and women are different from each other in their twenties, and they're still different from each other in their sixties. As the man, you're most likely the aggressor. Maybe you need to dial it back a bit and see how your wife responds.

Focus on making love to your wife outside the bedroom. As a man who has brought his wife a cup of coffee every morning of our married life and scratched her back (on top of the nightie only, according to her rule book), I've seen the response of a wife who feels cherished, loved, attended to, and listened to (not a bad deal for taking a few minutes to scratch her back and bring her coffee!). The joy of being married and pleasing your wife is knowing the kinds of things that will please her. If you work on finding those things, you'll find that she'll be much more responsive to you—both inside and outside the bedroom.

Now that's worth doing a little exploring.

Woo Her . . . All Over Again

Come away, my lover,
and be like a gazelle
or like a young stag
on the spice-laden mountains.

Song of Solomon 8:14

> **4 Ways to Show Him He's Still Sexy**
>
> 1. Call your unsuspecting husband into the laundry room of your home and delight him like he's never been delighted in all of his life.
> 2. Book the honeymoon suite—complete with hot tub and spa—at the local hotel.
> 3. Have sex with your dentures out.
> 4. Have sex every day for a week in a different room of the house. (That way you'll always have something to smile about. And if one of you dies? You'll die oh-so-happy.)

Q: I'm going to turn 70 soon. I guess I'm a little afraid that the bottom is going to fall out all of a sudden on my sex life. Any tips for my wife and me?

A: It's true that a man reaches his sexual peak at about age 18 to 20. As a lot of us get older, we slow down. I ought to know. I'm now in my sixth decade, and I've slowed down to sex just four times a week. But just because you're nearing the big 7-0 doesn't mean you can't enjoy an active, fulfilling, wonderful sex life. In fact, most couples say that as they age, the sex gets better! (After all, there are no ankle biters banging on the bedroom door to get your attention . . . or throwing up in the midst of your climax.)

It's important, though, that you are aware of changes that happen in your aging bodies. It may take longer for you to get an erection. But look on the bright side—that means longer to cuddle with your wife and enjoy her touch.

A woman's estrogen levels will drop, and as a result her skin will become drier and more sensitive, and her vagina will need more lubrication. What feels good on Friday may not feel good on Monday. Interestingly enough, though, many women report that they feel a more enthusiastic freedom in their sexuality after menopause. And that's something to celebrate!

Sure, your bodies are changing, but your most important sex organ—your mind—is still in charge. Use the coming years as an opportunity to explore the changes in a loving way with your spouse. A positive attitude makes all the difference.

Straight Talk

I got a chuckle out of the senior couple who found a way to get around their walkers and enjoy great sex on their living room floor.

"Help! I've fallen and I can't get up," the one called to the other, amid much laughter.

I hope that brought a smile to your face, as it did to mine.

My father once said, "Kevin, there's many a tune in an old viola." And now I—someone who qualifies for the senior discount for a cup of coffee at McDonald's—know what he meant. As couples grow older, love deepens and grows more mature. With so much practice, you're even better at sexual intimacy. It's really true that sex starts with a state of mind, and then the actions follow.

So go ahead, turn up the heat on your passion. A little long, slow simmering may be just what the doctor ordered . . . and now you have time for it.

Conclusion

Grow Old Along with Me

> The best is yet to be. So go ahead—turn up the heat!

Grow old along with me,
the best is yet to be.

Robert Browning (1812–1889)

Who would you rather grow old with? If you can think that about your wife or husband when you're 25, 35, 45, 55, 65, and 75, how wonderful! What do you want your relationship to look like now and in the future?

Don't waste another day, let alone a month, without giving everything you can to one of God almighty's best gifts—the joy of a great sex life with the person you love most.

I want to end with a story that truly is the essence of what "grow old along with me, the best is yet to be" really means.

An elderly gentleman always had his dental appointments early on Saturday mornings. One particular Saturday morning, the dentist was running behind schedule, and the elderly man became anxious.

"Is something wrong?" the dentist asked when he finally got the man into his chair.

"Well," the elderly gentleman said quietly, "I always meet my wife for breakfast, and I don't want to be late. You see, she's in a nursing home now."

"Oh, I get it," the dentist said, "she gets mad when you're late."

"Actually, she doesn't even recognize me anymore," the gentleman said. "It's been over three years now."

The dentist looked puzzled. "What's the big deal, then, about being late for breakfast? I mean, if she doesn't even know who you are?"

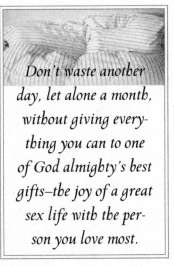

Don't waste another day, let alone a month, without giving everything you can to one of God almighty's best gifts–the joy of a great sex life with the person you love most.

"Yes," the older man said, "but I know who she is."

It's easy to get off to a great start in marriage. What is difficult to do is to finish the journey well. And that man was finishing it well.

Will there be some hills and valleys? Some rocks in the way? Admittedly, yes. You might even stumble a little.

But if you keep communication and commitment to each other as a high priority, and if you honor and respect each other, you will have love for a lifetime. And somewhere along the way, you'll find yourselves looking at each other, saying, "You know what? What a privilege this is—to share life's joys and heartbreaks with you, the person I know and love and understand more than anyone in the world."

Amazing, isn't it? That us strange men and you weird women were custom-made for each other? And that together you can have such a great ride?

You'll be glad you turned up the heat on your sex life. I promise.

Notes

1. Adapted from John Powell, *Why Am I Afraid to Tell You Who I Am?* (Niles, IL: Argus Communications, 1969). Also adapted from Dr. Kevin Leman, *Sex Begins in the Kitchen* (Grand Rapids: Revell, 1999), 123–26.

2. You can read the whole story in the Bible in Mark 11:15–17.

3. 1 Corinthians 7:3–5 (TLB).

4. Here is information you should know from the Alan Guttmacher Institute, "Facts in Brief: Teen Sex and Pregnancy," September 1999, http://www.agi-usa .org/pubs/fb_teen_sex.html:

Number of X's Partners	Number of Sexual Partners X Is Exposed To
1	1
2	3
3	7
4	15
5	31
6	63
7	127
8	255
9	511
10	1023
11	2047
12	4095

5. Ibid.

Suggested Resources
for Couples

Books

Sheet Music

Sex Begins in the Kitchen

Becoming a Couple of Promise

The Birth Order Book

Video Series

Making the Most of Marriage

Bringing Peace and Harmony to the Blended Family

Join us on our "Couples of Promise" annual cruise. Call 1-800-770-3830, or go to www.lemanbooksandvideos.com for more information.

About Dr. Kevin Leman

An internationally known psychologist, radio and television personality, and speaker, Dr. Kevin Leman has taught and entertained audiences worldwide with his wit and commonsense psychology.

The bestselling and award-winning author has made hundreds of house calls for radio and television programs, including *The View*, *Today*, *Oprah*, *Fox and Friends*, CBS's *The Early Show*, Janet Parshall's *America*, CNN's *American Morning*, *Focus on the Family*, and *Life Today* with James Robison. Dr. Leman has served as a contributing family psychologist to *Good Morning America*.

Dr. Leman is also the founder and president of Couples of Promise, an organization designed and committed to helping couples remain happily married.

Dr. Leman's professional affiliations include the American Psychological Association, the American Federation of Television and Radio Artists, and the North American Society of Adlerian Psychology.

In 1993, he was the recipient of the Distinguished Alumnus Award of North Park University in Chicago. In 2003, he received from the University of Arizona the highest award that a university can extend to its own: the Alumni Achievement Award.

Dr. Leman attended North Park University. He received his bachelor's degree in psychology from the University of Arizona, where he later earned his master's and doctorate degrees. Originally from Williamsville, New York, he and his wife, Sande, live in Tucson, Arizona. They have five children.

For information regarding speaking availability, business consultations, or seminars, please contact:

Dr. Kevin Leman
P.O. Box 35370
Tucson, Arizona 85740
Phone: (520) 797-3830
Fax: (520) 797-3809
www.lemanbooksandvideos.com

Resources by
Dr. Kevin Leman

Books for Adults

Have a New Kid by Friday

The Firstborn Advantage

The Birth Order Book

Sheet Music

Making Children Mind without Losing Yours

Sex Begins in the Kitchen

7 Things He'll Never Tell You . . . But You Need to Know

What Your Childhood Memories Say about You

Running the Rapids

What a Difference a Daddy Makes

The Way of the Shepherd (written with William Pentak)

Home Court Advantage

Becoming the Parent God Wants You to Be

Becoming a Couple of Promise

A Chicken's Guide to Talking Turkey with Your Kids about Sex
(written with Kathy Flores Bell)
First-Time Mom
Keeping Your Family Strong in a World Gone Wrong
Step-parenting 101
The Perfect Match
Be Your Own Shrink
Say Good-bye to Stress
Single Parenting That Works
When Your Best Isn't Good Enough
Pleasers

Books for Children, with Kevin Leman II

My Firstborn, There's No One Like You
My Middle Child, There's No One Like You
My Youngest, There's No One Like You
My Only Child, There's No One Like You
My Adopted Child, There's No One Like You
My Grandchild, There's No One Like You

DVD/Video Series

Making Children Mind without Losing Yours (Christian—
parenting edition)
Making Children Mind without Losing Yours (Mainstream—
public-school teacher edition)
Value-Packed Parenting

Making the Most of Marriage

Running the Rapids

Single Parenting That Works

Bringing Peace and Harmony to the Blended Family

Available at 1-800-770-3830 or www.lemanbooksandvideos.com

Make your marriage sizzle with advice from bestselling author Dr. Kevin Leman

Creating Intimacy
to Make Your
Marriage Sizzle

Sex Begins *in the* Kitchen

Dr. Kevin Leman
AUTHOR OF **THE BIRTH ORDER BOOK**

Learn to build communication, affection, consideration, and caring in your marriage to make it more emotionally— and physically—satisfying.

Revell
a division of Baker Publishing Group
www.RevellBooks.com

Available wherever books are sold

Change your life with these great new resources
from Dr. Kevin Leman

Reverse negative behavior in your children—fast! Internationally known child behavior expert Dr. Kevin Leman offers encouragement and practical strategies to change your child's behavior in under a week.

Firstborns were born to win. Dr. Kevin Leman helps firstborns understand their natural advantages for the highest level of personal success.